2025年度版

和歌山県の英語科

過去問

協同教育研究会 編

協同出版

本書には，和歌山県の教員採用試験の過去問題を収録しています。各問題ごとに，以下のように5段階表記で，難易度，頻出度を示しています。

難易度

非常に難しい	☆☆☆☆☆
やや難しい	☆☆☆☆
普通の難易度	☆☆☆
やや易しい	☆☆
非常に易しい	☆

頻出度

◎	ほとんど出題されない
◎◎	あまり出題されない
◎◎◎	普通の頻出度
◎◎◎◎	よく出題される
◎◎◎◎◎	非常によく出題される

※本書の過去問題における資料，法令文等の取り扱いについて

本書の過去問題で使用されている資料や法令文の表記や基準は，出題された当時の内容に準拠しているため，解答・解説も当時のものを使用しています。ご了承ください。

はじめに～「過去問」シリーズ利用に際して～

教育を取り巻く環境は変化しつつあり，日本の公教育そのものも，教員免許更新制の廃止やGIGAスクール構想の実現などの改革が進められています。また，現行の学習指導要領では「主体的・対話的で深い学び」を実現するため，指導方法や指導体制の工夫改善により，「個に応じた指導」の充実を図るとともに，コンピュータや情報通信ネットワーク等の情報手段を活用するために必要な環境を整えることが示されています。

一方で，いじめや体罰，不登校，暴力行為など，教育現場の問題もあいかわらず取り沙汰されており，教員に求められるスキルは，今後さらに高いものになっていくことが予想されます。

本書の基本構成としては，出題傾向と対策，過去5年間の出題傾向分析表，過去問題，解答および解説を掲載しています。各自治体や教科によって掲載年数をはじめ，「チェックテスト」や「問題演習」を掲載するなど，内容が異なります。

また原則的には一般受験を対象としております。特別選考等については対応していない場合があります。なお，実際に配布された問題の順番や構成を，編集の都合上，変更している場合があります。あらかじめご了承ください。

最後に，この「過去問」シリーズは，「参考書」シリーズとの併用を前提に編集されております。参考書で要点整理を行い，過去問で実力試しを行う，セットでの活用をおすすめいたします。

みなさまが，この書籍を徹底的に活用し，教員採用試験の合格を勝ち取って，教壇に立っていただければ，それはわたくしたちにとって最上の喜びです。

協同教育研究会

C O N T E N T S

第１部

和歌山県の
英語科
出題傾向分析

和歌山県の英語科　傾向と対策

2020年度までは，リスニングのみが共通問題であったが，2021年度からすべて中高共通問題となった。2024年度の問題構成は，2023年度と同様に，リスニング1，文法・語法問題1，自由英作文1，読解問題2であり，問題傾向も変わらなかった。文法・語法問題は誤文訂正問題である。リスニング問題の小問1問と読解問題の小問2問が短答式または記述式である。配点は，リスニング15点，文法・語法15点，自由英作文20点，1つ目の読解23点，そして2つ目の読解27点で合計100点である。

リスニング問題のスクリプトは公表されていない。2024年度は，食糧生産について，ワークシートにメモを取りながら，講義を聞いているという設定で，メモの空欄を埋める形式である。最初に，状況と問いを読む時間が1分間与えられるので，メモの空欄と選択肢に可能な限り目を通し，聞き取るべきところと聞き流すところを把握する。選択肢の英語は平易だが，放送は1回のみとなるので集中力が必要だ。リスニングについては，日頃から英語の音声に触れるとともに，問題演習などで必要な情報を聞き取る訓練をするとよい。問題形式については2023年度からの変更はほとんどなかったが，毎年同形式とは考えにくく，今後も様々な形式で出題されると思われるので，各種検定等の音声問題を幅広く入手し，いろいろな出題形式をこなしておくことを勧める。BBC 6 minutes EnglishやVOA learning Englishなどを活用しながら多くのインプットを受けることが重要である。

文法・語法問題として出題された誤文訂正では，高校レベルの基本的な文法が問われている。大学入試レベルの英文法の参考書をおさえておけば十分対応できるだろう。また，語彙を学習する際にはフレーズ単位で文法的な制約やコロケーションに着目し，知っている単語ほど英和辞典を引いて文法解説を読み込むことが重要である。

文章読解では，400語と600語程度の長文が出題された。内訳は空欄補充，内容一致語句，内容記述，タイトル選択と多岐にわたる。難解な語はないが，論理展開を把握しておかないと解答できない問題もある。英文のレベルとしては，本文全体の主張も大まかな流れをつかめば理解そのものはとりわけ困難ではないといえる。まずは過去問題を解くほか，他県の過去問題集にある同レベルの長文問題や，大学入試レベルの長文問題集を1冊仕上げておくことを勧める。長文の総合問題は時間を計りながら数多く解き，速読に慣れておくとよい。速読のためには語彙を素早く認知する能力が不可欠であるため，自分のレベルよりもやさしめの英文をたくさん読む多読も重要である。English e–Readerのような無料で読める多読のウェブサイトを活用しながら日々習慣的に英文に目を通すことを勧める。

自由英作文問題について，語数は2023年度と同様に100語程度とある程度の分量を求められている。2024年度では，直接的ではないものの学習指導要領に関わる内容を理解している前提でパフォーマンステストの実施方法と内容を自分の考えとして具体的にまとめさせる問題であった。英作文問題のトピックとしては幅広く英語教育に関するものが出題される傾向にあり，2020年度は中学校で「書くこと」の指導について，ある問題に解答するために必要な力とそれを育成するための授業実践の2つを書かせるというもの，高等学校では実際の指導に当たってどのような言語活動を行うかを記述する問題が出題された。共通問題となった2021年度からは，「機械翻訳の精度が増している中，義務教育として英語を学ぶ必要性」について意見を書くことが求められ，2023年度では「言語活動の充実を図るため，英語の授業において，生徒自身がICT機器をさらに活用することが望まれるとの分析がなされている。この分析を踏まえ，どのような授業を行うか」について論じることが求められた。

このような教育に関する内容をまとまった英文で論述するためには，日頃から教育関係の記事を読み自分なりの考えや方針をもっておくことが欠かせない。文部科学省からの公的文書や学会での実践報告など，アンテナを高く張って情報を収集することも重要である。また，学習指導要領及び解説をよく読み込んで，生徒たちにどのような授業展開を行っていきたいか具体的な案を多く持っておくことも大切である。英文の長さについては例年語数制限があり，時に30語程度と短い指定の場合もあったので，過去問題を参考に，様々な長さで自分の考えをまとめられるように対策しておくとよい。自由英作文は単問としては得点のウェートがかなり高い。先の読解問題に時間をとられて十分に書けずに試験終了になることがないように，全体の時間配分を考えておこう。

過去5年間の出題傾向分析

中学＝●　高校＝▲　中高共通＝◎

分類	設問形式	2020年度	2021年度	2022年度	2023年度	2024年度
リスニング	内容把握	◎	◎	◎	◎	◎
発音・アクセント	発音					
	アクセント					
	文強勢					
文法・語法	空所補充		◎			
	正誤判断	◎				
	一致語句					
	連立完成					
	その他			◎	◎	◎
会話文	短文会話					
	長文会話					
文章読解	空所補充	◎●▲	◎	◎	◎	◎
	内容一致文	▲	◎	◎	◎	◎
	内容一致語句	◎●		◎	◎	◎
	内容記述	◎●▲	◎	◎	◎	◎
	英文和訳					
	英問英答					
	その他	◎●▲	◎	◎	◎	◎
英作文	整序		◎			
	和文英訳					
	自由英作	●▲	◎	◎	◎	◎
	その他					
学習指導要領		▲				

第２部

和歌山県の
教員採用試験
実施問題

2024年度　実施問題

【中高共通】

【1】はリスニングテストです。

【1】リスニング問題は[問1]～[問4]までの4問です。

はじめに，状況，ワークシート及び問いに目を通しなさい。

【目を通す時間(約60秒)→リスニング(1回しか読まれません。)】

状況

あなたは食糧生産について，ワークシートにメモを取りながら，英語の講義を聞いています。

ワークシート

THE TRUE IMPACT OF WHAT WE EAT

●Food production is dependent on biological [A]

・The [B] of land for food production

= the biggest cause of loss of biological [A]

・[C] already occupies about 50% of the Earth's habitable land

⇒ a major threat to 80% of the mammal and bird species classified as close to extinction

We also use [D] % of available freshwater to produce food

The food system generates around [E] % of all greenhouse gas emissions

●The agricultural revolutions of the past have allowed us to feed more people

・With the global population projected to increase by over 2 billion by 2050, [F]

●It is important to see a sustainable approach to food production

WHAT WE CAN DO

①
②
③
④
⑤

[問1] ワークシート内の[A]～[C]にあてはまる適切な1語を，それぞれ書け。

[問2] ワークシート内の[D]，[E]にあてはまる最も適切な数値を，次の①～④の中から1つ選び，その番号を書け。

D ① 50 ② 55 ③ 70 ④ 75

E ① 25 ② 35 ③ 40 ④ 50

[問3] ワークシート内の[F]にあてはまる最も適切なものを，講義内容に基づいて，次の①～④の中から1つ選び，その番号を書け。

① other technological emissions can take us further.

② other technological exploitation can take us further.

③ expansion of food production will place our planet under even greater strains.

④ expansion of food regulation will place our planet under even greater strains.

[問4]　ワークシート内の“WHAT WE CAN DO”として講義の中で述べられている①～⑤の例のうち2つの例を日本語で書け。

(☆☆☆☆☆◎◎◎)

【２】以下の[問1]～[問5]の英文には，英文・語法的に誤っている箇所が1つずつある。次の(例)にならって，誤っている箇所を下線部①～④の中から1つずつ選び，その番号を書け。また，その箇所の語句を正しい形に直して書け。

(例)　Success is ①within ②reach if you ③are willed to ④put in the work.
番号：③　正しい形：are willing

[問1]　My brother ①is singing ②in ③a low voice with his eyes ④closing.

[問2]　We ①came to ②a fountain, ③which we rested ④for a short while.

[問3]　If I ①had not ②taken the pills this morning, I ③would have been suffering ④from carsickness now.

[問4]　The twins ①used to be so ②alike that even their friends found ③it difficult to tell one from ④other.

[問5]　①Since no one ②is at home ③during the day, our dog is ④taken care by our grandparents.

(☆☆◎◎◎◎◎)

【３】次の英文を読んで，以下の[問1]～[問5]に答えよ。

The world's population is more than three times larger than it was in the mid-twentieth century. The global human population reached 8.0 billion in mid-November 2022 from an estimated 2.5 billion people in 1950, adding 1 billion people since 2010 and 2 billion since 1998. The world's population is expected to increase by nearly 2 billion persons in the next 30 years, from the current 8 billion to 9.7 billion in 2050 and could peak at nearly 10.4 billion in the mid-2080s. ⓐThis dramatic growth has been driven largely by increasing numbers of people surviving to reproductive age, the gradual increase in human lifespan, increasing urbanization, and accelerating migration. These trends will have far-reaching implications for generations to come.

In the next three decades, the regions of the world will experience different growth rates of their populations. Consequently, ⓑthe regional distribution of the population in 2050 will significantly differ from that of today. Central and Southern Asia is expected to become the most populous region in the world by 2037 as the population of Eastern and South-Eastern Asia could start declining by the mid-2030s. Between 2022 and 2050, the population of sub-Saharan Africa is expected to almost double, surpassing 2 billion inhabitants by the late 2040s. With average fertility levels remaining close to 3 births per woman in 2050, sub-Saharan Africa is projected to account for more than half of the growth of the world's population between 2022 and 2050. In 2022, the size of the population in this region was growing at an annual rate of 2.5 per cent and more than three times the global average of 0.8 per cent per year.

Europe and Northern America is projected to reach its (1) population size and to begin experiencing population decline in the late 2030s due to sustained low levels of fertility, which has been below 2 births per woman since the mid-1970s and, in some countries, high emigration rates.

表

Regions	Population (in millions)		
	2022	2030	2050
①	1,152	1,401	2,094
②	1,120	1,129	1,125
③	2,075	2,248	2,575
Eastern and South-Eastern Asia	2,342	2,372	2,317

〔Adapted from GLOBAL ISSUES Population, World Population Prospects 2022 UNITED NATIONS...一部省略等がある〕

[問1]　本文中の下線部ⓐThis dramatic growthの理由として述べられているものを2つ日本語で書け。

[問2]　本文中の下線部ⓑthe regional distribution of the population in 2050 will significantly differ from that of today.の理由を30字程度の日本語で書け。

[問3]　表は，Central and Southern Asia，Eastern and South-Eastern Asia，Sub-Saharan Africa，Europe and Northern Americaの4つの地域の人口についてのものである。表中の①～③のうち，次のア，イの地域があてはまる箇所を1つずつ選び，その番号を書け。

ア　Central and Southern Asia　　イ　Sub-Saharan Africa

[問4]　本文中の(　1　)に入る最も適切なものを，次の①～④から1つ選び，その番号を書け。

①　peak　　②　surplus　　③　dense　　④　bottom

[問5]　この英文のタイトルとして最も適切なものを，次の①～④の中から1つ選び，その番号を書け。

①　History of Global Population Growth

②　History of Global Fertility Level

③　Trends of Global and Regional Population Growth

④　Trends of Global and Regional Emigration Rates

(☆☆☆☆◎◎◎◎◎)

【4】次の英文を読んで，以下の[問1]～[問7]に答えよ。

1) Assessment and Learning

Given the importance of assessment for student learning, it is important to consider how to best measure the learning that you want your students to achieve. Assessment should integrate grading, learning, and motivation for your students. Well-designed assessment methods provide <u>valuable information about student learning</u>. They tell us what students learned, how well they learned it, and where they struggled. Assessment then becomes a lens for understanding student learning, identifying invisible barriers, and helping us to improve our teaching approaches.

2) Formative and Summative Assessments

Assessment can serve many different purposes. Most instructors are familiar with the traditional way of assessing students, such as by mid-term and final exams (usually using multiple-choice questions). There is a reason that this type of assessment is so popular — it is cost efficient (as in the example of multiple choice exams), takes a relatively short amount of time to create and grade, and provides a numerical summary (grade) of how much a student has learned.

The (1) of this method is that it does not provide the learner or instructor any feedback on the learning process that has taken place, only a summative result. This lack of opportunity to apply new learning and receive formative feedback hinders student ability to learn.

Another type of assessment, known as formative assessment, has a different purpose from summative assessment. Formative assessments capture learning-in-process in order to identify gaps, misunderstanding, and evolving understanding before summative assessments. Formative assessment may take a variety of forms, such as informal questions, practice quizzes, one-minute papers, and clearest/muddiest point exercises. Paul Black (1998) described the difference between these terms using the analogy of cooking. As a cook is making her soup, she occasionally tastes it to decide if it needs a bit more spices or ingredients. With each taste she is assessing her soup, and using that feedback to change or improve it — (2), the cook is engaging in formative assessment. Once the soup is served to the customer, the customer tastes it and makes a final judgment about the quality of the soup — otherwise known as [A] assessment.

3) Diagnostic Assessment

Another type of assessment, which is given at the beginning of the course or the beginning of the unit/topic, is known as diagnostic assessment. This assessment is used to collect data on what students already know about the topic. Diagnostic assessments are sets of written questions (multiple choice or short answer) that assess a learner's current knowledge base or current views on a topic/issue to be studied in the course. The goal is to get a snapshot of (3) students currently stand - intellectually, emotionally or ideologically - allowing the instructor to make sound instructional choices as to (4) to teach the new course content and (　5　) teaching approach to use.

4) [B]

Formative assessment is a valuable tool that enables instructors to provide immediate and ongoing feedback to improve student learning. Formative assessment can involve providing feedback following an assessment, but more importantly, this feedback is delivered during instruction, allowing instructors to identify student misunderstandings and help them correct their errors. This formative feedback is crucial for improving knowledge, skills, and understanding, and is also a significant factor in motivating student learning. Students must use this feedback provided by the instructor to engage in the appropriate actions required to close the gap between the actual and desired level of performance. Therefore, for successful student learning, formative feedback must not be one-sided; instead it involves both the instructor and the students.

〔Adapted from QUEEN'S UNIVERSITY Teaching and Learning in Higher Education...一部省略等がある〕

[問1]　本文中の下線部valuable information about student learningについて，その具体的内容を50字程度の日本語で書け。

[問2]　本文中の(　1　)に入る最も適切なものを，次の①～④の中から1つ選び，その番号を書け。

①　upside　②　downside　③　uptrend　④　downtrend

[問3]　本文中の(　2　)に入る最も適切なものを，次の①～④の中から1つ選び，その番号を書け。

①　in addition　②　in any case　③　in the end

④　in other words

[問4]　本文中の[A]に入る適切な1語を書け。

[問5]　本文中の(　3　)～(　5　)に入る最も適切なものを，次の①～③の中からそれぞれ選び，その番号を書け。ただし，同じものを繰り返し選んではいけない。

①　how　②　what　③　where

[問6]　本文中4)のパラグラフの見出しとして [B] に入る最も適切なものを，次の①～④の中から1つ選び，その番号を書け。

① How Assessment Improves Formative Feedback?

② How Feedback Improves Three Types of Assessment?

③ Why Feedback is Important to Learning?

④ Why Assessment is Important to Feedback?

[問7]　本文の内容と一致するものを，次の①～⑤の中から2つ選び，その番号を書け。

① Students' motivation for learning should not be considered when instructors make assessment of them.

② Summative assessment is popular among instructors because it can take a variety of forms, such as informal questions and presentations.

③ Formative assessment provides feedback during the instructional process, which improves student learning.

④ Diagnostic assessment can help instructors identify students' current knowledge of an issue to be studied.

⑤ Successful summative assessment should be both-sided, involving both the instructor and the students.

(☆☆☆☆☆◎◎◎◎◎)

【5】パフォーマンステストを用いて，生徒の英語で「話すこと(やり取り)」の能力を評価したい。どのようなパフォーマンステストを実施するか。具体的な内容について，あなたの考えを100語程度の英語で書け。

なお，短縮形(I'mやdon'tなど)は1語と数え，符号(,や?など)は語数に含めない。

(例)　No,　I'm　not.　【3語】

(☆☆☆☆☆◎◎◎◎◎)

解答・解説

【中高共通】

【1】問1　A　diversity　B　conversion　C　Agriculture
問2　D　③　E　①　問3　③　問4　・食品がどこからもたらされているかを知る。　・生産地が，明確な企業(の製品)を選ぶ。　・魚や肉を食べるとき，それらが何を与えられて育てられたかを理解する。　・持続可能であると認定されている食品を買う。　・地元の小規模な農家をサポートする。　から2つ

〈解説〉スクリプトは非公開である。2024年度は，食糧生産に関する英語の講義を聞いて，内容のアウトラインをワークシート形式でまとめていくものとなっている。放送は1回のみだが，設問，選択肢が問題冊子に印刷されており，放送前に60秒間だけ目を通す時間が与えられている。内容理解に必要なキーワードはもちろん，統計的数値の聞き取りが必須である。また，問4のように，日本語に変換して解答する記述式の設問が含まれているので，日本語を介さずに英語で聞くことだけに慣れすぎていると，時間内に上手く表現できないことがあるので注意したい。このような，キーワードを英語で記述する形式の練習として，IELTS™試験の9段階評価(バンドスコア)のうち，5.0(Modest)レベルから6.0(Competent)レベルをターゲットにしたリスニングセクションの練習課題が役に立つと思われる。

【2】問1　番号…④　正しい形…closed　問2　番号…③　正しい形…where　問3　番号…③　正しい形…would be　問4　番号…④　正しい形…the other　問5　番号…④　正しい形…taken care of

〈解説〉誤っている個所を指摘し，正しい形にする問題。　問1　付帯状況with＋O＋C「OがCである状態で」の問題。O＋Cの関係は第5文型O＋Cの関係に準じる。C に動詞が来る主な形として，現在分詞を使っ

たwith＋O＋～ing「O が～している状態で」と過去分詞を使ったwith＋O＋p.p.「Oが～されている状態で」を押さえておくこと。私の兄弟が歌を歌っているときに目をつぶっている状態なので，He is closing his eyes.の意味を，状況説明的にwithを使って表現する。その際に，受動態に変換し，His eyes are being closed.からOとCの要素を抽出し，with his eyes closedとまとめる。　問2　関係代名詞と関係副詞の違いに関する問題。ここではWe came to a fountain.とWe rested beside the fountain for a short while.の2文を，関係詞を使って接合する。rest「休息する」は他動詞ではなく自動詞なので，前置詞の存在に気づくことが大切である。　問3　仮定法過去完了の構文。①If S had 過去分詞～, S' would have 過去分詞….「もし(過去に)～したら，(過去に)…しただろうに」と，②If S had 過去分詞～, S' would 動詞原形….「もし(過去に)～したら，(現在は)…だろう」の2パターンある。主節にnowがあるので，ここは②で考える。　問4　The twinsから2人の人間が存在し，不定代名詞を使って一方と他方を区別する時は，oneとthe otherの組合せを使う。so～that構文に注意。used to(動詞の原形)「過去に～だった」，be alike「似ている」，tell A from B「AとBを区別する」。　問5　群動詞の受動態の問題。能動態の文は，Our grandparents take care of our dog.である。take care ofを1つの動詞という視点でとらえれば，our dogはその群動詞の目的語となるので，our dogを主語にした受動態に変換できる。その際に前置詞of を忘れないこと。

【3】問1　・再生産年齢人口の増加　・漸進的な寿命の延伸　・都市化の進展　・加速する人々の移住　から2つ　問2　今後30年間，世界の各地域での人口増加率が異なると予想されるため。(33字)　問3　ア　③　イ　①　問4　①　問5　③

〈解説〉問1　This dramatic growth has been driven largly by～「このめざましい増加が促進されたのは～によって」とあるので，by 以下の4つの項目，1 increasing numbers of people surviving to reproductive age，2 the gradual increase in human lifespan，3 increasing urbanization，4

accelerating migrationがその理由となる。これらから2つの項目を選び日本語で書く。　問2　Consequently「その結果」とあるので，その前文In the next three decades,～their populations.が理由を表していることが分かる。日本語で30字程度と指定があるが，読点も字数内に入ることに注意。　問3　第2段落と第3段落で，4つの地域に関する今後の人口の推移について述べられている。Central and Southern Asiaでは「2037年までには世界で最も人口の多い地域になると推定されている」。Eastern and South-Eastern Asiaでは「2030年代中頃までに人口減少が始まる可能性がある」。sub-Saharan Africaでは「2022年から2050年の間に人口が約2倍になり，2040年代後半までに20億人を超えてくるだろう」。Europe and Northern Americaでは「2030年代後半には人口減少が始まると予想される」。以上より，与えられた表の人口推移のパターンと比べて表を完成させればよい。　問4　2030年代後半から人口減少に転じると述べており，それまでは上昇してピークに達していると読み取れるので①を選択。surplus「余り，余剰の」，dense「密集した」。
問5　第1段落で過去から今後についての世界人口の推移について，第2段落，第3段落で複数の地域での今後の人口推移について述べているので，それらをカバーしている内容をもったタイトルを選ぶ。①では地域の人口には触れていないので不適切。②は出生率しか触れていないので不適切。③は世界と地域の人口推移について触れているので適切。④は移民率をテーマにしていることになるので不適切。

【4】問1　生徒たちが何を学んだのか，どのように上手に学んだのか，そして，どこで学びにつまずいているのかということ。(52字)
問2　②　　問3　④　　問4　summative　　問5　3　③　　4　①
5　②　　問6　③　　問7　③，④
〈解説〉学習評価についての概念，特に形成的評価(formative assessment)，総括的評価(summative assessment)，診断的評価(diagnostic assessment)の3つの概念について述べられた英文だが，専門用語や概念が出てくる英文では，その定義や具体例について整理しながら読み進めることが内容理解につながる。　問1　下線部を含む文は「よく設計された評価方法は生徒の学習に関する貴重な情報を与えてくれる」の意であり，さらに「その方法により我々は～を理解する」と続いているので，下線部に後続する英文内のwhat students learned, how well they learned it, and where they struggled.を日本語に訳してまとめる。下線部は名詞句なので体言止め「～ということ」で締めくくること。　問2　空欄1のある第3段落では，学習する過程においてフィードバックを学習者や教師に与えることにより，新しい学習スタイルを適用し形成的フィードバックを受ける機会を創出し，生徒の学習能力を促すことにつながると読み取れる。つまり，学習上のフィードバックがないことが，伝統的評価法であるsummative assessmentの否定的側面であり，すなわち欠点となる。空欄1には，その意味を表すdownsideを選ぶ。　問3　空欄2の前では，「自分が作ったスープの味見を行い，そのフィードバックからスープの味を改良したり改善したりする」と述べている。改善を目指してフィードバックを行う評価方法はformative assessmentに他ならないことから，空欄2の前後は表現を変えて同じ内容を述べていると言える。in other words「言い換えれば」が正解。　問4　第4段落では，formative assessmentとsummative assessmentの違いについて対比的に説明していることを念頭に置く。料理として出されたスープを客が食し，その客が最終的にそのスープの味の評価結果を出すことは，教師が生徒の学習結果を数値で評定することと類似しているのでsummative assessmentと言える。otherwise known as～「別名～として知られている」。　問5　疑問詞を挿入する問題で，繰り返し同じ疑問詞を使わない前提であることに注意。空欄4について，whereなら「どこで教えるか」となり不可解。また，他動詞teachに目的語the new courseが後続するのでwhatは不可。よって，howを選び，「どのようにその新しい授業を教えるべきか」と考える。as to「～に関して」。空欄5にもwhereは不可解。whatなら「何の教授法を使うべきか」となり意味を成す。結果として，空欄3にはwhereを当て，「生徒の今の(学習上の)立ち位置がどこかという全体像を得ること」と読み解く。　問6　第6段落では，formative assessmentがa valuable toolであるという書き出しで始まり，後続するmore importantly，crucial，a significant factorの語句から，フィードバックの重要性について説明しているのが見えてくる。assessmentが重要なのではなく，feedbackが重要であることから，③「なぜ学習にフィードバックが重要なのか」を選ぶ。　問7　①「教師が生徒を評価する時，生徒の学習意欲は考慮に入れるべきではない」は第1段落2文目より不一致。　②「総括的評価は教師に人気がある。なぜならばインフォーマルクエスチョンやプレゼンテーションなど様々な形式をとることができるからだ」は第4段落3文目より不一致。③「形成的評価では，授業が進行している間にフィードバックを与えることで生徒の学習効果が上がる」は第6段落1文目と一致する。④「診断的評価を実施することで教師は生徒が学習項目に関する知識を現状どの程度持っているかを確認することができる」は第5段落2文目と一致する。　⑤「総括的評価が効果を発揮するには，教師と生徒を含め双方向的であるべきだ」は第3段落と第6段落最終文より不一致。

【5】First, I will tell my students about two goals in the conversation test. One is to give correct information about their school life to their FLT. The other goal is to get information about those in other countries. Then a student will have a conversation with their FLT. The FLT will begin with some questions about their timetable, school rules, or school events so that the student can answer to them based on facts, using easy words. Then, I will check if the student can exchange information with the FLT, if they can use proper vocabulary, and if they have a positive attitude to communicating with others in English. (109 words)

〈解説〉「話すこと[やり取り]」の能力評価のためにパフォーマンステストを実施するにあたり，その実施方法や内容を英文100語程度でまとめる問題である。この設問の配点は20点となっており，点数評価の詳細は不明だが，学習指導要領の「話すこと[やり取り]」の内容を意識した内容になっているか，英文として論理的に内容を整理して書いているか，文法的な間違いがないか，という点には注意すべきである。また，テスト内容は「話すこと[やり取り]」であって，プレゼンテーションやスピーチなどの「話すこと[発表]」ではないので誤解しないように注意すること。難しく考える必要はなく，自分が生徒に対して具体的にどのような作業をさせたいか，話題は何か，資料を活用するのか，評価者は誰か，評価のポイントをどこに置くかなどに思いを巡らせ，内容のアウトラインをまとめてから英文に仕上げることになる。解答例では，生徒に2つのテスト目標を示し，英語教員(FLT)との対話を行わせて，情報伝達力，語彙力，英語によるコミュニケーションにおける積極性を見ようとしていることが窺われる。英文を書く際には，ディスコースマーカーを十分駆使して分かりやすくまとめることを忘れないように。

2023年度　実施問題

【中高共通】

【1】はリスニングテストです。

【１】リスニング問題は[問1]～[問4]までの4問です。

はじめに，状況，ワークシート及び問いに目を通しなさい。

【目を通す時間(約60秒)→リスニング(1回しか読まれません。)】

状況

あなたは気候変動について，ワークシートにメモを取りながら，英語の講義を聞いています。

ワークシート

Climate change

Current situation

Measurements show that the average temperature at the Earth's surface has risen by about (A)℃ since the pre-industrial period.

●Change in temperature

In the 21 century : 17 of the 18 warmest years on record have occurred.

The last (B) decades : have been hotter than the previous one.

●The UK is already affected by rising temperatures.

→The most recent decade (2008-2017) has been on average (C)℃ warmer than the 1961-1990 average.

●The change in temperature has been particularly fast (D).

●Natural fluctuations will still cause (E).

Along with warming at the Earth's surface

Many other changes in the climate like (F), (G) are occurring.

To make the situations better

At the Paris climate conference (COP21) in December 2015.

195 countries adopted the first-ever universal global climate deal.

⇩

Global action plan limiting global warming well below 2℃ above pre-industrial levels and pursue efforts towards limiting to 1.5℃.

⇩

The country commitments are predicted to give rise to global temperature increases of around 3℃.

⇩

(H)

[問1] ワークシート内の A ～ C にあてはまる適切な数値を，それぞれ書け。

[問2] ワークシート内の D ， E にあてはまる最も適切なものを，次の①～④の中から1つ選び，その番号を書け。

D ① in the Antarctic ② in the Arctic
③ over the oceans ④ over the land

E ① rising temperatures ② long-term climate changes
③ warmer years and seasons ④ cold years and seasons

[問3] ワークシート内の F ， G にあてはまる例を，講義で述べられていることから2つ選び，英語で書け。

[問4] ワークシート内の H にあてはまる最も適切なものを，講義内容に基づいて，次の①～④の中から1つ選び，その番号を書け。

① Further urgent action is needed to put us on track to well below 1.5℃.

② Further urgent action is needed to put us on track to well below 2℃.

③　By limiting global warming, it impossible to avoid temperature increases of around 3℃.

④　By limiting global warming to well above 2℃, we will see a dramatic improvement.

(☆☆☆◎◎◎)

【2】以下の[問1]～[問4]の英文には，文法・語法的に誤っている箇所が1つずつある。例にならって，誤っている箇所を下線部①～④の中から1つずつ選び，その番号を書け。また，その箇所の語句を正しい形に直して書け。

(例)　Success is ①within ②reach if you ③are willed to ④put in the work.
　番号：③　正しい形：are willing

[問1]　①It is no doubt ②that it ③is going to rain ④this evening.

[問2]　When we ①considered the matter in all ②aspects, one of us ③mentioned about a ④problem.

[問3]　My sister found ①so a beautiful shell ②that I ③wanted ④it.

[問4]　The temple is ①said ②to ③have built four hundred years ④ago.

[問5]　①Acccording to this book, we can reduce stress ②by accepting events ③what they are, rather than as you would like them ④to be.

(☆☆◎◎◎◎◎)

【3】次の英文を読んで，あとの[問1]～[問6]に答えよ。

When the COVID-19 pandemic broke out earlier this year, much of the world moved online, accelerating a digital transformation that has been underway for decades. Children with at-home Internet access began attending class remotely; many employees started [A] from home; and numerous firms adopted digital business models to maintain operations and preserve some revenue flows. Meanwhile, mobile applications were developed to help "track and trace" the development of the pandemic; and researchers employed artificial intelligence to learn more about the virus and (1) the search for a vaccine. Internet traffic in some countries increased by up to 60% shortly after the outbreak, underscoring the digital acceleration that the pandemic sparked.

While these activities demonstrate the tremendous potential of the digital transformation, the pandemic has also accentuated the gaps that remain. Although some digital divides have narrowed fast in recent years, [B], leaving some behind in the COVID-induced digital acceleration. Moreover, the increased reliance on digital solutions has added new urgency to concerns around privacy and digital security.

This presents countries with a major challenge. It is unlikely that economies and societies will return to "pre-COVID" patterns; the crisis has vividly demonstrated the potential of digital technologies and some changes may now be too deep to reverse. Faced with a future where jobs, education, health, government services and even social interactions may be more dependent on digital technologies than ever before, failing to ensure widespread and trustworthy digital access and effective use risks deepening inequalities, and may hinder countries' efforts to emerge stronger from the pandemic.

The OECD Digital Economy Outlook 2020 highlights the growing importance of digital technologies and communications infrastructures in our daily lives, and reveals that governments are increasingly putting digital strategies at the centre of their policy agendas. Widespread connectivity has allowed many businesses and individuals to adapt to the crisis. Connectivity has steadily improved over time. (Figure 1) Though rising at a slower pace, by June 2019 fibre accounted for (2) of all fixed broadband subscriptions in the OECD, and no less than (3) in nine OECD countries.

Figure. 1 Fibre broadband connections, June 2019
As a percentage of total fixed broadband subscriptions

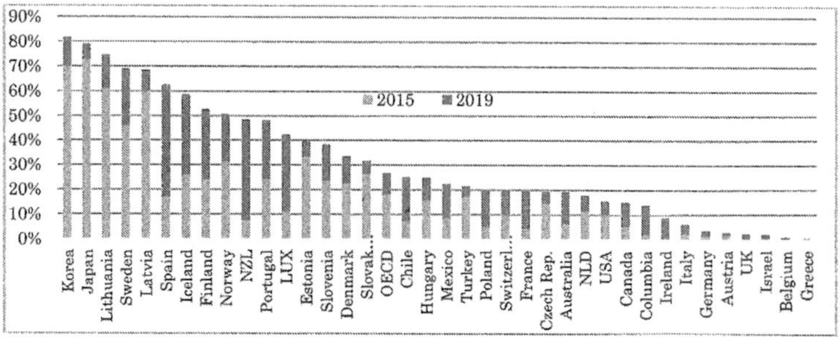

〔Adapted from OECD DIGITAL ECONOMY OUTLOOK 2020…一部省略等がある〕

[問1]　本文中の A にあてはまる最も適切な1語を書け。

[問2]　本文中の(　1　)にあてはまる最も適切な語を，次の①～④の中から1つ選び，その番号を書け。

①　invent　　②　solve　　③　apply　　④　accelerate

[問3]　本文中の B にあてはまる最も適切なものを，次の①～④の中から1つ選び，その番号を書け。

①　others have followed the same pace

②　others have not followed the same pace

③　others have attempted the same pace

④　others have not attempted the same pace

[問4]　本文中の下線部a majour challengeを解決するために必要なことは何か。本文中に述べられている内容を50字程度(句読点を含む。)の日本語で書け。

[問5]　Figure 1を参考にして，本文中の(　2　)，(　3　)にあてはまる最も適切なものを，次の①～④の中から1つずつ選び，その番号を書け。

①　27%　　②　33%　　③　50%　　④　60%

[問6]　この英文のタイトルとして最もふさわしいものを，次の①～④の中から1つ選び，その番号を書け。

① Impact of COVID-19 Pandemic on Digital Transformation
② Impact of COVID-19 Pandemic on Digital Business Models
③ The Rise of Online Learning during COVID-19 Pandemic
④ The Rise of New Types of Artificial Intelligence during COVID-19 Pandemic

(☆☆☆◎◎◎◎◎)

【4】次の英文を読んで，以下の[問1]～[問6]に答えよ。

Inquiry-based learning (IBL) is often employed in math and science classrooms, which naturally lend themselves to a problem-solving approach. However, the framework certainly has potential for other disciplines as well, including [A]. Of course, balancing inquiry-based learning with language learning means that teachers must also attend to the language and vocabulary skills students need to be effective inquisitors. Tweaks to the traditional model can make this become a reality.

Below are four key principles that distinguish an inquiry-based approach, and suggestions on how teachers can scaffold them for the English language classroom.

1) Students as Researchers

In a typical inquiry-based learning framework, students are introduced to a topic and tasked with developing their own research questions to guide their process of discovery. In an English language setting, one way to model this is to provide a leading question for the students, choosing one that is (1) and can lead students in more than one direction. Even (2) questions can provide such ambiguity, for by doing deeper research, students begin to realize that the answer is not always (3).

Students can use WebQuests to find relevant articles and videos to look at the question from multiple perspectives. In a more scaffolded setting, instructors can provide articles and videos to discuss as a class, and ask students to draw out the relevant ideas and identify connections. (4), the goal is to have students revisit the question each time new information is learned so they can elaborate on and refine their answers, and in doing so, slowly become experts on the topic.

2) Teachers as Research Assistants

An inquiry-based learning model often flips the roles of the teacher and student. Students become the researchers, and teachers assume the role of the assistant or guide to their learning. One way to encourage this is to <u>flip the classroom itself</u> so that instructional lessons are delivered online, and class time is devoted to students applying what they have learned through practice and collaborative activities.

As language teachers, we can direct students to instructional videos on skills they'll need to understand and respond to the texts they encounter. An instructional video on how to classify information could support a text about different kinds of problem solvers, for example. Teachers can then use class time not to present the material, but to attend to students' questions and curiosities.

3) [B]

Learning from peers and sharing ideas with others is another core principle of inquiry-based learning. Students in an IBL classroom become each other's soundboards, which gives them an authentic audience from which to draw alternative perspectives from their own and test the validity of their ideas. Students are meant to collaborate throughout the entire process, from their initial response to the question to the final project. To do this, teachers can pose the leading question on an online discussion board and require peers to respond to each other's ideas. To scaffold, teachers can provide language used to respond to posts, such how to acknowledge someone else's ideas (*I think you're saying that...*) or show agreement or disagreement (I see your point, but I also wonder...).

4) Reflecting on Learning

The final principle is asking students to reflect on their learning. This can be achieved by posing the leading question on the discussion board at the end of the cycle, to see how students' responses have evolved based on what they've learned. Language teachers can also encourage reflection through assessment feedback. If giving a test on the language and skills students have studied, they can go a step further by posing questions about the experience. This helps students identify areas for improvement, and it gives teachers guidance in tailoring their instruction in the future.

〔Adapted from OXFORD UNIVERSITY PRESS ELT Global Blog...一部省略等がある〕

[問1] 本文中の[A]にあてはまる最も適切な1語を書け。

[問2] 本文中の(1)~(3)にあてはまる最も適切なものを，次の①~③の中から1つずつ選び，その番号を書け。ただし，同じものを繰り返し選んではいけない。

① yes-no ② black-and-white ③ open-ended

[問3] 本文中の(4)にあてはまる最も適切なものを，次の①~④の中から1つ選び，その番号を書け。

① On the contrary ② In addition ③ Whereas
④ Either way

[問4] 本文中の下線部flip the classroom itselfについて，教室ではどのような活動を行うと述べられているか。40字程度(句読点を含む。)の日本語で具体的に書け。

[問5] 本文中の[B]にあてはまるパラグラフの見出しとして最も適切なものを，次の①~④の中から1つ選び，その番号を書け。

① Student-to-Teacher Agreement
② Peer-to-Peer Agreement
③ Student-to-Teacher Collaboration
④ Peer-to-Peer Collaboration

[問6] 本文の内容と一致するものを，次の①~④の中から1つ選び，その番号を書け。

① Inquiry-based learning is best suited for language learning if teachers maintain traditional models.

② Instructional videos help teachers present the instructional material in the classroom.

③ Teachers can encourage students to reflect on what they've learned by asking them about their learning experience.

④ Giving a test on the language and skills students have studied should not be introduced into inquiry-based learning.

(☆☆☆☆◎◎◎◎◎)

【5】文部科学省による英語教育実施状況調査結果から，言語活動の充実を図るため，英語の授業において，生徒自身がICT機器をさらに活用することが望まれるとの分析がなされている。この分析を踏まえ，どのような授業を行うか。あなたの考えを100語程度の英語で書け。

なお，短縮形(I'mやdon'tなど)は1語と数え，符号(,や?など)は語数に含めない。

(例)　No.　I'm　not.　【3語】

(☆☆☆☆☆◎◎◎◎◎)

解答・解説

【中高共通】

【1】問1　A　1　B　3　C　0.8　問2　D　②　E　④

問3　F　・warming oceans　・melting polar ice and glaciers

G　・rising sea levels　・more extreme weather events　問4　②

〈解説〉スクリプトは非公開で，気候変動についての英語の講義を聞きながら，ワークシートにメモを取るという設定である。放送前に60秒間だけワークシートに目を通す時間が与えられるので，聞き取るべきポイントを迅速に押さえておくこと。数値の正確な聞き取りが求められ，問3のようなディクテーションに近い記述式出題もある。放送は1回のみなので，聞き逃さないように集中して臨みたい。

【2】問1　番号…①　　正しい形…There　　問2　番号…③　　正しい形…mentioned　　問3　番号…①　　正しい形…such　　問4　番号…③　　正しい形…have been built　　問5　番号…③　　正しい形…as

〈解説〉誤っている箇所を指摘し，正しい形にする問題。　問1　there is no doubt that S「Sということに疑いの余地はない」の構文。形式主語itを用いる場合にはit is not doubtful that Sのように形容詞であれば容認されるが，使用頻度は低い。that節の内容は「今夜雨が降るだろう」という未来形であり，主節の時制が現在であるため，一致しており適切である。　問2　mention「～について言及する」は他動詞であるため，aboutは不要である。consider A in all aspects「Aについてあらゆる観点から考慮する」。　問3　強調を表すsuchの用法である。「such a＋比較変化する形容詞＋名詞＋that」の形で「とても～な…なので」という意味になる。　問4　受動態に関する問題。「建てられた」が適切な意味となる。発話時は現在のことであるが，建設されたのは発話時よりも過去であるため完了形が用いられる。　問5　as it is「(文末で)そのままの，そのままで」を複数形にした形である。rather thanの直後にあるasが手がかりとなる。後半のasもas SVの形を取っている。

【3】問1　working　　問2　④　　問3　②　　問4　信頼してデジタル情報にアクセスできる環境を広く普及させ，それを効果的に活用できるようにすること。(48字)　　問5　2　①　　3　③　　問6　①

〈解説〉COVID-19とデジタルデバイドに関する長文読解である。

問1　子どもたちが自宅からリモートで出席し始めていることの対比で，多くの会社員はリモートで働き始めていることが推測できる。動詞startは動名詞を選択するため，workingが適切。　問2　研究者はAIを用いてウイルスについて学ぶようになったことが示されているため，ワクチンに関する調査が増えたことがわかる。invent「～を開発する」，solve「～を解決する」，apply「～を応用する」，accelerate「～を加速させる」。　問3　近年デジタルデバイドが改善されてきたが，COVIDによってもたらされた急速なデジタル化に取り残される人もいる。このことから，空所にはペースについていけない人が入る。
問4　下線部の内容は仕事や教育，医療などがデジタル化され，コロナ禍前の状態に戻ることはないにもかかわらず，信頼できるデジタル技術が普及せずに，不平等が拡大し，パンデミックから立ち上がるための国の努力を阻害することである。対策としてまとめる内容はfailing to以下の内容である。　問5　①はOECDのラベルで2019年時点のインターネット契約数の割合を確認すればよい。③は契約者数の多い上位9カ国(韓国からノルウェー)に着目すると，その割合は50%を下回っていない。本文のno less thanは「～ほども多く」と肯定的な意味であり，OECD加盟国の9カ国は50%もインターネット契約があることを表している。　問6　英文の内容はCOVID-19によってもたらされたデジタルデバイドに関する内容であることから①が適切。ポジティブな内容のみを表している③と④はネガティブな面を表す語が含まれていないため不適切。②はニュートラルであるが，ビジネスに限定している点が不適切。

【4】問1　English(languages)　　問2　1　③　　2　①　　3　②
問3　④　　問4　生徒が実践練習や生徒同士の協働作業を通して学んだ内容を応用するための活動を行う。(40字)　　問5　④　　問6　③
〈解説〉英文はinquiry-based learning (IBL; 探究型学習) と呼ばれる指導法について述べたものである。　問1　IBLは数学や理科で採用されている指導法であるが，他の分野でも応用できると述べられている。空所の直後には言語学習とバランスを取ることが述べられていることから，空所に入るのは「英語の授業や言語に関する授業」であることがわかる。　問2　空所1は生徒の意見を一方に偏らせないことが述べられているため，open-ended (答えが1つに収束しないもの)が適切。空所2は直後にquestionがあるため，コロケーションとしてyes-noが適切。

空所3は物事が常にblack-and-white (白黒はっきりする)ではないと気づき始めると述べている。　問3　空所4の前では(a)生徒自身が質問に関連する様々な観点の記事やビデオを見つける，(b)指導者が生徒に対して足がかりとなる記事やビデオなどを提示し，生徒がそれに関連する考えを引き出したりつながりを確認したりする，という2つの方法が挙げられている。その目標は，新しい情報を得るたびに問いに立ち返り，答えを練り直すことで，生徒が次第にそのトピックのエキスパートになることである。空所4の後で述べられている目標は(a)と(b)で共通していることであるため，either way (いずれの方法でも)が適切である。　問4　IBLでは教師と生徒の役割が逆転することがあり，下線部の状態では，指導的な授業はオンラインで配信され，授業時間は生徒が練習や協働的な活動を通して学んだ内容を応用することに充てる。class time is devoted to以下の部分を日本語でまとめればよい。なお，この形式は反転授業・反転学習と呼ばれる。　問5　該当のパラグラフで導入されているトピックセンテンスにはキーワードとなるpeersがあり，具体例としてagreementやdisagreementを主張するときに使える言語表現を提示することが教師の役割であることが述べられている。そのため，賛成か反対かを決定することよりも協働的に活動することが重要であることがわかる。　問6　①　第1パラグラフにて，伝統的なモデルを微調整すれば，IBLの実現が可能であるとあることから，「伝統的なモデルを維持すること」は不適切。　②　第4パラグラフにて，問いに関するビデオは，生徒が情報を集めたり考えを引き出したりする手助けとなるものと述べられているので不適切。　④　最終パラグラフに言語教師がテストを行うことを述べている点と矛盾するため不適切。

【5】In my classes, I want students to use ICT effectively so that students can interact with foreign students. For example, through online meetings, students can enjoy talking about themselves or their own cultures with foreign students. Using email or SNS is a good way to be exposed to authentic materials and to enhance students' ability of reading and writing. Providing opportunities to interact with foreign students will raise students' motivation to learn English. I think what is important in English class is to learn through communication. I will provide students the activities that involve authentic communication by using ICT. (99 words)

〈解説〉ICT(Information Communication Technology; 情報通信技術)は時間的・空間的制約を超えること，双方向性を有すること，カスタマイズが容易であることなどが特徴である。生徒1人に1台の端末，教室に電子黒板や無線LANなどの環境を整備することが前提となるが，生徒1人1人の能力や特性に応じた個別学習や生徒同士が教え合い学び合う協働学習を促進でき，一斉指導による学習を相互に組み合わせた学びの場を形成できる。活用例としては，インターネットを用いた情報収集や，シミュレーションなどのデジタル教材による学習，マルチメディアを用いた資料・作品の制作，評価のためのポートフォリオ作成などが挙げられる。英語の授業では特に遠隔地や海外の学校と交流する機会を提供することができ，プレゼンテーション能力の伸長なども見込める。解答例では海外の学生と交流することが述べられている。設問では100語程度の英語で書けという指示があるため，適切な量を論理的に述べる必要がある。

2022年度　実施問題

【中高共通】

【1】はリスニングテストです。

【１】リスニング問題は[問1]～[問5]までの5問です。

はじめに，状況，ワークシート及び問いに目を通しなさい。

【目を通す時間(約60秒)→リスニング(1回しか読まれません)】

状況

> あなたは，日本のエネルギー事情について，ワークシートにメモを取りながら，英語の講義を聞いています。

ワークシート

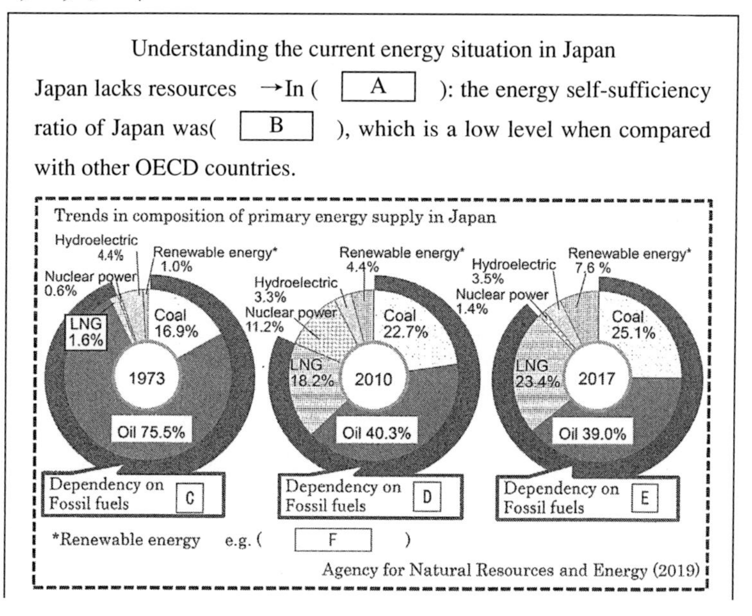

Understanding the current energy situation in Japan

Japan lacks resources →In (A): the energy self-sufficiency ratio of Japan was(B), which is a low level when compared with other OECD countries.

〇Electricity rates influenced largely by power sources
Factor 1: Thermal power: influenced by changes in international energy prices
Factor 2: ([G]): influenced by the rise of purchase costs.
〇Reducing greenhouse emissions
Japan's energy policy: ([H])

[問1]　ワークシート内の [A], [B] にあてはまる最も適切なものを，次の①～④の中から1つずつ選び，その番号を書け。

A	B
①　1973	① 0.96%
②　2010	②　9.6%
③　2017	③ 90.6%
④　2019	④　96%

[問2]　ワークシート内の [C] ～ [E] にあてはまる最も適切なものを，次の①～④の中から1つずつ選び，その番号を書け。

C	D	E
①　81.2%	①　81.2%	①　81.2%
②　87.5%	②　87.5%	②　87.5%
③　94.0%	③　94.0%	③　94.0%
④　96.0%	④　96.0%	④　96.0%

[問3]　ワークシート内の [F] にあてはまる例を，講義で述べられているものから1つ選び，英語で書け。

[問4]　ワークシート内の [G] にあてはまる最も適切なものを，講義内容に基づいて，次の①～④の中から1つ選び，その番号を書け。

①　Fossil fuels

②　Hydroelectric

③　Nuclear power

④　Renewable energy

[問5]　ワークシート内の H にあてはまる最も適切なものを，講義内容に基づいて，次の①～④の中から1つ選び，その番号を書け。

① Having too many power sources is a major headache for Japan.

② Having too many nuclear power plants is a major issue in Japan.

③ It is essential for Japan to have various means of energy supply.

④ It is essential for Japan to replace renewable energy with fossil fuels.

(☆☆☆◎◎◎◎◎)

【2】次の[問1]～[問5]の英文には文法・語法的に誤っている箇所が1つずつある。例にならって，誤っている箇所を下線部①～④の中から1つ選び，その番号を書け。また，その箇所の語句を正しい形に直して書け。

(例)　Success is ①within ②reach if you ③are willed to ④put in the work.
番号：③　正しい形：are willing

[問1]　We ①discussed about the issue ②until a ③solution ④was found.

[問2]　No one could argue that the ①Internet is one of the ②most important ③electrical ④invention of all time.

[問3]　You ①cannot imagine ②how different Kanako ③is from ④whom she was ten years ago.

[問4]　You ①had better ②clean your room, ③and your mother will ④get angry.

[問5]　Our softball game ①will be ②put off ③if it ④will rain tomorrow.

(☆☆☆◎◎◎◎)

【3】次の英文を読んで，以下の[問1]～[問6]に答えよ。

If British people have not traditionally worried about their identity, the Japanese, at least since the Meiji period, seem to have been obsessed with the issue. Is Japan part of the West or part of Asia? Is Japan a backward country, a modern country or a post-modern country? Is modernization the same as Westernization? Should the Japanese stay true to their traditions or should they aim to (1) a new kind of society? Issues such as these have worried many of Japan's leading thinkers, writers and academics, and have led to the writing of an enormous number of books about the character of Japanese culture and the differences between the Japanese and other people.

At the heart of these worries, I think, we find an interesting tension. On the one hand, the Japanese have been very anxious to 'catch up' , as they have seen it, with the wealthier countries of Europe and the United States. [A] This has stimulated an immense interest in all aspects of those countries and a determined effort on the part of the Japanese to master and absorb the cultures of those countries. [B] This is obviously true in the areas of science, industry, technology, medicine and scholarship, but it has also been the case in music, literature, art, fashion and other purely cultural fields.

On the other hand, at the very same time as struggling to absorb and keep up-to-date with European and American culture, the Japanese have also been very anxious to insist upon their difference from the West. [C] Moreover, the Japanese have been extremely creative in applying the methods of Western scholarship and philosophy to the study of their own cultural heritage. [D] Whereas most non-Western cultures have, until recently, been dominated by Western scholarship on their histories and cultures, Japan has uniquely been able to define for itself the study of its own past. But Japanese have only been able to do this precisely because they have been so ready to learn from Western developments in scholarship and theory. It is easy, I think, for foreigners to miss this tension, or to <u>emphasize only one side or the other of it</u>. To some, the Japanese seem thoroughly Westernized and to have lost touch with their own traditions. To others, the Japanese seem uniquely self-obsessed and interested mainly in insisting on the differences between themselves and other people and on the impossibility of outsiders truly understanding the Japanese language or culture. Certainly, it is very easy to find individual Japanese who exemplify one or other of these attitudes. The truth about Japan, however, is that it has tried continually to do two (2) things at once — to absorb Western culture and to preserve its difference from the West.

〔Adapted from Adrian J.Pinnington, Here and There, KINSEIDO...一部省略等がある〕

[問1] 本文中の(1)に入る最も適切な語を，次の①～④の中から1つ選び，その番号を書け。

① invent　② deny　③ modify　④ continue

[問2] 本文の流れに合うように，次の英文が入る箇所としてどこがふさわしいか，本文中の［A］～［D］の中から最も適切なものを1つ選び，その記号を書け。

This has meant that the Japanese have also devoted an enormous amount of effort to the study, preservation and retrieval of their own history and culture.

[問3] 本文中の下線部について，その具体的な内容がわかるように，次の〔 X 〕，〔 Y 〕にふさわしい日本語をそれぞれ10字程度で書け。

日本が〔 X 〕あるいは日本が〔 Y 〕のどちらか一方しか強調しない

[問4] 本文中の(2)に入る最も適切な語を，次の①～④の中から1つ選び，その番号を書け。

① sensible　② opposing　③ similar　④ harmonious

[問5] 本文の内容と一致するものを，次の①～④の中から1つ選び，その番号を書け。

① The Japanese were so superior in such fields as music, literature, art and fashion that many Western people were interested in them.

② The tendency in Japanese society to maintain their identity has been stronger and stronger since the Meiji period.

③ Some foreigners tend to think only of the Japanese interest in their Westernization, while missing their efforts to emphasize the differences from the West.

④　Japanese identity has been one of the most important issues among Westerners as well as Japanese.

[問6]　この文章のタイトルとして最もふさわしいものを，次の①～④の中から1つ選び，その番号を書け。

①　Great Japanese Culture

②　The Tradition of Japan

③　The Japanese and Westernization

④　Japan's Identity

(☆☆☆◎◎◎◎◎)

【4】次の英文を読んで，以下の[問1]～[問5]に答えよ。

While the debate regarding how much screen time is appropriate for children rages on among educators, psychologists, and parents, it's another emerging technology in the form of artificial intelligence and machine learning that is beginning to alter education tools and institutions and changing what the future might look like in education. It is expected that artificial intelligence in U.S. Education will grow by 47.5% from 2017-2021 according to the Artificial Intelligence Market in the US Education Sector report. Even though most experts believe the critical presence of [A] is irreplaceable, there will be many changes to a teacher's job and to educational best practices.

[B]

AI has already been applied to education primarily in some tools that help develop skills and testing systems. As AI educational solutions continue to mature, the hope is that AI can help fill needs gaps in learning and teaching and allow schools and teachers to do more than ever before. AI can drive efficiency, personalization and streamline admin tasks to allow teachers the time and freedom to provide understanding and adaptability — uniquely human capabilities where machines would struggle. By leveraging the best attributes of machines and teachers, the vision for AI in education is one where they work together for the best outcome for students. Since the students of today will need to work in a future where AI is the reality, it's important that our educational institutions expose students to and use the technology.

Differentiated and individualized learning

Adjusting learning based on an individual student's particular needs has been a priority for educators for years, but AI will allow a level of differentiation that's impossible for teachers who have to manage 30 students in each class. There are several companies currently developing intelligent instruction design and digital platforms that use AI to provide learning, testing and feedback to students from pre-kindergarten to college level that gives them the challenges they are ready for, identifies gaps in knowledge and redirects to new topics when appropriate. As AI gets more sophisticated, it might be possible for a machine to read the expression that passes on a student's face that indicates they are struggling to grasp a subject and will modify a lesson to respond to <u>that</u>. The idea of customizing curriculum for every student's needs is not viable today, but it will be for AI-powered machines.

Universal access for all students

Artificial intelligence tools can help make global classrooms available to all including those who speak different languages or who might have visual or hearing impairments. A presentation software can create subtitles in real time for what the teacher is saying. This also opens up possibilities for students who might not be able to attend school due to illness or who require learning at a different level or on a particular subject that isn't available in their own school. AI can help break down <u>silos</u> between schools and between traditional grade levels.

Tutoring and support outside the classroom

Ask any parent who has struggled to help their teenager with algebra, and they will be very excited about the potential of AI to support their children when they are struggling at home with homework or test preparations. Tutoring and studying programs are becoming more advanced thanks to artificial intelligence, and soon they will be more available and able to respond to a range of learning styles.

There are many more AI applications for education that are being developed including AI mentors for learners, further development of smart content and a new method of personal development for educators through virtual global conferences. Education might be a bit slower to the adoption of artificial intelligence and machine learning, but the changes are beginning and will continue.

〔Adapted from Bernard Marr, How Is AI Used In Education...
一部省略等がある〕

[問1]　本文中の A に入る適切な1語を書け。

[問2]　本文中の B に入るパラグラフの見出しとして最も適切なものを，次の①～④の中から1つ選び，その番号を書け。

① Teacher and AI collaboration

② Saving time and improving human capabilities

③ Automating admin tasks

④ Bridging gaps between schools and teachers

[問3]　本文中の下線部thatはどのようなことをさすか，日本語で具体的に書け。

[問4]　本文中の下線部silosが本文で表す意味に最も近い意味の語を，次の①～④の中から1つ選び，その番号を書け。

① diversities　② barriers　③ challenges　④ deficiencies

[問5]　本文の内容と一致するものを，次の①～④の中から1つ選び，その番号を書け。

① As AI can streamline administration tasks, it might be a future problem for teachers to secure more time to spend with each student.

② Educators have classified differentiated and individual learning as high priority for years.

③ AI-powered machines have already put personalized learning into practical use.

④ The adoption of artificial intelligence and machine learning is most advanced in education.

(☆☆☆◎◎◎◎)

【5】高等学校1年生を対象とした英語学習に関するある調査において，「英語があまり好きではない」・「英語が全く好きではない」と答えた生徒は4割を超えた。

このように答えた生徒たちが中学校または高等学校で英語を好きになるように，どのようなことを取り入れて，授業を行うか。あなたの考えを100語程度の英語で書け。

なお，短縮形(I'mやdon'tなど)は1語と数え，符号(, や？など)は語数に含めない。

(例) No, I'm not. 【3語】

(☆☆☆☆☆◎◎◎◎)

解答・解説

【中高共通】

【1】問1 A ③ B ② 問2 C ③ D ① E ②

問3 geothermal power, wind power, solar power から一つ 問4 ④

問5 ③

〈解説〉スクリプトは公開されていない。「日本のエネルギー事情について，ワークシートにメモを取りながら，英語の講義を聞いている」という状況設定で，放送は1回のみである。放送前に60秒間だけ，問題冊子に印刷された選択肢に目を通す時間が与えられている。例えば，問1と問2は数字の正確な聞き取りが求められていることに留意しておくとよいだろう。

【2】問1　番号…①　　正しい形…discussed　　問2　番号…④　　正しい形…inventions　　問3　番号…④　　正しい形…what　　問4　番号…③　　正しい形…or　　問5　番号…④　　正しい形…rains

〈解説〉問1　英文は「私たちは解決策が見つかるまでその問題について議論した」の意である。discussは他動詞であるため，前置詞のaboutは不要である。　問2　英文は「インターネットが，歴史上もっとも重要な電気関連の発明品であることに異論を唱える人はいないだろう」の意である。“one of～”を用いる際は続く名詞を複数形にする必要がある。問3　英文は「カナコが10年前(の姿)とどれくらい違うかを想像することはできないでしょう」の意である。先行詞を含んだ関係代名詞のwhatを用いた“what＋S＋be動詞”で「現在(過去)のSの姿・様子」のような意味になる。　問4　英文は「部屋を掃除した方がいい。そうしないとお母さんに怒られるよ」の意である。“had better”は命令文のような強い表現である。命令文と同様に，肯定的な内容を続ける場合はandで節を続けることで「そうすれば」の意味になり，否定的な内容が続く場合はorで節を続けることで「そうしないと(さもないと)」の意味になる。　問5　英文は「明日雨が降ったら私たちのソフトボールの試合は延期だ」の意である。時や条件を示す副詞節では動詞は現在形を用いることになっている。

【3】問1　①　　問2　C　　問3　X　西洋化すること　　Y　自国文化を維持すること(順不同)　　問4　②　　問5　③　　問6　④

〈解説〉問1　空欄を含んだ英文は「日本人は伝統を重んじるべきか，それとも新しい社会を(　　)ことを目指すべきか」の意であるため，invent「創造する」が適切。　問2　挿入する英文は「このことは，日本人も自分たちの歴史や文化の研究，保存そして復元のために膨大な労力を割いてきたことを意味している」の意である。第2パラグラフでは日本が欧米に追いつきたいと思っているという内容が書かれていることから，第2パラグラフにあるAとBは不適切である。また，挿入する英文が“This has meant”で始まっていることに着目すると，挿入する英文は前の英文を説明するような形になっていることがわかる。よって，直前に「日本人が西洋との違いを主張したいと思っていた」と述べているCが適切である。　問3　下線部の後の2文に着目すると，「日本人が，完全に西洋化され，自身の伝統との接点を失っているように見える人もいる。その一方で，日本人が，自分たちと他国の人たちが異なっていること，そして，他国の人たちが自分たちの言語や文化を理解できないことを主張することに，比類ないほど取りつかれたり関心を持っていたりするように見える人もいる」とある。これらを簡潔にまとめればよい。　問4　空欄を含んだ文は「しかしながら，日本に関する真実としては日本がこれらの(　　)である2つのこと，すなわち，西洋文化の吸収と西洋との違いを保護することを継続的に同時に行おうとしてきたことである」の意である。問3にあるとおり，西洋化することと自国の文化を守ることは対立するものであるから，opposing「対立する，正反対の」が適切。　問5　第3段落6文目より，③「外国人の中には，日本が西洋との違いを強調するために努力していることを見ずに，日本の西洋化に対する関心だけを考えがちな人もいる」が適切。　問6　第1段落で，明治時代以降，日本人がアイデンティティの問題に取りつかれてきたことが述べられていることから考えるとよい。

【4】問1　teachers　　問2　①　　問3　ある問題を把握するのに苦労していること　　問4　②　　問5　②

〈解説〉問1　空欄を含んだ文は「ほとんどの専門家が(　　)の重要な存在はかけがえのないものだと信じていても，教師の仕事や教育の最高の取り組みには多くの変化が生じるだろう」の意である。主節にある

「教師の仕事」に着目するとよい。　問2　当該パラグラフではAIに何度も言及しており，AIによって教育が大きく改善されることが述べられている。　問3　下線部を含んだ文は「AIがさらに洗練されていくにつれて，ある課題を理解するのに苦労していることを示す生徒の表情を機械が読み取り，それに応じて授業を修正することができるかもしれない」の意であり，thatの意味する内容は下線部を含んだ同じ文中にある。　問4　break down silos「(部署や組織間などの)壁を取り払う」。下線部直前の文に着目する。AIは，授業に参加できない生徒に加え，個々のレベルに応じた学習や自分の学校では学べない科目の学習を必要としている生徒たちに，教育の門戸を広げる可能性がある旨が述べられている。　問5　第3段落1文目より，②「教育者たちは何年もの間，差別化された個別の学習を優先事項として分類してきた」が適切。

【5】Experiencing the joy of learning English is important for such students. In my opinion, they will feel more confident and happy when they get a sense of achievement or share ideas with their classmates. Providing pair work or group work in class is a good way. By exchanging various ideas with others, they can enjoy discovering new things. Using ICT is also a big help, which will let them learn at their own pace. They can tackle their tasks at their own speed or repeat them as often as possible. I expect these types of learning will give them the joy of learning English. (104 words)

〈解説〉英語が好きではない生徒たちに対する授業実践を100語程度の英語で書くことが求められている。内容として絶対的な答えがあるわけではないが，学習指導要領や英語科教育法の理論に基づいた指導法などを踏まえた方が書きやすいかもしれない。解答例で挙げられている協働学習やICTの活用のほかにも，現実のコミュニケーションに即した(目的・場面・状況が整った)言語活動や，生徒の興味・関心に基づくトピックの導入なども挙げられるだろう。また，生徒に言語形式の正確さだけを求めるのではなく，意味内容や言語機能も評価するといったことも考えられる。ただし，目安となる語数が100語であるため，思いついた授業実践の方法を列挙するのではなく，具体的に説明できる方法に焦点を当て，ポイントを整理しながら論じたい。

2021年度　実施問題

【中高共通】

【1】はリスニングテストです。

【１】リスニング問題は[1]～[5]までの5問です。
状況と問いが問題冊子に書かれているので，今，読みなさい。
【状況と問いを読む時間(約60秒)→リスニング(1回しか読まれません)→解答】

状況
あなたはアメリカの大学で，SDGsについて，ワークシートにメモを取りながら，講義を聞いています。

ワークシート

What are the SDGs? → Sustainable Development Goals

SDGs: adopted by all UN Member states in 2015
a universal call to action
to end poverty, to protect the planet and（ 1 ）by 2030

The 17 SDGs are **integrated**.
Development must balance（ 2 ）sustainability.

Leave No One Behind
Designed to bring the world to several life-changing 'zeros'
0 zero
- Poverty
- Hunger
- AIDS
- （ 3 ）

Everyone is needed to reach these ambitious targets.
We need the creativity, knowhow, technology and financial resources from all of

society to achieve the SDGs.

Goal 1: End poverty in all its forms everywhere

In 2015, about ([A]) million people still lived on less than ([B]) a day; many lack food, clean drinking water and sanitation.

[C]	2010	2015	2018	2030
36 %	16 %	10 %	8.6 %	6 %

[1]～[3]について，ワークシート中の[1]～[3]にあてはまる最も適切なものを，①～④から1つずつ選び，その番号を書け。

[1] [1]

① to ascertain there are no wars and enough food for everyone

② to be certain that we have access to clean water

③ to ensure inclusive and equitable quality education

④ to make sure that everyone enjoys peace and prosperity

[2] [2]

① social, economic and educational

② social, educational and ecological

③ social, economic and environmental

④ social, environmental and educational

[3] [3]

① age discrimination

② gender discrimination

③ racial discrimination

④ religious discrimination

[4] ワークシート中の[A]～[C]にあてはまる最も適切なものを，次の①～④から1つずつ選び，その番号を書け。

A	B	C
① 736	① US$1.60	① 1900
② 756	② US$1.70	② 1950
③ 776	③ US$1.80	③ 1990
④ 796	④ US$1.90	④ 1995

[5] Goal 1についての講義内容から言えることとして最も適切なものを，次の①～④から1つ選び，その番号を書け。

① We will realize the goal earlier before the due date.

② The world is not on track to achieve the target.

③ The goal will be achieved as planned.

④ We have experienced the ups and downs of poverty rate.

(☆☆☆◎◎◎◎)

【2】次の[1]～[3]の会話文について，(　　)に入る最も適切なものを，①～④から1つずつ選び，その番号を書け。

[1]

A : I wish I were rich and could buy that latest model of computer!

B : If you (　　) that insane amount of money on your new bicycle, you would have enough money for two!

① hadn't spent　② haven't spent　③ couldn't spend

④ shouldn't spend

[2]

A : Mr. Smith, do you think the economy will recover next year?

B : Well, I am not very optimistic about that. Fewer people are buying new things, such as houses and cars, and that usually (　　) a worse economy in the future.

① acts on　② comes out　③ leads off　④ points to

[3]

A : No wonder Professor Grey received so many awards! I just came back from the conference where she spoke and her speech was incredible.

B：I agree. She (　　) herself among her peers through hard work and outstanding achievements.

① committed　② distinguished　③ enveloped
④ finalized

(☆☆☆◎◎◎◎)

【3】次の[1]～[4]の英文の(　　)に意味が通るように[　　]内の語を入れるとき，(①)，(②)に入る語の組み合わせとして最も適切なものを，1～4から1つずつ選び，その番号を書け。

[1] The songs written by the (　　)(①)(　　)(②)(　　).
[worth / to / composer / listening / are]

1 ① are ② to　2 ① are ② listening
3 ① to ② listening　4 ① listening ② composer

[2] The new machine that (　　)(①)(　　)(②)(　　) did not function properly.
[would / was / I / told / work]

1 ① told ② I　2 ① was ② would
3 ① work ② told　4 ① would ② told

[3] The research members focused mainly on the (　　)(①)(　　)(②)(　　) the economy.
[global / has / impact / warming / on]

1 ① impact ② warming　2 ① warming ② has
3 ① global ② has　4 ① global ② impact

[4] As soon as the rain stopped, the moon (　　)(①)(　　)(②)(　　) thick clouds.
[came / behind / the / out / from]

1 ① out ② behind　2 ① out ② from
3 ① from ② behind　4 ① from ② out

(☆☆◎◎◎◎)

【4】次の英文を読んで，あとの[1]～[5]に答えよ。

SEATTLE ― In Laurie Pearson's kindergarten classroom at Lake Forest Park Elementary, students stand at attention. Pearson knows the silence won't last long and that she needs to be quick with her instructions.

"Everyone must wash your hands," Pearson says, "because baby Claire will be here soon."

The 20 or so kindergartners are already well acquainted with Claire, a seven-month- old infant who visits the classroom regularly as part of the social and emotional learning program Roots of Empathy.

Roots of Empathy, first started in 1996 in Toronto and introduced into U.S. schools in 2007, aims to build more peaceful and caring societies by increasing the level of empathy in children. In the last six years, the program has spread to California, New York and other parts of Washington.

Some teachers at the school, including Pearson, say they were initially nervous about the safety of the babies in classrooms full of students.

"I thought they were crazy," Pearson said, "but it was just amazing to see the kids respond and light up."

Roots of Empathy instructor Marilyn Enloe visits the classroom 27 times over the course of the year and for nine of those visits baby Claire will be there as well with her mother, Jenny Fitzpatrick. It's Enloe's job to help students observe the baby's development and to label Claire's feelings.

The class then reflects on why Claire is either happy or sad and discusses how the children often have similar feelings.

At the heart of the program, which targets the students from kindergarten to 8th grade, is a mission to decrease aggressive behavior patterns at an early age and therefore curb bullying. Roughly 160,000 children miss school every day "due to fear of an attack or intimidation by other students," according to the National Education Association.

A recent study by the University of Virginia also found that the dropout rate was 29 percent above average in schools with high levels of teasing and bullying.

Kim Schonert-Reichl, a professor at the University of British Columbia, has studied the effects of Roots of Empathy and says that the program offers teachers a springboard to talk about emotions.

"It helps children learn to identify emotions, to become self aware and to develop relationship skills," Schonert-Reichl said.

A 2011 study in the publication Child Development looked at research involving 270,000 students — comparing those who participated in social and emotional learning programs, like Roots of Empathy, with those who had not.

Their findings showed that students who received the training not only increased in social and emotional skills but also had an 11 percentage point increase in standardized achievement test scores.

As for Jenny Fitzpatrick, Claire's mother, she says she was never worried about bringing her daughter into a classroom and that she enjoys watching the kindergartners'reactions.

"The tone of the room changes when Claire comes in," Fitzpatrick said, "and I think kids start to think about how it feels to be treated a certain way, because they don't like it when she gets upset." 〔Adapted from an article from PBS NewsHour, March 2013〕

[1] Why was Roots of Empathy established? Choose one statement from ① to ④.

① To spread its program in California and New York and other parts of the U.S.

② To lighten the burdens of teachers and improve the academic achievement of children.

③ To let children have compassion for others and build a society where people care about each other.

④ To adopt children in need and to reduce the number of abandoned babies.

[2] What are the students expected to do when a baby is in class? Choose

one statement from ① to ④.

① They talk about the baby's feelings after monitoring his or her growth and emotions.

② They care for the baby in class and keep the baby's feelings as stable as possible.

③ They try to soothe the baby when he or she is crying crazily.

④ The students ensure the safety of the baby and decrease his or her risk of injury.

[3] According to the passage, how does the program help reduce bullying? Answer in English concretely.

[4] Regarding the underlined part, what are the results of the study? Choose TWO appropriate statements from ① to ④.

① Students improved their relationship skills and the ability to care about the feelings of others.

② The level of empathy in teachers increased by observing how babies develop.

③ It showed there are some improvements in students' academic achievements.

④ The dropout rate decreased while the number of bullying incidents increased.

[5] Choose the appropriate title for this passage from ① to ④.

① Seattle fights for the negative influence of the modern educational system.

② Bringing babies to the classroom to teach empathy, prevent bullying.

③ Abandoned babies are adopted in local elementary schools and kindergartens.

④ Children can experience the empathy between a baby and her mother.

(☆☆◎◎◎◎)

【5】次の英文を読んで，あとの[1]～[3]に答えよ。

Dörnyei proposed that a learner's self-image as a second language speaker is partly based on actual experiences of the second language community and partly on imagination. The theory also recognized the impact that environmental conditions can have on motivation. There are three components to the *L2 Motivational Self System*:

1. *Ideal L2 Self.* 'If the person we would like to become speaks an L2, the "ideal L2 self" is a powerful motivator to learn the L2 because of the desire to reduce the discrepancy between our actual and ideal selves'. This component incorporates both integrative and instrumental aspirations relating to a desired end state, such as a better job. The ideal self also facilitates the self-regulation needed to succeed.
2. [A]. This 'concerns the attributes that one believes one ought to possess to meet expectations and to avoid possible negative outcomes'. Instrumentality is involved here but is preventive — directed at preventing negative outcomes (for example, performing poorly in an examination).
3. *L2 Learning Experience.* This refers to the 'executive motives related to the immediate learning environment and experience'. Important factors here are the impact of the teacher, the curriculum, the peer group, and the experience of success. This component, therefore, incorporates insights from self-determination and attribution theories.

Dörnyei claimed that the results of a number of early studies provided 'solid confirmation' of the L2 Motivational Self System. He noted that the Ideal L2 Self was closely related to integrativeness, but that it explained a higher percentage of variance in measures of learners' intended effort. The Ideal L2 Self also correlated with measures of promotional instrumentality while the [A] correlated with measures of preventive instrumentality, as predicted by the theory.

Later studies, however, have not always supported the important role the theory attaches to the Ideal L2 Self. Lamb (2012) investigated the motivation of adolescent Indonesian learners in three contexts — a metropolitan city, a provincial city, and a rural district in Indonesia. Using a questionnaire based on Dörnyei's own research, he was unable to obtain a satisfactory measure of the [A]. Of the other two components, it was L2 Learning Experience rather than the Ideal L2 Self that was found to be of greater importance in motivating the learners. Interestingly, the Ideal L2 Self was found to contribute significantly to learning in the metropolitan context (but less so than L2 Learning Experience), but did not contribute at all in the provincial and rural contexts.

The L2 Motivational Self System has been shown to work well with learners in Hungary and in a number of other foreign language contexts (for example, Japan and Chile), but Lamb's study suggests that [X]. Perhaps the drive to develop a theory of L2 motivation that is applicable to every context is mistaken as separate theories may be needed to take account of contextual differences.

〔Adapted from Rod Ellis, Understanding Second Language Acquisition, Oxford University Press, 2015〕

※注　L2…the second language

[1] This is the simple table of Dörnyei's L2 Motivational Self System. Answer the following questions.

Dörnyei's L2 Motivational Self System

Component's name		Example
1	Ideal L2 Self	[a]
2	[A]	I don't like English very much. But it's too embarrassing if I fail the exam next week.
3	L2 Learning Experience	[b]

(1) Choose one appropriate component's name for [A] from ① to ④.

① Language Engagement　② Confidence in the Future

③ Ought-to Self　④ Curriculum Focus

(2) Choose an appropriate example from ① to ④ for each blank [a], [b].

① I'm studying English very hard because I want to become a pilot. I want to play an important role in a globalized world.

② I got low scores on my last English test. My parents were disappointed very much. I don't want to disappoint them again.

③ I gave an English speech for the first time in class. I was very nervous at first, but my classmates enjoyed my speech a lot!

④ I want to enter university to study English because it is an international language. I want to use English in my future job.

[2] Choose one appropriate statement which is suitable for [X] from ① to ④.

① the theory does not apply to all learning contexts

② all learners hope to improve their English skills

③ teachers should not force students to have any motivation

④ a questionnaire based on a research study was used for the theory

[3] Dörnyei recently wrote his view on the L2 Learning Experience as below. Read the passage and answer the following question.

> There is no doubt that the refinement/reconceptualization of the L2 Learning Experience component of the L2 Motivational Self System is a timely task. The challenge of this endeavor is to find an appropriate theoretical framework within which the notion of learning experience can be interpreted. Tapping into the domain of engagement in educational psychology might be a fruitful way forward in this respect, as student engagement offers a well-defined and sufficiently specific conceptual area that can be customized for use in L2 motivation research. Accordingly, I have proposed a definition of the L2 Learning Experience as the perceived quality of the learners' engagement with various aspects of the language learning process. Besides offering a theoretical base, the adoption of an engagement-centered approach may

also be beneficial for allowing researchers to draw on the relevant measurement resources developed in educational psychology.

〔Adapted from Zoltán Dörnyei, Towards a better understanding of the L2 Learning Experience, the Cinderella of the L2 Motivational Self System, SSLLT, 2019〕

Question:
Choose one statement from ① to ④ which would be consistent with the author's idea.

① Focusing on future student aspirations may be beneficial for researchers to develop an appropriate measurement in educational psychology.

② We should focus on developing new learner identities that can lead to the development of possible future L2 selves.

③ Understanding concrete aspects of future student aspirations could contribute to the relevant measurement resources of L2 Learning Experience.

④ To set and focus on a theoretical framework of learners' experience could be beneficial for promoting the measurement resources of L2 learning motivation.

(☆☆☆◎◎◎◎)

【６】次の意見に対するあなたの考えを，100語程度の英文で書け。
ただし，賛成か反対かの立場を明らかにするとともに，そのように考える理由を2つ挙げること。
なお，短縮形(I'mやdon'tなど)は1語と数え，符号(, や ? など)は語数に含めない。
(例) No, I'm not. 【3語】

Even with the increasing accuracy of machine translation, students at junior and senior high schools still need to learn a foreign language as a compulsory subject.

(☆☆☆☆◎◎◎◎)

解答・解説

【中高共通】

【1】(1) ④ (2) ③ (3) ② (4) A ① B ④ C ③ (5) ②

〈解説〉スクリプトは非公開である。「SDGsについてアメリカの大学で講義を受けている」という状況設定である。放送は1回のみだが，設問，選択肢が冊子に印刷されており，60秒間だけ目を通す時間が与えられている。講義の長さは不明であるが，かなりの情報を事前に得た状態で音声を聞くことができ，取り組みやすい。聞き取るべきところ，聞き流してもよいところをざっと把握することが大切となる。なお，SDGs(Sustainable Development Goals：持続可能な開発目標)は，2015年9月の国連サミットにおいて採択された，2030年までに持続可能でよりよい世界を目指す17の国際目標のこと。SDGsは「経済・社会・環境の3つの側面を含み，「誰一人取り残さない」持続可能で多様性と包摂性のある社会の実現を目指している。

【2】(1) ① (2) ④ (3) ②

〈解説〉(1) 仮定法過去完了の文。空所を含む文は，「あなたが正気ではない額のお金を新しい自転車に費やしていなければ，2つ買う十分なお金があっただろうに」の意味となる。 (2) point to ～「～の傾向を示す，～を暗示する」。空所を含む文は，「家，車などの新しいものを買う人はより少なくなっており，通常こうしたことは，将来の景気悪化の傾向を示す」の意味となる。　(3)　distinguish oneself「名をあげる，功を立てる」。空所を含む文は，「彼女は多大な努力と優れた功績で同僚の中で頭角を現した」の意味となる。

【3】(1)　2　　(2)　2　　(3)　3　　(4)　1

〈解説〉(1)　be worth ～ing「～する価値がある」。整序すると，The songs written by the composer are worth listening to.となる。　(2)　関係代名詞の後に，I was toldが挿入された形。整序すると，The new machine that I was told would work did not function properly.となる。「作動すると私が言われた新しい機械は，正常に動かなかった」。　(3)　has an impact on ～「～に影響を与える」。整序すると，The research members focused mainly on the impact global warming has on the economy.「研究メンバーは，地球温暖化が経済に与える影響に主として焦点を合わせた」。

(4)　from behind ～「～の後ろから」。整序すると，As soon as the rain stopped, the moon came out from behind the thick clouds.となる。

【4】(1)　③　　(2)　①　　(3)　By decreasing aggressive behavior patterns at an early age.　　(4)　①，③　　(5)　②

〈解説〉(1)　設問は「Roots of Empathyはなぜ開設されたのか」。第4段落1文目の記述が，③「子どもたちに他人への思いやりの気持ちを持たせ，人々がお互いを気づかう社会を作らせるため」と合致する。

(2)　設問は「赤ちゃんが教室にいるとき，生徒たちは何をすることになっているか」。第7段落2文目と第8段落の記述が，①「赤ちゃんの成長と喜怒哀楽を観察した後，赤ちゃんの感情について話をする」と合致する。　(3)　設問は「そのプログラムはいじめを減らすのにどのように役立っているか。具体的に英語で答えよ」。第9段落の1文目後半で，「幼いときに攻撃的な行動様式を減らすことによって」いじめを抑えると述べている。　(4)　設問は，「Child Developmentという出版物の2011年の研究結果は何か」。第14段落でnot only ～ but also …という形で2つの成果，すなわち「社会的・感情的スキルの向上」と「標準入学検定試験のスコアが11%上がった」と述べている。よって，①「生徒は人間関係能力と他人の感情を気づかう能力を向上させた」と③「生徒の学業成績に改善があることが示された」が適切。 (5) 本文は，Roots of Empathyのねらい，手法，その成果について書かれていることから，タイトルとして②の「共感することを教え，いじめを防止するため，赤ちゃんを教室に連れてくること」が適切。

【5】(1) ③ (2) a ① b ③ (2) ① (3) ④

〈解説〉言語学者Zoltán Dörnyei(ゾルタン・ドルニェイ)が提唱するL2 Motivation Self System(L2[＝第2言語]動機づけ自己システム)についての記述である。 (1) 空所Aがどのような学習者かは，第1段落2項の1文目「期待に応えたり，起こり得るネガティブな結果を避けたりするため，自分がそうあるべきだと信じる特質」に注目する。他者が自分に期待している自己，そうならなければいけない自己のことであるから，③のOught-to Self「義務自己」が適切。 (2) a 第1段落1項参照。Ideal L2 Self「L2理想自己」とは，第2言語を使って将来どのような自分になりたいかという理想の自己像で，現実の自分と理想の自己の差を埋める願望が第2言語を学ぶ動機づけ要因となる。よって，①の「パイロットになりたいのでとても一生懸命に英語を勉強している。グローバル化した世界で重要な役割を果たしたい」が適切。 b 第1段落3項参照。L2 Learning experience「L2学習経験」は，直接的な学習環境や経験に関わる動機を指し，要因として教師の影響，カリキュラム，仲間，成功体験などが挙げられる。よって，③「初めて授業で英語のスピーチをした。最初はとても緊張したが，クラスメートは私のスピーチをとても楽しんでくれた」が適切。 (2) 第3段落に，2012年にLambがインドネシアの成人学習者(大都市，地方都市，農村地域)を対象に行った研究では，「『L2理想自己』より『L2学習経験』が動機づけとして重要であった。また『L2理想自己』は大都市では動機づけにかなり関与したが，地方都市や農村地域では全くそうではなかった」

と述べられている。よって，Lambの研究は，①「その理論が全ての学習状況にあてはまるのではないことを示している」が適切。　(3)　問題文はDörnyeiが最近示したL2学習経験についての英文。L2動機づけ自己システムの構成要素である学習経験を改良，再概念化することはタイムリーな課題であり，それは学習経験の考え方を解釈する適切な理論上の枠組みを見つけることだとしている。よって，④の「学習経験の理論上の枠組みを定め焦点を当てることは，L2学習の動機づけを測る手段を促進するのに有益だろう」が適切。

【６】I agree with the idea that students should learn a foreign language as a compulsory subject. First, if they have a good command of a foreign language, it is easier to communicate with other people, making a conversation more natural. However, with machine translation, they would have unnatural pauses, and would not have real-life communication. Second, they can broaden their horizons. Through language learning, they can learn about the essential parts of different cultures such as history, lifestyle, and food. This experience will open up future possibilities for students. For those reasons, I think learning a foreign language should be a requirement. (102 words)

〈解説〉「機械翻訳の正確性が高まっているが，中学生や高校生は必修科目として英語を学ばなければならない」という意見に対して，「2つの理由を挙げ自分の意見を述べよ」という設問。機械翻訳のデメリットや英語を学ぶことのメリットを挙げる。解答例では，言語学習により「容易にコミュニケーションがとれ，視野を広げられること」を理由として挙げている。どんなに優れた翻訳機でも限界がある。例えば翻訳機が，人間の心の機微に触れることは不可能であろう。人間関係を築いていく上でも言葉は欠かせない。翻訳機を作っているのは人間で，誤訳をチェックできるのも人間しかいない。

2020年度　実施問題

【中高共通】

【1】はリスニングテストです。放送の指示に従ってください。

【1】放送を聞いて，次の〔Part 1〕～〔Part 3〕に答えよ。

〔Part 1〕

No.1

(A) 10:00

(B) 10:20

(C) 11:00

(D) 12:30

No.2

(A) A bed.

(B) A bookshelf.

(C) A TV.

(D) A picture.

No.3

(A) 4,000 yen in cash.

(B) 4,000 yen by credit card.

(C) 2,000 yen in cash.

(D) 2,000 yen by credit card.

No.4

(A) Go to a movie with Bill.

(B) Attend a conference.

(C) Stay home.

(D) Call the shop to change the schedule.

No.5

(A) The room is too small for her.

(B) The available room costs too much.

(C) All the rooms in the hotel are booked on that day.

(D) The available room is a smoking room.

No.6

(A) Buy the leather jacket.

(B) Take the leather jacket to the second-hand shop.

(C) Ask her friend how to sell the leather jacket.

(D) Sell the leather jacket online instead of him.

〔Part 2〕

No.1 The woman wanted to speak with Professor Smith because...

(A) she had some questions about grammar.

(B) she wanted to thank him for her grade.

(C) she wanted to know the topic of her next essay.

(D) she wanted to improve her writing skills.

No.2 The woman wrote the essay...

(A) the night before the deadline.

(B) last night.

(C) several days before the deadline.

(D) earlier than the professor expected.

No.3 Professor Smith advised the woman...

(A) to study the format of the essay.

(B) to finish her paper earlier.

(C) to ask someone to check the grammar.

(D) to go to a seminar on studying English.

No.4 To take a seminar at the Study Support Center, she has to ...

(A) apply for admission in advance.

(B) go there today.

(C) bring her student ID.

(D) pay for it.

〔Part 3〕

No.1 How has the Japanese dietary habit changed in the last 50 years?

No.2 What enabled us to get food from foreign countries?

No.3 What might prevent us from importing food from other countries?

No.4 What is good about Japanese dietary patterns?

No.5 What are three things that hit the highest records as exports?

(☆☆◎◎◎◎)

【2】次の英文は *"That Doesn't Mean What You Think It Means"* という本のIntroductionとContentsの一部である。英文を読み，あとの[問1]～[問7]に答えよ。

This book is about words that aren't doing what they want to do because we're not letting them. It's really a word liberation book — letting those words be the words they were meant to be.

It's about how we misuse the English language and use the wrong words that don't mean what we think they mean. It's not only about mistakes, but about correcting those mistakes, and discussing if they're even mistakes at all. In short, it's about the 150 most commonly confused, abused, questioned, and misused words and phrases in the English language, according to surveys, dictionaries like *Merriam-Webster's*, and top word experts like Steven Pinker and Bryan Garner.

These are the words that educated people most often misuse, are embarrassed about misusing, and want to use correctly. Some of them are what are sometimes called ⓐ<u>bubble words</u> — words of which you are sure you know the meaning, but you actually don't.

Before we begin, we want to say emphatically that we're not absolute, antiquarian-style prescriptivists who speak in funny quasi-British accents, stare over our glasses, and insist on old definitions of words and refuse to acknowledge changes in English. [A], we've made mistakes ourselves — and it would be more than hypocritical to criticize other people for doing what we've done. [B], the latest *Oxford English Dictionary* lists 171,476 words in current usage. That's a myriad, plethora, staggering number, enormity, or a real load of words. [C], many of them are words most of us don't use, but the point is that it's impossible for anyone to be fully conversant with all the words in English, or even the most common ones, and use each one of them correctly. We found examples of mistaken usage from national newspapers such as *The New York Times* and *Washington Post*, from eminent authors and magazines, as well as from blogs, Wikipedia, newscasts, and popular magazines. [D], yeah, we ALL make mistakes.

More to the point, words change, times change, and meanings change, and we're not going to halt the flow of time. We're not going to be struthious (resembling an ostrich) and ⓑstick our heads in the sand. But who gets to decide what's right and wrong? France has a national academy, the Académie française, that rules on what's good French and what's not. English is more [　あ　]: we all decide. We yell, argue, talk, and write, and eventually some sort of consensus is reached; and then, of course, things change once move. Naturally, in different parts of the English-speaking world, different words are sometimes considered correct. You want to "prepone" a meeting? You don't say that in the United States, but it's considered correct by many in India. This book is about what's generally considered correct right now by educated people in the generally accepted standard dialect of North America called GA (General American). We try to tack our way through the stormy seas of linguistic confusion and arrive at reasonable conclusions of what to say and what not to say. [E]

Like it or not, words can be dangerous, humiliating, and anger inducing. People can get absolutely infuriated over words. Just recently in an online argument over politics, a writer criticized someone over the "tenants of his beliefs." The guy fired back and ridiculed the writer for choosing the wrong word — it should have been "tenets," and instead of talking about the criticism (in our opinion justified), the internet was buzzing with talk about the "dumb" guy (that's the most polite pejorative, you can imagine the others) who couldn't write English correctly. It was unfair, and detracted from an important debate, but ⓒit happened. And that's also why we wrote this book, so it doesn't happen to you; or in a lesser way, so people don't simply look at you quizzically when you use the wrong word. Who wants to sound like they don't know what they're talking about? (Hint: rhetorical question.)

But most of all, words are fun. It's fascinating to delve into the complicated histories of words and see how they came to mean what they do. As Steve Martin said," Some people have a way with words, and other people ...oh, uh, not have way." This book is for all of us, who at least occasionally, uh, "not have way" with words.

historic / historical

"It was an historical day on Wall Street, the biggest intraday drop ever!"

— FOX BUSINESS NETWORK ANCHOR

The example above is technically correct, but that's pushing it. *Every* past day is a (①) day. But only a few days are (②). (③) merely means "based in history," so anything that happened in the past is (③) and not necessarily news. Yesterday when I ate a chicken salad sandwich on rye bread — that was (③). (④) means "significant or famous in history," or "having a long history." Yesterday when I ate that chicken salad sandwich — no, that wasn't (④). A huge drop in the stock market, on the other hand, is big news, and that is (⑤). We're sure the Fox anchor wasn't trying to say it was just another day on the Street with the biggest intraday drop ever — she was talking about a big down day that should go down in history. This distinction between *historic* and *historical* is interesting because it's recent. In Shakespeare's day, you could easily use *historical* to mean *historic* and vice versa without arousing attention.

〔Ross Petras and Kathryn Petras, 2018. *That Doesn't Mean What You Think It Means*, TEN SPEED PRESS. 一部編集等あり〕

[問1]　下線部ⓐはどのようなものか，日本語で説明せよ。

[問2]　本文中の［ A ］～［ D ］に入る最も適切な語(句)を，次の(ア)～(エ)からそれぞれ1つ選び，その記号を書け。ただし，すべての記号を使用すること。

(ア)　True　　(イ)　For one thing　　(ウ)　And after all　　(エ)　So

[問3]　下線部ⓑの意味を表す最も適切なものを，次の(ア)～(エ)から1つ選び，その記号を書け。

(ア)　argue with other people about it
(イ)　take the truth for granted
(ウ)　pretend to know the truth
(エ)　ignore the things happening around us

[問4]　本文中の[　あ　]に入る最も適切な語を，次の(ア)～(エ)から1つ選び，その記号を書け。

(ア)　authoritative　　(イ)　democratic　　(ウ)　decisive
(エ)　conclusive

[問5]　本文中の［ E ］に，意味の通った文章となるように次の(ア)～(エ)の文を並べかえて入れると，どのような順番になるか。その記号を書け。

(ア)　Most of all, it's designed to give you some "word armor" in speaking and writing.
(イ)　It's designed to be fun.
(ウ)　We also throw in a little word history and etymology.
(エ)　But it's also designed to educate.

[問6]　次の英文は下線部ⓒが指している内容である。(　a　)，(　b　)に入る適切な一語を，下線部ⓒのある段落の中から抜き出し

てそれぞれ書け。

This "it" refers to the situation where internet commenters criticized a writer's (a) rather than the writer's (b).

[問7] 本文中の(①)~(⑤)に入る最も適切な語を，次の(ア)，(イ)からそれぞれ1つ選び，その記号を書け。ただし，文頭にくる場合も小文字としている。

(ア) historic (イ) historical

(☆☆☆☆◎◎◎◎)

【3】下の(1)~(7)の英文には，それぞれ誤りがある。次の例にならって誤りをすべて直して書け。ただし，できるだけ元の英文を生かすこと。

(例) 彼女はお母さんに似ている。
She <u>is resembling</u> her mother.
resembles

(1) 私はレストランにスマートフォンを忘れてきたことに気付きませんでした。

I didn't realize that I left my smartphone at the restaurant.

(2) 私達は，その問題について何度も話し合いました。

We discussed about the problem many times.

(3) 彼が選挙で勝つ可能性はほとんどない。

There is few possibility that he will win the next election.

(4) 来週の火曜日までに書類を提出してください。

Please submit the documents until next Tuesday.

(5) 君たちはそれぞれ自分の昼食を持っていかなければならない。

Each of you have to bring your own lunch.

(6) 私はそんなに早く起きることに慣れていない。

I'm not used to get up so early.

(7) もしもっとお金があれば，海外旅行に行くのに。

If I have more money, I would travel abroad.

(☆☆◎◎◎◎)

【中学校】

【１】次の英文を読み，あとの[問1]～[問5]に答えよ。

The tale of tea-ceremony master Sen no Rikyū and the morning glories is well known. When Toyotomi Hideyoshi came to see Rikyū's famous garden of morning glories, he was (　①　) and angered to find that Rikyū had plucked every flower in the garden before his arrival. However, upon entering Rikyū's tea-ceremony room, Hideyoshi saw that a single morning glory bloom had been arranged in the *tokonoma* alcove, and this was more than enough to satisfy him.

This story is a good illustration of Rikyū's philosophy of beauty. A garden full of morning glories in bloom is, of course, an appealing scene in its own right. But Rikyū sacrificed that beauty to concentrate it all into a single point in the *tokonoma*. To heighten the impact of a single flower's beauty, all the other flowers are unnecessary — in fact, they only get in the way. The excision of unnecessary and unwanted elements is what allows Rikyū's aesthetics to take form.

However, picking all the flowers in the garden was not simply about eliminating the unnecessary. The bare garden played an important role in forming the aesthetic world Hideyoshi entered that day. The high expectations he brought with him were dashed when he saw the empty garden. He surely still felt that disappointment as he entered the tea-ceremony room, and coming face-to-face with the flower in the *tokonoma* in that state was a much greater shock than simply seeing a single flower with no particular meaning would have been. The deeper his initial dissatisfaction, the bigger the surprise, and the more powerful the impression left. This, we may be sure, was all part of Rikyū's plan.

The flower in the tea-ceremony room, (　②　) by the absence of flowers in the garden: to create an aesthetic world like this in a painting, simply placing a flower at the center of the tableau would not be enough. The composition would need a flower on one side and, on the other side, empty space — exactly the kind of space created by the margins in Japanese ink wash painting.

The word *margin* here corresponds to *yohaku* in Japanese. This word is difficult to translate into English or French, but literally means "leftover blank." In Western oil painting, be it landscape or still life, the entire canvas is expected to be covered in paint, corner to corner: a bare patch ③【it / painted / on / as / with / would / be / viewed / nothing / an incomplete section】. But in a Japanese work like Hasegawa Tōhaku's *Pine Trees*, between the stands of dark pines and the stands of pines so light they seem to be fading away, there is a space containing nothing at all. It is this space that gives the painting its mystical depth; the atmosphere of the painting seems to come from the empty space itself.

Even in the most dazzling, (④) works of Japanese art, however, we can detect a strong tendency to exclude everything outside the central motif. Consider the well-known *Irises* by Ogata Kōrin. A Western artist painting irises blooming by a river would seek to recreate the scene in its entirety: the surface of the pond, the riverbank, the meadow, probably even the clouds in the sky. I have even been asked by a Westerner exactly where these irises are supposed to be blooming. But just as Rikyū cleared his garden of flowers, Kōrin has eliminated all peripheral elements from his painting and replaced them with a gorgeous field of gold. This gold field is both a way of covering up unnecessary elements and a background in and of itself.

Even today, gold screens are often arranged at wedding receptions and other celebrations in Japan. But these screens are always plain gold. When I attended a party at the Japanese Embassy in Seoul late last year, a gold screen had been erected near the entrance, and the ambassador stood before this to welcome guests as they arrived. A Korean friend I was with remarked at how Japanese the scene was. My curiosity aroused, I asked what my friend meant, and learned that, while gold screens are often deployed at Korean celebrations, in Korea the screen will always have a vivid fortuitous motif on it as well: a pine tree, perhaps, or a crane. To my friend, ⑤ a plain gold screen seemed to be lacking something, even to have a melancholy, lonely air. One nation's melancholy, however, is another's simplicity. Look closely at a field of plain gold, and the Japanese aesthetic consciousness begins to come into view.

〔THE JAPANESE SENSE OF BEAUTY　一部編集等あり〕

[問1]　本文中の(　①　), (　②　), (　④　)に入る最も適切な語を, 次から選び, 必要であれば形を変えて書け。

delight　　highlight　　obscure　　florid　　dismay　　plain

[問2]　下線部③【　　】内の語句を本文の流れに合うように正しく並べかえよ。

[問3]　本文の内容について, 次の(1), (2)の質問に対する答えを, それぞれ日本語で書け。

(1)　What effects did Rikyū produce by removing all the flowers in the garden?

(2)　What are the roles of the gold field in "*Irises*" ?

[問4]　下線部⑤について, なぜ筆者の友人はそう思ったのか, 日本語で書け。

[問5]　この本文のタイトルとして最も適切なものを, 次の(ア)～(エ)から1つ選び, 記号で書け。

(ア)　The Aesthetics of the Margin

(イ)　The Contrasting Shade of Paintings

(ウ)　The Transient Beauty of Art

(エ)　The Magnificence of Japanese Art

(☆☆◎◎◎◎)

【2】次の資料は, 平成31年4月に実施された全国学力・学習状況調査(英語)の「書くこと」の領域に出題された調査問題である。

生徒がこの問題に解答するためには, どのような力が必要だと考えるか。また, その力を育成するため, あなたは, 授業においてどのような実践を行うか。

必要だと考える力を2つ挙げ，それぞれの力を育成するため，授業でどのような実践を行うか英文で書け。

なお，語数は120語から150語とすることとし，語数を記入すること。

資料

> [10] 海外のある町が，外国人旅行客にも分かりやすいタウン・ガイドを作成するために，「学校」を表す2つのピクトグラム(案内用図記号)のうち，どちらがよいかウェブサイトで意見を募集しています。どちらかの案を選び，2つの案について触れながら，あなたの考えを理由とともに25語以上の英語で書きなさい。
>
> 【A】
>
> 
>
> 【B】
>
> 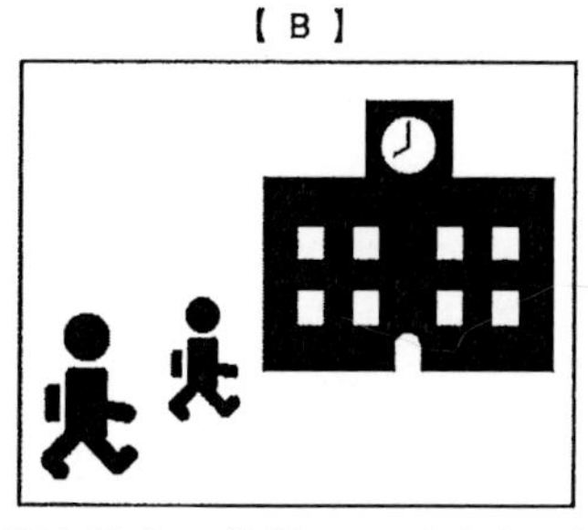
>
> ※　短縮形(I'mやdon'tなど)は1語と数え，符号(, や？など)は語数に含めません。
>
> (例) No, I'm not. 【3語】

(☆☆☆◎◎◎◎)

【高等学校】

【1】次の英文を読み，あとの[問1]～[問8]に答えよ.

A veteran police dog handler and his toy poodle — a rather unusual breed for a police dog — have been busy lately, not only at crime scenes or searching for missing persons, but also with community outreach. The message from handler Hirofusa Suzuki to parents: Don't give up on your children's dreams or limit their career choices based on preconceived notions or prejudice. There should be many ways for them to live their lives by maximizing their talent and potential — just like he never gave up on his toy poodle, Anzu.

At a lecture last month in Ibaraki Prefecture, Suzuki said he hopes people learn from the success story of his once abandoned pooch now excelling as a police dog. This lecture was organized as part of the Hitachinaka Municipal Government's family education classes, targeting parents of local elementary school students. Suzuki said, "(①) being caught up in stereotypes, like small dogs should live their lives as pets, we ought to help maximize their potential. If we become aware of their potential, it is important for us to prepare an (②) where they can blossom. This notion of not stereotyping also applies to people."

The 4-year-old Anzu has been working with big dogs on police activities, developing her abilities since Suzuki adopted her when she was 3 months old. Anzu was saved by Suzuki when she ⓐ[be / put / was / to / down / about]. Her owner had abandoned her because she barked at night. The dog appeared to have been abused because she was really (③) of people, especially women, Suzuki said, noting her healing process started with building a trusting relationship with his family, including other dogs.

Suzuki, 66, lives with Anzu and some German shepherds, also police dogs, in the village of Tokai. He has been involved in training police dogs for about 30 years. While he was training the other dogs to track footprints, Anzu showed an interest in the exercise. Anzu also honed her sense of smell; she began digging up the ground and sniffing around by watching and learning from the behavior of the German shepherds, Suzuki said. "ⓑShe began behaving [ア] [イ] she were a German shepherd. So probably, it is more like my dogs, rather than myself, that made Anzu into a police dog," he said.

"What I would like to underscore is the importance of environment. It is probably the same for your children, too. There are many ways for them to live their lives," Suzuki said, arguing that like dogs, children benefit from a variety of stimuli.

During a trial program by the Ibaraki Prefectural Police to expand the scope of police dog recruitment to all breeds, Anzu passed the test on her first try and was commissioned as a police dog in January 2016. There are two kinds of police dogs in Japan — those that are kept and trained by police, and those that are managed by civilians. The latter are called commissioned police dogs and are ready to be dispatched to crime scenes when (④). The Ibaraki Prefectural Force relies exclusively on civilian-owned dogs, according to Suzuki and the police website. Anzu was mobilized last year for around 10 cases, including searches for missing persons and finding evidence at crime scenes.

Since fewer households keep big dogs these days, the trend of employing small and medium-size canines as police dogs will increase, Suzuki said, noting a division of labor based on size and breed characteristics can be (⑤) in investigations. Small dogs' advantages include being good at finding small objects large dogs tend to overlook, investigating in public spaces without drawing attention and fitting into narrow spaces. Anzu has ⓒ[felt / been / presence / her / making] in searches for evidence and missing persons by playing on her strengths and characteristics, according to Suzuki.

Mari Takebayashi, a mother of a fifth-grader who attended the lecture, said she found ⓓsomething important in common between caring for and training dogs and raising and educating children: finding their hidden talents and trying not to be judgmental about their strengths and weaknesses.

〔*THE JAPAN TIMES March 15, 2017* 一部編集等あり〕

[問1] 本文中の(①)に入る最も適切な語句を，次の(ア)～(エ)から1つ選び，その記号を書け。

(ア) Instead of　(イ) By means of　(ウ) Owing to

(エ) In addition to

[問2]　本文中の(　②　)に入る最も適切な一語を，本文中から抜き出して書け。

[問3]　下線部ⓐ，ⓒについて，[　　]内の語を本文の流れに合うように正しく並べかえよ。

[問4]　本文中の(　③　)，(　④　)に入る最も適切な語の組み合わせを，次の(ア)～(エ)から1つ選び，その記号を書け。

(ア)　③　frightening　　④　needing

(イ)　③　frightened　　④　needed

(ウ)　③　frightening　　④　needed

(エ)　③　frightened　　④　needing

[問5]　下線部ⓑについて，文意が通じるように[　ア　]，[　イ　]に入る最も適切な語をそれぞれ書け。

[問6]　本文中の(　⑤　)に入る最も適切な語を，次の(ア)～(エ)から1つ選び，その記号を書け。

(ア)　vague　　(イ)　objective　　(ウ)　effective　　(エ)　impractical

[問7]　下線部ⓓは，どのようなことか。40字程度の日本語で具体的に書け。

[問8]　本文の内容と一致するものを，次の(ア)～(エ)から1つ選び，その記号を書け。

(ア)　Before Anzu was adopted by Suzuki, she had already started to be trained as a police dog.

(イ)　Suzuki said that it was not so much his dogs as his training that made Anzu a police dog.

(ウ)　Anzu took a trial program test to work as a police dog over and over, and finally she passed it.

(エ)　Small police dogs are good at finding small things large police dogs usually fail to notice.

(☆☆◎◎◎◎)

【2】現行の高等学校学習指導要領「外国語」における「第2款　各科目　第2　コミュニケーション英語Ⅰ　2　内容」の中に「聞いたり読んだりしたこと，学んだことや経験したことに基づき，情報や考えなどについて，話し合ったり意見の交換をしたりする。」という項目がある。

この内容を踏まえて，あなたならどのような授業を行うか。既に与えられている英文に続いて，120語程度の英文で書け。なお，語数を記入すること。

Students have just learned about environmental issues in the English Communication Ⅰ class. They have already learned about this issue in the Contemporary Society class.

Based on what they have already learned, I would like...

(☆☆☆☆◎◎◎◎)

解答・解説

【中高共通】

【1】Part 1　No.1　(C)　No.2　(D)　No.3　(C)　No.4　(A)　No.5　(B)　No.6　(C)　Part 2　No.1　(D)　No.2　(A)　No.3　(B)　No.4　(C)　Part 3　No.1　People have preferred western dishes (to traditional Japanese dishes).　No.2　The progress of means of transportation and methods of food preservation.　No.3　Unseasonal weather. / Troubles with transportation.　No.4　Nutritional balance.　No.5　Beef, green tea, and rice.

〈解説〉本自治体では，リスニングスクリプトが公開されていない。Part 1とPart 2は選択問題である。Part 1では設問が与えられていないため，リスニング中に単語レベルの簡単なメモをとるとよい。時刻や値段，今後の予定など身近な場面での話だと想定される。Part 2では，設問に続く内容を答えるという形式であるため，事前に聞き取りに必要な情報を明確にしておくとよい。Part 3は英問英答であるが，大まかな流れを理解できれば解答できる問題が多いと考えられる。ただし，No. 5のように具体的な名詞など詳細な情報を書かせる問題もあるため，事前に設問の内容を確認しておくとよい。

【2】問1　自分では意味がわかっていると確信しているが，実は意味がわかっていない語。　問2　A　(イ)　　B　(ウ)　　C　(ア)　D　(エ)　　問3　(エ)　　問4　(イ)　　問5　(ウ)→(イ)→(エ)→(ア)　問6　a　English　　b　argument / opinion　　問7　①　(イ)　②　(ア)　　③　(イ)　　④　(ア)　　⑤　(ア)

〈解説〉問1　bubble wordsの意味は，下線部後のダッシュ (—) に続く部分を訳出すればよい。ダッシュは前の語句に情報を追加したりするときなどに用いられる。　問2　設問は文と文をつなぐ副詞の意味を問うものである。　A　空欄の前に，私たちは完全でなく，規範主義者でもないなどの内容があり，空欄の後では私たち自身間違いをしてきたとある。この空欄の後の部分はその前の主張をサポートする具体的な根拠であるため，空欄にはFor one thing「その一例として」が入る。　B　空欄の後で，*Oxford English Dictionary*が171,476語という非常に多くの語を収録していることを示しており，すべてを正しく使用することは困難であると続く。そのため，空欄には私たちが誤りをすることが必然であることを強調するAnd after all「そしてなんといっても，結局のところ」が入る。　C　空欄の後に「それらの多くは私たちの多くが使用しない単語である」とあるが，これはその前にある非常に多くの英単語が存在するということのTrue「事実」をさらに説明するためのものである。　D　空欄の前では，全国紙，著名な作家，雑誌などでも誤用が見られ，その後，私たちはみな誤りを犯すとある。したがって，空欄には2文をつなぐ順接の接続詞であるSo「そのため」が入る。　問3　第5段落1文目に単語，時代，意味は変わり，時間の流れを止めることはないとある。下線部ⓑの意味する内容は，そのような変わりゆく状況下でしないこと (we are not going to …) であり，(エ)

の「私たちの周りで起きていることを無視すること」であると言える。stick one's heads in the sandは直訳すると「頭を砂の中に突き刺す」で，比喩的に「現実や困難を直視しようとしない」という意味がある。
問4　第5段落3文目に「何が正しくて何が誤りであると，だれが決めるのか」との問いかけがある。空欄を含む文以下には，アメリカではみなが議論し，話したりすることで徐々に合意を形成するとある。そのようなプロセスはdemocratic「民主的な」である。　問5　空欄部Eの前文からこの本の目的を述べており，まず「何と言うべきで，何と言わないべきかに関する合理的な結論に達すること」とある。したがって，次に続くのはもう一つ別の目的でもある「少しの単語の歴史と語源を差しはさむ」とする(ウ)である。残りの3つの選択肢はすべて"its's designed to ～" を含んでおり，それらの2つの目的を達成するためにどのように本が設計されているかを示すと考えられる。その中で，(ア)にはmost of all「何よりも」があることから最後に位置し，(エ)にはalso「また」とあることから，(イ)の後に続くと推測できる。
問6　この段落では，政治に関しての議論でtenetsと言うべきところをtenantsと言った書き手が中傷された例を取り上げている。ネットはその書き手が英語を正しく書けなかったとして騒然としたが，それは不公平であり，重要な議論から注意をそらしたと書かれている。設問はその結果としてどのようなことが起こったかについてである。設問の英語の意味は「この『それ』はインターネットのコメンテーターが書き手の（　b　）というよりは（　a　）のことで非難した」である。（　b　）に入るのは政治の議論において本来重要となるものであるため，argument「主張」またはopinion「意見」である。一方，（　a　）は本来重要ではない書き手が誤用した英語 (English) である。
問7　historic「歴史に残る，歴史上重要な」とhistorical「歴史(上)の，史実に基づく，過去に使われた」の使い方を問う問題。historicalは単に過去に起きた出来事を指すため，過去の日，歴史上のこと，過去に起きた何か，サンドイッチを食べたことなどはすべてhistoricalなものである。一方で，歴史上重要または有名であること，長い歴史を持つことなどに対してはhistoricを使用する。

【3】(1)　I didn't realize that I left my smartphone at the restaurant.
had left

(2)　We discussed about the problem many times.
discussed (aboutは不要である事が示されていれば可。)

(3)　There is few possibility that he will win the next election.
little

(4)　Please submit the documents until next Tuesday.
by

(5)　Each of you have to bring your own lunch.
has

(6)　I'm not used to get up so early.
getting

(7)　If I have more money, I would travel abroad.
had

〈解説〉(1)　スマートフォンを置き忘れたのは，(that節の内容に) 気づかなかったという過去のある一時点よりも以前のことであるため過去完了 (had + 過去分詞) を用いる。　(2)　discuss「～について議論する」は他動詞であるため前置詞のaboutは不要。　(3)　possibility that ～は「～という可能性」で，その際possibilityは不可算名詞であるためfewではなくlittleが用いられる。　(4)　untilは「まで(ずっと)」という意味で，期限を表す場合はby「～までに」。　(5)　代名詞のeachは単数扱いのため動詞には3単現のsがつく (everyも同様)。　(6)　be used to ～「～に慣れている」のtoは不定詞ではなく前置詞であるため，動詞が続く場合には動名詞にする必要がある。　(7)「もしもっとお金があれば」という仮定法過去であるため動詞は現在形ではなく過去形にする。

【中学校】

【1】問1　①　dismayed　②　highlighted　④　florid　問2　with nothing painted on it would be viewed as an incomplete section

問3　(1)　庭の花をすべて抜くことで，茶室の一輪の花の美しさを際立たせたとともに秀吉を失望させ，その後，茶室の花を見たときに受ける印象をより強くさせた。　(2)　余計なものを隠しているとともに，それ自体が背景にもなっている。　問4　韓国では，金屛風にはたいてい松や鶴などの縁起のいいものが色とりどりに描かれているため。　問5　(ア)

〈解説〉問1　①　豊臣秀吉が千利休による庭を見た際の反応を問うものである。空欄の後に「すべての花が摘まれたのを知って怒った」とあるため，選択肢から考えると秀吉はがっかりした (dismayed) と言える。dismayは「がっかりさせる」という意味の他動詞であるため「(主語が) ～がっかりする」と言う場合は過去分詞を用いる。　②　千利休による茶室の特性を問うものである。空欄以後の意味は「庭に花がないことによって」で，前の段落で「最初の不満が深ければ深いほど驚きは大きく，強烈な印象を残す」とあるため，空欄にはhighlight「強調する」が入る。本文では「～によって強調される」となるため過去分詞を用いる。　④　第6段落は尾形光琳による金屛風についてである。彼はすべての周辺的な (peripheral) 要素を削除し豪華な金の野としたとある。そのため，空欄部は，そのような「めまいのするような (dazzling) 日本の芸術においても，中心となるモチーフ以外のものはすべて排除する傾向がある」とあり，空欄にはdazzlingと同様のflorid「華麗な」が入る。　問2　第5段落は，日本と西洋での芸術や美における余白 (margin) のとらえ方を問うものである。第4段落から日本では空白のスペースが用いられることがあると書かれており，第5段落最終文でも何も書かれていないスペースが不思議な奥深さを与えるとある。一方で，西洋では下線部③の前文に「すべてのキャンバスは絵具で端から端まで塗られていると想定される」とある。そのため，それに続く内容は (a bare patch) with nothing painted on it would be viewed as an incomplete section「何も描かれていないむき出しの部分は不完全な部分として見られるだろう」となる。withからitまでは付帯状況のwithである。　問3　(1)　庭のすべての花を取り除くことの効果については，第2段落及び第3段落に述べられており，第2段落3文目にある一輪の花の印象を際立たせることと，第3段落5文目で述べられている失望が印象を強力にするということを含めればよい。　(2)　“Irises”における金の部分の役割は，第6段落最終文の内容である。backgroundは「背景化する」という意味。　問4　下線部⑤の意味は「単純な金の仕切りは何か欠いているようで，さらには憂鬱で，孤独な様子である」である。韓国の友人がそう思った理由としては，その前文で金の仕切りは韓国でも用いられるが，縁起物が描かれているとあり，解答にはこの部分の具体的な内容を含めればよい。　問5　本文全体の内容は，庭の花を取り除いたり，中心のもの以外の周辺的なものを排除したりして余白 (margin) を作ること，そしてその芸術的な役割を述べているため，(ア)の「余白の美学」が正答となる。(イ)は「絵画の対照的な影」，(ウ)は「芸術の儚い美」，(エ)は「日本の芸術の壮大さ」の意味。

【2】I think students need the following abilities.

First, each student must think of his or her opinion for the given themes and some reasons.

Second, each student can write his or her own opinion in English.

So I want my students to practice writing their own opinions in English at the end of every class. The topic is “the things you learned in the class”. I will check their English after every class.

Once a month, I will give a writing test. Students must give their own opinions and the reasons in the test. The topic is, for example, “What can you do for your town?” The students practice writing English sentences while thinking about their grammar, and they can make progress in expressing their ideas in English.(128 words)

〈解説〉解答例では，必要だと考える力について，「与えられたテーマに基づいて意見と理由を考えること」と「意見を英語で書くことができること」の2つを挙げている。それらを達成するための指導として，意見を書く練習を授業に取り入れたり，ライティングテストを行ったりすることが書かれている。日頃の指導とテストの内容を一貫させることは重要であり，授業で扱うだけではなく，その内容をテストや評価の内容にも反映することは，何が重要なのかを教師と生徒の両者が共有し，その目的に向かって指導・学習するために必要なことである。

【高等学校】

【1】問1 (ア) 問2 environment 問3 ⓐ was about to be put down ⓒ been making her presence felt 問4 (イ)
問5 ア as イ if／though 問6 (ウ) 問7 隠れた才能を見つけることと長所短所について早急な判断をしないようにすること。(38字) 問8 (エ)

〈解説〉問1 ①を含む箇所の意味は「小さな犬はペットとして生きるべきであるような固定観念にとらわれる(①)彼らの可能性を最大限にするのを手助けすべきである」となり，文意からinstead of「～の代わりに」が入る。 問2 ②を含む箇所の意味は「彼らの可能性に気づいたら私たちがそれらを開花する(②)を用意することは重要である」となる。空欄の後に関係副詞の“where”があることから空欄には才能を開花させるための場所で，さらに直前に“an”があることからも母音で始まることもわかる。したがって，空欄には第5段落1文目にあるenvironment「環境」が入る。 問3 ⓐ be about toは「まさに～しようとする」，この文におけるput downの意味は「見放す」で，文全体の意味「見捨てられそうな時にアンズは鈴木さんに救われた」となる。 ⓒ make one's presence feltは「自分の存在を注目させる」という意味。下線部の後に述べられている「強みや特性を生かすことで，証拠や行方不明の人を探した」という内容からも，文意が推測できる。問4 ③にはアンズが虐待(abuse) されていたように見えた理由が入るため，それはアンズが人々を怖がっていたためであると考えられる。

動詞のfrightenは「怖がらせる」という意味の他動詞で「(主語が) 怖がっている」と言う場合，受動態(be動詞 + 過去分詞)の形をとる。④を含む部分の意味は「必要な時」となりneededが入る。これはwhen it is neededの “it is” が省略されたものである。　問5　第4段落ではアンズが警察犬のジャーマンシェパードとともに生活し，彼らへの訓練に興味を示したり，行動を観察したりすることで嗅覚を磨いたとある。そのため，空欄を含む文の意味としては「アンズはまるでジャーマンシェパードであるかのようにふるまい始めた」となり，as ifが入る(she wereからも仮定法過去を使用していることがわかる)。　問6　大きさや血統に応じて労働を分けることが捜査においてどのようなものであるかを問う問題。空欄に続く文で，「小さな犬の利点として大きな犬が見逃すような小さなものを見つけるのが得意である」と述べていることからも，そのような分業はeffective「効果的である」と言える。問7　下線部の意味は「共通して重要な何か」であり，犬の世話・訓練と子育て・教育における共通点を答えればよい。その具体的内容は：(コロン)の後に述べられている。judgmental「決めつける」。
問8　(ア)　鈴木さんに拾われる前に訓練を始めたかどうかは記述されていない。　(イ)　第4段落最終文にアンズを警察犬にしたのは鈴木さんの犬とある。　(ウ)　第6段落1文目に最初のテストで合格したとある。　(エ)　第7段落2文目の内容と一致する。

【2】(Students have just learned about environmental issues in the English Communication Ⅰ class. They have already learned about this issue in the Contemporary Society class.

Based on what they have already learned, I would like...) them to make a presentation. First, they decide on what issue to focus on. Then, they are divided into groups according to their topics and discuss what to include in their presentation such as their background knowledge; the present situation and how to solve the problem. Their solution should be what they can actually work on. They are encouraged to use the vocabulary they have learned in the

English lesson and the background knowledge from the Contemporary Society class.

On the presentation day, they are divided into groups of four students with different topics. One student makes a presentation, and the rest ask questions or make comments. They take turns. After the presentations, they share what they have discussed in their original groups. (123 words)

〈解説〉英語の授業では，単に聞いたり，書いたりなど個々の技能の向上だけでなく，聞いたり読んだりしたこと，学んだことや経験したことなどの背景知識をもとに話し合うなど複数の技能を統合するような活動を行うことが求められている。与えられている条件では英語コミュニケーションⅠで学習した内容が「聞いたり読んだりしたこと」，現代社会の授業での学習内容が主に「学んだこと」にあたると考えられる。解答例ではトピックごとにグループを形成し，発表内容について話し合い，発表では各グループ内で発表・質問したのち全体で共有するという授業例を示している。このような授業は既習事項を有効に活用しているため，生徒にとっての負荷も高くなく，話し合いの中でこれまで聞いたり読んだりするだけでは得られなかった情報を得ることが期待される。

2019年度　実施問題

【中高共通】

【1】はリスニングテストです。放送の指示に従ってください。

【１】放送を聞いて，次の[Part 1]～[Part 3]に答えよ。

[Part 1]

No. 1

(A) By taxi.

(B) By subway.

(C) In thirty minutes.

(D) In ten minutes.

No. 2

(A) By eight.

(B) By eight thirty.

(C) By nine.

(D) By nine thirty.

No. 3

(A) She doesn't like her job.

(B) She is not satisfied with her salary.

(C) She will move abroad.

(D) She will be fired.

No. 4

(A) He will eat dinner.

(B) He will write in his diary.

(C) He will prepare for tomorrow's classes.

(D) He will do his homework.

No. 5

(A) In an Italian restaurant.

(B) In a Chinese restaurant.

(C) In the woman's house.

(D) In the man's house.

No. 6

(A) His house key.

(B) His room key.

(C) His cellphone.

(D) His wallet.

[Part 2]

No. 1 The man and the woman are most likely ...

(A) classmates.

(B) a shopkeeper and a customer.

(C) husband and wife.

(D) co-workers.

No. 2 The man and the woman are ...

(A) at their desks.

(B) in a kitchen.

(C) in a restaurant.

(D) in a coffee shop.

No. 3 The article the woman read says drinking too much coffee can ...

(A) damage our cells.

(B) be a cause of cancer.

(C) raise our blood pressure.

(D) increase blood cholesterol level.

No. 4 In the afternoon, the woman ...

(A) will prepare for the presentation.

(B) will send some messages.

(C) will go out with the man.

(D) will see a doctor.

[Part 3]

No. 1 What does Bea Johnson use to clean in her zero-waste lifestyle?

No. 2 Bea Johnson proposes "5R's" in her book *Zero Waste Home*. One of them is "Rot". What are the other four R's?

No. 3 How does the speaker help to reduce the amount of trash when eating out?

No. 4 When did the speaker decide to give the zero-waste lifestyle another try?

No. 5 What is a good place to buy fresh food without packaging?

(☆☆◎◎◎◎)

【２】次の英文を読み，あとの[問1]～[問8]に答えよ。

Notions such as accuracy, clarity, and the avoidance of ambiguity are what we want our children to learn about grammar, and how we want to be able to use grammar ourselves. They have ⓐone thing in common: they are all to do with the expression of meaning. Meaning is at the heart of everything we want children (and adults) to do in their interactions. Speakers and writers need to express their meaning clearly and precisely, and listeners and readers need to understand the meaning of those communicating with them.

However, most people don't immediately associate meaning with grammar, but with (①). The more 'word power' we have, it is said (and I'm now recalling the famous column in *Reader's Digest*, 'It pays to increase your word power'), the better we will be able to express what we mean. That is why people use dictionaries: in principle, they contain all the meanings of all the words in a language. But words by themselves are not enough for meaningful communication. A word by itself may have meaning, but it will not always make sense. For that to happen it needs to be put into a sentence. It needs

(②).

This is because the vast majority of words in English are inherently ambiguous: we look them up in a dictionary and find they have more than one meaning (they are *polysemous*). *Charge* can be something to do with money, energy, or military activity (to name just three of its meanings). Some words have over a dozen meanings. A common verb such as *take* or *do* might have several dozen. How can we use language meaningfully when there is so much polysemy?

The answer, of course, is that (③) sorts it out. By putting words into a sentence, we combine them in ways that enable us to select just one of those meanings:

The theatre charged for the tickets.
The cavalry charged along the valley.
I charged the battery in my phone.

The ambiguity has disappeared. The sentences have created sense out of the words they contain.

That is what sentences are for: to make sense of words. And that is what every grammatical construction is for — from the largest sentence patterns to the smallest word inflections: they are there to help us, literally, to make — construct, create — sense. There are over 3,500 index entries to the various features explained in the biggest descriptive grammar to come out of the twentieth century: *A Comprehensive Grammar of the English Language*, published in 1985. Each one is there for ⓑa reason: to help us express an aspect of our thinking in a way that others will understand. And because our thoughts are often complex, grammar is complex too. If all we ever wanted to say was at the level of 'Me Jane; you Tarzan,' grammar would be easy.

What this amounts to is that grammar should never be studied or taught divorced from the meaning that the sentence patterns convey. To teach grammar without reference to meaning is the strategy that has given grammar a bad name. Anyone who has ever felt that grammar is boring, dull, pointless, and irrelevant has almost certainly been taught it in ⓒthis way.

I was taught it like that. The teacher would put a sentence on the board (*The man sat on a chair*) and engage me in a dialogue that went something like this. I was aged about eleven or twelve at the time.

Teacher: [④]

Me: *The man* is the subject and *sat on a chair* is the predicate.

Teacher: [⑤]

Me: *Sat*, sir.

Teacher: [⑥]

Me: The verb, sir.

Teacher: Good boy. [⑦]

Me: The object, sir.

Teacher: Crystal, Crystal, Crystal... It is not an object. Does anyone else know what it is?

[*silence*]

Teacher: Have you all forgotten the lesson we had about adverb phrases?

[*more silence*]

Teacher: It's an adverb phrase of place. [*pause*] Can anyone tell me any other kinds of adverb phrase?

And that led to more silence, which meant that we all had to write out ten times the names of all the adverb phrases in English — of time, place, concession, result, and so on — with an example of each.

I remember thinking — but never having the courage to ask — 'why are we doing this?' And today I know the three kinds of answer that would have been given:

・Because (Crystal) the analysis of grammar has had a long and revered history that dates back to Plato, Aristotle, and the Stoics, and what was good enough for Plato should be good enough for you, so you will write out one hundred times …

・Because when you learn to analyse sentences you will become a better user of your language — a better listener, speaker, reader, and writer.

・Because this will teach you the terms you will need when you start learning a foreign language.

None of these answers helped eliminate the boredom. The first was [A] The second might or might not have been [B] And the third was [C]

To this day I have no idea why those early grammatical experiences didn't put me off grammar for life, as ⓓthey did so many others. Probably, deep down, it was a predilection, for analysing things. (I liked jigsaw puzzles too.) But I do clearly remember the day at university when in a lecture I understood for the first time what grammar analysis was really about, and in so doing learned the term *semantics*.

〔Crystal, David, 2017. *Making Sense: The Glamorous Story of English Grammar*, PROFILE BOOKS LTD.　一部編集等あり〕

[問1]　下線部ⓐについて，具体的内容を日本語で説明せよ。

[問2]　本文中の(　①　)に入る最も適切な語を，次の(ア)～(エ)から1つ選び，その記号を書け。

(ア)　communication　(イ)　ambiguity　(ウ)　vocabulary

(エ)　accuracy

[問3]　本文中の(　②　)，(　③　)に共通して入る最も適切な一語を，本文中から抜き出して書け。

[問4]　下線部ⓑについて，具体的内容を日本語で説明せよ。

[問5]　下線部ⓒはどのようなやり方か。具体的に日本語で説明せよ。

[問6]　本文中の[　④　]～[　⑦　]に入る最も適切なせりふを，次の(ア)～(エ)からそれぞれ1つ選び，その記号を書け。

(ア)　Good, and what's the most important word in the predicate?

(イ)　And what is *on a chair*?

(ウ)　Which is called ...?

(エ)　Can you name the two parts of this sentence, Crystal?

[問7]　本文中の[A]～[C]には，その直前で述べられている3つの理由についての著者の解釈が入る。空欄に入る最も適切なものを，次の(ア)～(ウ)からそれぞれ1つ選び，その記号を書け。

(ア)　an offer of manna to feed in a future French-language heaven, which sounded like a good idea — but was it worth making the present English class a mother-tongue purgatory?

(イ)　intellectually respectable, as part of the study of the history of ideas, but perhaps not a very relevant response for an eleven-year-old.

(ウ)　true, but it was difficult to see such analyses producing any immediate benefit.

[問8]　下線部ⓓはどのようなことか，具体的に日本語で書け。

(☆☆☆◎◎◎◎)

【中学校】

【1】次の英文を読んで，あとの[問1]～[問5]に答えよ。

Lafcadio Hearn, an English man of letters who adopted Japanese citizenship and lived in Japan from 1890 until his death in 1904, wrote the following in his essay, *The Japanese Smile*.

"A Japanese can smile in the face of death, and usually does... There is neither defiance nor hypocrisy in the smile; nor is it to be confounded with that smile of sickly resignation which we are apt to (　①　) with weakness of character. It is an elaborate and long cultivated etiquette. ②It is also a silent language. But any effort to (　③　) it according to Western notions of physiognomical expression would not be successful.

The first impression is, in most cases, wonderfully pleasant. The Japanese smile at first charms. It is only at a later day, when one has observed the same smile under extraordinary circumstances — in moments of pain, shame, disappointment — ④【 one / of / that / it / becomes / suspicious 】. Its apparent inopportuneness may even, on certain occasions, cause violent anger.

To comprehend the Japanese smile, one must be able to enter a little into the ancient, natural, and popular life of Japan.

The Japanese child is born with this happy tendency, which is fostered through all the period of home education... The smile is taught like the bow; like the prostration;... But the smile is to be used upon all pleasant occasions, when speaking to a superior or to an equal, and even upon occasions which are not pleasant; ⑤it is part of deportment. The most agreeable face is the smiling face; and to present always the most agreeable face possible to parents, relatives, teachers, friends, well-wishers, is a rule of life... Even though the heart is breaking, it is a social duty to smile bravely." (From The Writings of Lafcadio Hearn, *Glimpses of Unfamiliar Japan*, published by Houghton Mifflin Co.)

Here, then, Lafcadio Hearn refers to the Japanese smile as a form of the self-control rooted in the culture of the Japanese. Smiles to indicate affection, agreement, sympathy etc. are the same wherever one goes; but this smile of self-control is something that on occasion seems to (⑥) people from other countries.

〔*NIPPON THE LAND AND ITS PEOPLE* (1996)　一部編集等あり〕

[問1]　本文中の(①), (③), (⑥)に入る最も適切な語句を，次の(ア)～(オ)からそれぞれ1つずつ選び，その記号を書け。

(ア) interpret　(イ) please　(ウ) puzzle　(エ) compare
(オ) associate

[問2]　下線部②を，Itがさす内容を具体的にして日本語に訳せ。

[問3]　下線部④の【　】内の語句を本文の流れに合うように正しく

並べかえよ。

[問4]　下線部⑤は，どのようなことをさすか，日本語で具体的に書け。

[問5]　本文の内容と一致するものを，次の(ア)～(エ)から1つ選び，その記号を書け。

(ア)　Lafcadio Hearn wrote that the Japanese smile has a lot of meanings and they were common in the world.

(イ)　When Lafcadio Hearn lived in Japan, the Japanese smile was regarded as a virtue in Western countries.

(ウ)　Lafcadio Hearn wrote Western people admired Japanese who could always smile under unusual circumstances.

(エ)　Lafcadio Hearn wrote that the Japanese smile was strongly influenced by the culture of the Japanese.

(☆☆◎◎◎◎)

【2】次の[問1]，[問2]に答えよ。

[問1]　次の(1)～(7)について，下線部と最も近い意味を表す語句を，ア～エからそれぞれ1つずつ選び，その記号を書け。

(1)　If it rains, the game will be <u>postponed</u>.

ア　cut off　　イ　called off　　ウ　put off　　エ　showed off

(2)　The old man <u>experienced</u> a lot of hardships when he was young.

ア　went through　　イ　used up　　ウ　stopped by

エ　faced up to

(3)　We should <u>do away with</u> such old rules.

ア　despise　　イ　reject　　ウ　criticize　　エ　abolish

(4)　Ichiro and Kenji are <u>industrious</u> students.

ア　intelligent　　イ　indolent　　ウ　cheerful　　エ　diligent

(5)　Come and eat lunch with me <u>once in a while</u>.

ア　generally　　イ　occasionally　　ウ　repeatedly

エ　immediately

(6)　He said that <u>on purpose</u>, knowing it would annoy his mother.

ア unexpectedly　イ deliberately　ウ secretly
エ frequently

(7) I have <u>almost</u> finished the book.

ア more and more　イ more than a little　ウ more or less
エ less and less

[問2] 下の(1)～(7)の英文には，それぞれ誤りがある。できるだけ元の英文を生かすという観点で，正しい英文にするには，どのように直せばよいか。次の例にならって書け。

> (例) オリンピックは2020年に日本で開催される。
> The 2020 Olympics will <u>be taken place</u> in Japan.
> take place

(1) 私は彼がその建物に入るのを見た。
I saw him enter into the building.

(2) 彼女はお母さんに似ている。
She is resembling her mother.

(3) 映画に行くのはどうですか。
What do you say to go to a movie?

(4) 富士山は，海抜3776メートルの高さであり，日本で一番高い山である。
Mt. Fuji, that rises 3776 meters above sea level, is the highest mountain in Japan.

(5) あなたの都合のよい時にいつでも私に電話してください。
Please call me whenever you are convenient.

(6) 私は，母が帰ってくるまでには部屋の掃除を終えます。
I will finish cleaning my room until my mother comes home.

(7) あなたは食べ過ぎないほうがよいですよ。
You had not better eat too much.

(☆☆◎◎◎◎)

【3】「平成30年度学校教育指導の方針と重点(和歌山県教育委員会)」において，グローバル人材の育成のための指導の重点として，「小学校教員と中・高等学校の英語科教員が連携を図り，一貫性のある英語教育の充実や，表現力や発信力を高める授業づくりをめざす。」としている。

あなたは，中学校英語科教員として，小学校の学びを中学校へ円滑に接続させるためにどのような取組を行っていくか，英文で2つ以上書け。ただし，それぞれの取組について，その内容と目的を具体的に書くこと。

なお，英文の語数は120語から150語とすることとし，語数を記入すること。

(☆☆☆☆◎◎◎◎)

【高等学校】

【1】次の英文を読み，あとの[問1]～[問8]に答えよ。

Escalators are convenient to ride, but if something goes wrong they can be the scene of serious accidents. The practice has become established of keeping to the left side of an escalator in Tokyo and to the right side in Osaka, while leaving the other side open for people in a hurry. However, many are unaware that an industry group is calling for people not to walk on escalators and not to leave one side open as a rule to prevent accidents. Railway companies are also appealing to people to ensure compliance with ⓐthe rule.

According to the Consumer Affairs Agency, a total of 3,865 people were taken to hospitals (　①　) escalator accidents in Tokyo from 2011 to 2013. The majority of the cases were injuries caused by falls. The cases included “toppled over by losing balance while walking up an escalator” and “toppled over as their cane was jostled by a person who was walking up an escalator.”

The agency warns that if people [　　A　　], they run the risk of an accident not only by losing their balance themselves but also by jostling other people.

According to the Japan Elevator Association, comprising elevator and escalator makers, escalators are designed based on the assumption that people will not walk on them and the correct way of using an escalator is by standing still and holding the handrail. "It's not necessary to leave one side open. There are some people who have an arm or a hand that is incapable of functioning and ⓑ[specific side / keeping / have / a / open / difficulty]," said an official at the association.

Major railway companies started a campaign calling for people not to leave one side open and not to walk on escalators about five years ago. This year, a total of 51 railway operators and companies related to Haneda and Narita airports are participating in the campaign.

A public relations official at East Japan Railway Co., one of the participating companies, said: "The number of accidents decreases during the campaign period but the practice of keeping one side open is strongly rooted. We'd like to positively appeal to people to change the practice."

Meanwhile, the rule of keeping one step empty behind each person taking an escalator is spreading.

The rule was established from a lesson (②) from an escalator accident at Tokyo Big Sight, a major exhibition hall in Tokyo's Koto Ward, in August 2008. At that time, about 50 people toppled over and 10 of them were injured in the accident when a major event for manga enthusiasts was being held. An ascending escalator about 30 meters long, linking the first and fourth floors of the building, suddenly stopped and began to slide backward, (③) about 50 people to topple over.

An accident investigation committee at the Land, Infrastructure, Transport and Tourism Ministry announced its report on the accident in January this year, attributing the accident to improper maintenance. (④), it is also believed that the escalator became overloaded with people at the time of the accident. Tokyo Big Sight began playing recorded announcements the month following the accident in Japanese and English ⓒ[escalators / people /

using / to / urging] keep one empty step between themselves and the person ahead for safety.

About 15 million people visit Tokyo Big Sight annually, and there are 38 escalators in the facility. A public relations official at the facility stressed the effect of the announcement, saying, "As fewer people now stand on the very next step after the person ahead of them, (⑤) has improved."

〔*The Japan News by The Yomiuri Shimbun August 26, 2015* 一部編集等あり〕

[問1] 下線部ⓐの内容を日本語で具体的に書け。

[問2] 本文中の(①)に入る最も適切な語句を，次の(ア)～(エ)から1つ選び，その記号を書け。

(ア) in spite of　(イ) for the sake of　(ウ) for the purpose of

(エ) due to

[問3] [A]に入る語句を，本文の流れに合うように4語で書け。

[問4] 下線部ⓑ，ⓒについて，[ ]内の語または語句を本文の流れに合うように正しく並べかえよ。

[問5] 本文中の(②)，(③)に入る最も適切な語の組み合わせを，次の(ア)～(エ)から1つ選び，その記号を書け。

(ア) ② learning ③ causing

(イ) ② learning ③ caused

(ウ) ② learned ③ causing

(エ) ② learned ③ caused

[問6] 本文中の(④)に入る最も適切な語を，次の(ア)～(エ)から1つ選び，その記号を書け。

(ア) However　(イ) Therefore　(ウ) Namely

(エ) Consequently

[問7] 本文中の(⑤)に入る最も適切な一語を，本文中から抜き出して書け。

[問8] 本文の内容と一致するものを，次の(ア)～(エ)から1つ選び，その記号を書け。

(ア) People in Osaka and Tokyo leave the left side open for people in haste on an escalator.

(イ) According to the Japan Elevator Association, it is appropriate to stand unmoving and grip the handrail on an escalator.

(ウ) A public relations official at East Japan Railway Co. stated the way people used an escalator left nothing to be desired.

(エ) An accident investigation committee at the Land, Infrastructure, Transport and Tourism Ministry reported: "The escalator accident at Tokyo Big Sight had little to do with improper maintenance."

(☆☆☆◎◎◎◎)

【2】下の(1)～(7)の英文には，それぞれ誤りがある。できるだけ元の英文を生かすという観点で，正しい英文にするには，どのように直せばよいか。次の例にならって書け。

(例) オリンピックは2020年に日本で開催される。 The 2020 Olympics will <u>be taken place</u> in Japan. take place

(1) 私は彼がその建物に入るのを見た。

I saw him enter into the building.

(2) 彼女はお母さんに似ている。

She is resembling her mother.

(3) 映画に行くのはどうですか。

What do you say to go to a movie?

(4) 富士山は，海抜3776メートルの高さであり，日本で一番高い山である。

Mt. Fuji, that rises 3776 meters above sea level, is the highest mountain in Japan.

(5) あなたの都合のよい時にいつでも私に電話してください。

Please call me whenever you are convenient.

(6)　私は，母が帰ってくるまでには部屋の掃除を終えます。

I will finish cleaning my room until my mother comes home.

(7)　あなたは食べ過ぎないほうがよいですよ。

You had not better eat too much.

(☆☆◎◎◎◎)

【3】現行の高等学校学習指導要領「外国語」における「第2款　各科目　第5　英語表現Ⅰ　2　内容」の項目のひとつに「読み手や目的に応じて，簡潔に書く。」という記述がある。

この内容を踏まえて，あなたならどのような点に留意して指導を行うか。既に与えられている英文に続いて，120語程度の英文で書け。なお，語数を記入すること。

Writing style differs according to the reader or purpose. To teach students how to write effectively, we need to give them a specific purpose for writing.

For example, ...

(☆☆☆☆◎◎◎◎)

解答・解説

【中高共通】

【1】Part1　No.1　(B)　No.2　(A)　No.3　(C)　No.4　(B)　No.5　(A)　No.6　(C)　Part2　No.1　(D)　No.2　(D)　No.3　(C)　No.4　(A)　Part3　No.1　Vinegar and baking soda.　No.2　“Refuse,” “Reduce,” “Reuse,” and “Recycle.”　No.3　By using his own chopsticks.　No.4　After Johnson’s talk.　No.5　The farmers’ markets.

〈解説〉スクリプトは公開されていない。Part1及びPart2は選択問題である。選択肢から，ともに簡単な日常会話の内容であると推察できる。

Part3は記述式の問題であるのでスペルミスには気をつけたい。設問から，トピックはzero-waste lifestyle「無駄をゼロに近づける生活様式」とわかる。解答を見る限り難しい内容ではなさそうだが，固有名詞など聞きなれない語に戸惑って後の重要な箇所を聞き逃してしまわないように注意しよう。また，リスニングだけでなくディクテーションの練習をしておくのも有効であろう。

【2】問1　正確さや明瞭さ，曖昧さの回避という概念はすべて，意味を表現することに関係しているということ。　問2　(ウ)
問3　grammar　問4　(文法は)自分の考えを，他人が理解できるように表現するのに役立つということ。　問5　意味を無視した文法の教え方。　問6　④　(エ)　⑤　(ア)　⑥　(ウ)　⑦　(イ)
問7　A　(イ)　B　(ウ)　C　(ア)　問8　文法を学び始めた頃の経験のせいで，非常に多くの人が文法嫌いになってしまったということ。(文法を学ぶ気をなくしてしまったということ。)

〈解説〉問1　They have one thing in common:「それら(正確さや明瞭さ，曖昧さの回避という概念)には1つ共通点がある」。コロン(:)以下に，その共通点が具体的に書かれている。do with ～「～を扱う」。　問2　たいていの人が意味と何を結びつけるか考える。「たいていの人はすぐに，意味と文法ではなく，意味と語彙を結びつけて考えるのである」。問3　空欄②と空欄③を含む文の直前の文意に注目する。「単語が文の中に入れられることによって必要となるもの」,「多義語が多い言語を，意味あるように使うために必要となるもの」を考えればよい。polysemy「多義，多義語」。　問4　下線部ⓑを含む文の意味は「それぞれ(3500を超える文法の検索項目)には存在理由がある」。コロン以下が具体的内容にあたる。　問5　文法は退屈で，無意味で，重要でないと感じている人が，どのようにして文法を教えられたかを答える。前文のTo teach grammar without reference to meaningが解答にあたる部分。without reference to～「～と関係なく，～をかまわず」。
問6　④　教師の最初の発話。(エ)「この文の2つのパートの名前を言うことができますか」。　⑤　筆者が「主語」と「述部」と答えた後の教師の発話。(ア)「よろしい。では述部の中で最も大切な言葉は何ですか」。　⑥　筆者が「座った」と答えた後の教師の発話。(ウ)「それは何と呼ばれている」。　⑦　筆者が「動詞」と答えた後の教師の発話。(イ)「では椅子の上には何がある」。　問7　1つ目の理由は「文法の分析はプラトン，アリストテレスやストア派までさかのぼる長く尊い歴史を持っている。そしてプラトンにとって十分価値のあるものはあなたにも十分価値があるのだから100回書いて…」。筆者の解釈は(イ)「考え方の歴史の勉強の一部として頭では尊敬するが，おそらく11歳(の生徒)にはあまり適切な返答ではない」。2つ目の理由は「文を分析することを学ぶと言語のよい使用者，よい聞き手，話し手，読み手，書き手になれるだろうから」。筆者の解釈は(ウ)「その通りだが，そのような分析がすぐに助けになると認めるのは難しかった」。3つ目の理由は「外国語を学び始める時，このことが必要な用語を教えることになるから」。筆者の解釈は(ア)。mannaは聖書に出てくる神の賜物である食物。文意は「将来外国語(フランス語)を学ぶときに役立つから，という考えはよさそうであるが，将来のために，母国語(英語)の授業を苦行にする価値はあったのか」となる。　問8　下線部ⓓはearly grammatical experiences put so many others offということ。put ～ off「～を遠ざける，～を寄せつけない」。この場合は「意欲をなくさせる」という意味で使用している。

【中学校】

【1】問1　①　(オ)　③　(ア)　⑥　(ウ)　問2　日本人の微笑は物言わぬ言語でもある。　問3　that one becomes suspicious of it
問4　目上の人に話す時でも，対等の相手と話す時でも，愉快な場合はもちろんのこと不快な場合にでさえ，微笑むこと。　問5　(エ)

〈解説〉問1　①「微笑の中には軽蔑も偽善もない。性格の弱さを連想しがちな病的なあきらめの微笑と混同すべきでもない」とする。confound「混同する」。associate with「～と関連づける」。　③「表情で感情表現する西洋人の考え方に従うと，それを解釈しようとするどんな努力もうまくいかないだろう」。physiognomical「人相の」だが，ここでは感情を顔に出すという意味。interpret「解釈する」。
⑥「自制の微笑は，時折他国からの人々を困惑させるものである」。puzzle「困らせる」。　問2　下線部②の直前にもIt is an elaborate and long cultivated etiquette.「それは手の込んだ，長期にわたり作り上げられたエチケットである」とあるが，itはすべて同じJapanese smileを指している。　問3　下線部④を含む文は，It is only at a later day, when one has observed the same smile under extraordinary circumstances … that one becomes suspicious of it.となり，「人がそれを疑うのは後日，特異な状況下で同様の微笑に気づいたときである」。It is～thatの強調構文である。　問4　下線部⑤を含む文は，「それは(人前での)振る舞いの一部である」。deportment「行儀」。具体的には前文の内容を指す。
問5　(ア)「日本人の微笑はたくさんの意味を持ち，それらは世界中で共通だと，ラフカディオ・ハーンは書いた」，(イ)「ラフカディオ・ハーンが日本に住んでいた時，日本人の微笑は西洋の国で美徳と見なされていた」，(ウ)「西洋人は普通でない状況でもいつも微笑むことのできる日本人を称賛していると，ラフカディオ・ハーンは書いた」はいずれも，日本人の微笑が西洋では理解されにくいとする本文の内容に合致しない。(エ)「日本人の微笑は日本の文化に強く影響されていると，ラフカディオ・ハーンは書いた」は第6段落の内容に合っている。

【2】問1　(1)　ウ　(2)　ア　(3)　エ　(4)　エ　(5)　イ
(6)　イ　(7)　ウ

問2　(1)　I saw him enter <u>into</u> the building.
intoをとる

(2)　She <u>is resembling</u> her mother.
resembles

(3)　What do you say to <u>go</u> to a movie?
going

(4)　Mt. Fuji, <u>that</u> rises 3776 meters above sea level, is the highest mountain
　　　　which
in Japan.

(5)　Please call me whenever <u>you are convenient</u>.
　　　　it is convenient (for you)

(6)　I will finish cleaning my room <u>until</u> my mother comes home.
　　　　by the time

(7)　You <u>had not better</u> eat too much.
　　　　had better not

〈解説〉問1　(1)　postpone「延期する」。put offと同意。　(2)　experience「経験する」。go throughと同意。　(3)　do away with「廃止する」。abolishと同意。　(4)　industrious「勤勉な」。diligentと同意。　(5)　once in a while「時々」。occasionallyと同意。　(6)　on purpose「わざと，故意に」。deliberatelyと同意。　(7)　almost「ほとんど」。more or less「多かれ少なかれ，だいたい」と同意。　問2　(1)　enter「～に入る」は他動詞。よって前置詞intoは不要。　(2)　resemble「～に似ている」は状態を表す動詞なので進行形にしない。　(3)　What do you say to ～？「～に対してあなたは何と言いますか？，～はどうですか？」。toは前置詞。よって後ろは名詞(動名詞)にする。　(4)　関係代名詞の継続用法にthatは用いない。　(5)　convenient「都合のよい」は人を主語にとらない。　(6)　untilは「～までずっと」という意味。by the time SVで接続詞的に「SがVするまでに」となる。　(7)　had better「～したほうがいい」。否定は，had better not「～しないほうがいい」。

【３】Teachers in junior high schools and elementary schools should cooperate in teaching English to children. I would like to explain what to do as an English teacher of a junior high school.

First, I think it is important to know what the students have learned in their elementary schools. So I want to watch the foreign language activities in elementary schools. Also I want teachers in elementary schools to watch my

English classes. After watching, we would be able to discuss the classes.

Second, we should make a CAN-DO list in elementary schools and junior high schools. If we make a CAN-DO list, we can understand the aim of each grade clearly, and can check the level of understanding the children have attained. By knowing that, we can make better lesson plans than before.(134語)

〈解説〉解答例では「小中相互の授業交流や小中のCAN-DO listを共同作成」を挙げている。小学校で英語の教科化は大きな変革であり，小中連携は重要かつ時間を要する課題である。特に受け取る側となる中学校では，小学校学習指導要領を熟読し児童が学んできたことを把握するのはもちろんである。特に入門期には指導内容や指導方法に関して，継続や反復が円滑な接続となることを目指したい。長期的には，小学校中学年からの通算7年間を見据えた指導を目指すことが求められている。

【高等学校】

【1】問1　エスカレーターでは歩かず，片側を空けないこと。

問2　(エ)　　問3　walk on an escalator / walk up an escalator

問4　ⓑ　have difficulty keeping a specific side open　　ⓒ　urging people using escalators to　　問5　(ウ)　　問6　(ア)　　問7　safety

問8　(イ)

〈解説〉問1　下線部ⓐを含む文の意味は「鉄道会社もこのルールを確実に守るよう人々に求めている」。この前の文に，業界団体が求めているとしてルールが具体的に書かれている。　問2　空欄①の前後の文である「消費者庁によると全部で3,865人の人が病院に運ばれた」と「2011年から2013年までに東京のエスカレーターの事故」をつなぐのはdue to～「～の原因で」。　問3　空欄Aの後は「人々は，自身のバランスを失うことによってだけでなく，ほかの人を押しのけて進むことよっても事故の危険を冒すことになる」。そのようなことが起きる原因となる動作を本文中から探す。第2段落3文目walk up an escalatorや第

5段落1文目walk on escalatorsなどに注目する。　問4　ⓑ　手や腕が不自由な人の説明にあたる部分。よってhave difficulty keeping a specific side open「特定の側を空けておくのが難しい」。　ⓒ　東京ビッグサイトが流したアナウンスの内容にあたる部分。urging people using escalators to ～「～するようエスカレーター利用者に強く勧める」。urge O to ～「Oに～するよう説得する」。　問5　②「東京ビッグサイトでのエスカレーター事故から学ばれた教訓」。過去分詞の後置修飾。③「…突然停止し，逆走した。そして約50人が転倒した」。cause O to ～「Oに～させる(…が原因でOは～する)」。causingは分詞構文。
問6　空欄④の前では「事故原因は不適切な整備」と述べながらも，空欄の後では「人員超過もまた…」と述べているので，適切な接続詞はhowever「しかしながら」。　問7　エスカレーターに乗る時，自分の前方の人の次の段に人が立たなくなったことで，何が改善されたかを考える。第9段落の最後の文からsafetyを抜き出す。　問8　第1段落2文目の内容より，東京と大阪では空けておく側が逆なので，(ア)は誤り。(イ)「日本エレベーター協会によると，エスカレーターで動かずに立ち，手すりを握るのがふさわしい」は第4段落1文目の内容より正解。第6段落1文目の内容より，片側を空けておくという習慣は強く定着していることから，(ウ)は誤り。leave nothing to be desired「申し分ない」。第9段落1文目より，国土交通省は東京ビッグサイトの事故原因を不適切な整備と発表したので(エ)は誤り。have little to do with ～「～とほとんど関係ない」。

【２】(1)　I saw him enter <u>into</u> the building.

intoをとる

(2)　She <u>is resembling</u> her mother.

resembles

(3)　What do you say to <u>go</u> to a movie?

going

(4)　Mt. Fuji, <u>that</u> rises 3776 meters above sea level, is the highest mountain

which

in Japan.

(5) Please call me whenever you are convenient.

it is convenient (for you)

(6) I will finish cleaning my room until my mother comes home.

by the time

(7) You had not better eat too much.

had better not

〈解説〉(1) enter「～に入る」は他動詞。よって前置詞intoは不要。

(2) resemble「～に似ている」は状態を表す動詞なので進行形にしない。 (3) What do you say to ～?「～に対してあなたは何と言いますか?，～はどうですか?」。toは前置詞。よって後ろは名詞(動名詞)にする。 (4) 関係代名詞の継続用法にthatは用いない。

(5) convenient「都合のよい」は人を主語にとらない。 (6) untilは「～までずっと」という意味。by the time SVで接続詞的に「SがVするまでに」となる。 (7) had better「～したほうがいい」。否定は，had better not「～しないほうがいい」。

【3】(Writing style differs according to the reader or purpose. To teach students how to write effectively, we need to give them a specific purpose for writing.

For example,) I would have students write to an FLT to ask to put off the deadline of their assignment.

Here are three things students should consider: what to write, how to write, and how effectively they can achieve their goal. First, as for the content, they should write about how much more time they need and why. Is the reason good enough? It should not be a long, stupid excuse. Second, they need to use formal, polite expressions, since their teacher will read it. Third, they should judge the letter from the FLT's point of view. Some students can play the role of the FLT and decide if they will be persuaded or not. Based on this, students can rewrite their letters. (121語)

〈解説〉「高等学校学習指導要領解説　外国語編　英語編」(平成21年12月)における「第2章　第5節　英語表現I　2　内容　(1)イ」では，「読み手に応じて書く」とは読み手が持っている知識，興味・関心や態度，年齢などを考慮すること，「目的に応じて書く」とは情報や知識を与えるため，説得するため，論証するため，楽しませるため，記録を行うため，自分自身の思索を深めるため，など具体例が述べられている。解答例はFLTが読み手，宿題の提出期限を延ばしてもらえるよう説得するという目的設定となっている。生徒が読み手と目的の両方を考慮し，実際に英文を書く経験を重ねることが重要である。「地域のことを観光客に紹介するパンフレットを作成する」，「学校の話題をホームページ上で紹介する」など教師はその場となる題材を適切に設定し指導することが求められている。なお，今回は現行版からの出題であるが，「高等学校学習指導要領」についてはすでに改訂版が告示されている(平成30年3月)。念のため同解説(平成30年7月)と併せて入手し，今回の改訂箇所を確認しておきたい。

2018年度　実施問題

【中高共通】

【1】はリスニングテストです。放送の指示に従ってください。

【1】放送を聞いて，次の[Part1]～[Part3]に答えよ。

[Part 1]

No.1

(A) Three dollars.

(B) Ten dollars.

(C) Twenty dollars.

(D) Thirty dollars.

No.2

(A) Spaghetti.

(B) Beef stew.

(C) Fried fish.

(D) Indian curry.

No.3

(A) Writing a report.

(B) Eating dinner.

(C) Reading a comic book.

(D) Watching a DVD.

No.4

(A) A movie star.

(B) A veterinarian.

(C) A police officer.

(D) A doctor.

No.5

(A) At two.

(B) At two thirty.

(C) At four thirty.

(D) At five.

No.6

(A) In the car.

(B) On the shelf by the window.

(C) In the pocket of the jacket.

(D) On the sofa.

[Part 2]

No.1 Takao is...

(A) a teacher.

(B) a friend.

(C) a student.

(D) a traveler.

No.2 This morning, Ms. Smith came here...

(A) by bike.

(B) by car.

(C) by train.

(D) on foot.

No.3 Takao will go...

(A) cycling next Sunday.

(B) fishing next Sunday.

(C) cycling next Saturday.

(D) fishing next Saturday.

No.4 Ms. Smith says that she likes traveling by bike, because...

(A) she can eat at different restaurants.

(B) she can meet people and make friends.

(C) she can enjoy beautiful scenery.

(D) she can go fishing in the sea.

[Part 3]

No.1　How many natural world heritage sites are considered to have "outstanding universal values"?

No.2　According to the new study, what are 63% of the sites under increased pressure from? Give two examples.

No.3　Which continent was home to sites with the most intense increases in human pressure?

No.4　Where did human pressure on natural world heritage sites decrease significantly?

No.5　The forest losses in North America were mostly caused by pine beetle outbreaks. What caused the pine beetle outbreaks?

(☆☆◎◎◎◎)

【中学校】

【1】次の英文を読んで，あとの[問1]～[問7]に答えよ。

I have been a writer of historical fiction. I have always liked history. I love history the way I love my parents. Whenever I am asked what history is, I always reply that it's a big world, a world crammed with the lives of the billions of people who lived before us.

I am lucky in having many wonderful friends in this world.

[　①　] There are wonderful people there, people it would be hard to find in this world, and they encourage me and comfort me in my daily life. As a result, I feel I am living within a period of time over two thousand years long, at the very least. I would like to share this pleasure with you, if that is what you'd like.

[　②　] There is something big which I don't have but you do: a future. I don't have much longer to live. For example, I am sure I won't be able to see the 21st century.

But you will. You will not only live to see your fill of the 21st century, but you will be its splendid leaders.

[③] I would like to ask you a question like that and learn the answer from you, but unfortunately I will no longer be on that street corner called the future. That's why it's only now, while I'm still here, that I can talk with you.

[④] But there is something I can speak on. This is the basic way for a human being to live, which I have learned from history.

In the ancient past and today, as well as in the future, there are ⑤<u>some things that do not change</u>. Among them is the existence of Nature－air, water, soil and such－and the fact that man, other animals, plants and even microorganisms rely on it to live. Nature has unchanging value. This is because man cannot live without breathing air, and unless he consumes water he becomes parched and dies. Here, I would like to think about man, using Nature, this "unchanging thing," as ⑥<u>a yardstick</u>.

Humans－though I may seem to repeat myself－are kept alive by Nature. In ancient times and in the Middle Ages, Nature was equated with gods. This is not wrong even slightly. People in history always feared Nature, respected its power, and behaved cautiously in the belief that Nature was something that is above them. This attitude wavered a little in modern and contemporary times. The conceited notion that it is man who is the greatest thing in existence reared its head. This contemporary era called the 20th century in a sense might be called the period in which the fear of Nature weakened.

At the same time, man is by no means a fool. He also thought almost the exact opposite of being conceited: namely, the idea that we human beings are merely one part of Nature.

This was what the wise men of ancient days also thought, and how 19th-century medical science thought of it too. This idea, which in a sense is nothing more than a common fact, was unfolded before people as scientific fact by 20th-century science.

People of the late 20th century, with knowledge of this fact, again came to fear Nature in the way people feared gods in ancient times and the Middle Ages. Probably, the period in which man lorded it over Nature will surely come to an end as time draws increasingly close to the 21st century.

"⑦Human beings do not live on their own, but are kept alive by a great presence."

This is how people in the Middle Ages, both in Europe and in the Orient, humbly thought. Although this thinking wavered after the arrival of modern times, in recent times human beings appear to be returning again to this good idea. This humble attitude toward Nature represents hope for the 21st century and the aspiration I have for you. I want you to have that kind of humility and to spread that feeling around. If you do, then the human beings of the 21st century will have even more respect for Nature. Then between humans, who are a part of Nature, there will surely be greater respect than in the previous century. For this to happen is also my aspiration for you.

Now, I will turn to you, yourselves. You, as has been so in all ages, must establish a self—a self that must be strict toward yourself, and kind toward others. And a self that is honest and wise. This will be especially important in the 21st century. In the 21st century, science and technology will develop further. ⑧Science and technology cannot be allowed to swallow up human beings like a flood. I want that your firm selves will take control over science and technology and take it in the right direction, like setting the course of a river properly.

Above, I frequently spoke about the "self." But though I have spoken of a self, it is wrong to slip into self-centeredness. Humans live by helping one another. When I look at the character for person, *hito*, I am frequently moved.

It is composed of two slanting lines supporting each other. As we can understand from this too, human beings live by forming a society. A society refers to an arrangement of mutual support. The society of primitive times was small. It was a society centered on the family. It gradually became a big society, and now we form societies called nations and the world, and we live by helping one another.

Man, as a natural being, was definitely not made to be able to live in (⑨).

Because of this, helping one another is a great moral virtue for human beings. The original origin of feelings and actions of helping one another is the sentiment called compassion. We might also speak of it as feeling the pain of others. Another way to call it might be kindness. "Compassion." "Feeling the pain of others." "Kindness." They are all similar types of expression. All three expressions originally derive from one root.

Though I say root, it isn't an instinct. That's why we have to train to acquire it.

The training is simple. For example, a friend stumbles. ⑩[develop / you / to do / to / all / is / have] within you, each time, a feeling that "Oh, that must have hurt." When that root of sentiment takes firm root within your self, a feeling of compassion toward other races will spring forth. So long as you make that kind of self, [⑪].

〔*To You Who Will Live in the 21st Century* (1999)　一部編集等あり〕

[問1]　本文中の[①]～[④]に入る最も適切な文を，次のア～エからそれぞれ1つずつ選び，その記号を書け。

ア　One thing makes me sad, though.

イ　Of course, I am altogether unable to predict what the 21st century will be like.

ウ　I have some in history too.

エ　How nice it would be if I could stop you on a street corner called "the future" and say, "Excuse me, young Mr. Tanaka. What kind of world is the 21st century where you are living now?"

[問2]　下線部⑤について，本文中に明記されているものをすべて日本語で書け。

[問3]　下線部⑥の説明として最も適切なものを，次のア～ウから1つ選び，その記号を書け。

ア　a level of quality or attainment

イ　a standard used for comparison

ウ　a significant stage or event in the development of something

[問4]　下線部⑦，⑧を日本語に直せ。

[問5]　文脈から考えて，本文中の(　⑨　)に入る最も適切な語を書け。ただし，その語は，iから始まるものとする。

[問6]　下線部⑩について，[　　]内の語句を，本文の流れに合うように正しく並べかえよ。ただし，文頭にくる語句も小文字にしている。

[問7]　文脈から考えて，本文中の[　⑪　]に入る最も適切なものを，次のア～ウから1つ選び，その記号を書け。

ア　the 21st century will surely become an age in which science and technology help us from stronger relationships with each other

イ　the 21st century will surely become an age in which mankind will be able to live in harmony

ウ　the 21st century will surely become an age in which people use the same unit of currency

(☆☆◎◎◎)

【2】次の[問1]，[問2]に答えよ。

[問1]　次の(1)～(10)について，(　　)に入る最も適切な語句を，ア～エからそれぞれ1つずつ選び，その記号を書け。

(1)　The party will not be held next Sunday, (　　)?

ア　won't it　　イ　will it　　ウ　shall we　　エ　will you

(2)　Tommy made him angry, (　　) I would never do.

ア that　イ who　ウ what　エ which

(3) If I had kept my word, I (　　) happy now.

ア am　イ will be　ウ would be　エ have been

(4) Mr. Tanaka told the secretary that he wouldn't be able to return to work (　　) September 5th.

ア before　イ within　ウ above　エ between

(5) The train (　　) from Wakayama to Tanabe is 1,660 yen.

ア fare　イ charge　ウ cost　エ fee

(6) He was in (　　) a hurry then that he left his wallet at home.

ア such　イ so　ウ quite　エ much

(7) It would (　　) me a lot of trouble if you could write more legibly.

ア find　イ take　ウ spend　エ save

(8) A: "It's very hot. What do you say to a glass of beer?"
B: "OK, (　　) not?"

ア could　イ why　ウ certainly　エ if

(9) He had a dream of becoming an actor even though he didn't know how to (　　) it.

ア perform　イ become　ウ realize　エ play

(10) We greatly (　　) the memory of the Reverend King.

ア polish　イ perish　ウ diminish　エ cherish

[問2] 次の(1)～(6)の英文は，生徒の作文の一部である。それぞれの英文の下線部のうち，誤っている箇所をア～エから1つ選び，その記号を書け。また，その箇所を正しい表現に書き直せ。

(1) When she heard the news, she was ア<u>too</u> sad イ<u>to</u> say ウ<u>something</u> エ<u>else</u>.

(2) I ア<u>enjoyed</u> イ<u>reading</u> the novel which I ウ<u>had</u> エ<u>lent</u> from the library the other day.

(3) I'm ア<u>going</u> to イ<u>talk</u> you ウ<u>about</u> my school エ<u>life</u>.

(4) I know this horse can run ア<u>very</u> イ<u>faster</u> ウ<u>than</u> that エ<u>one</u>.

(5) The students were ア<u>exciting</u> イ<u>to see</u> the ウ<u>gorgeous</u> fireworks

display $_{エ}$<u>held by</u> the lake.

(6) I'm looking $_{ア}$<u>forward</u> $_{イ}$<u>to see</u> you $_{ウ}$<u>at</u> the party $_{エ}$<u>next Sunday</u>.

(☆☆◎◎◎)

【3】次の英文を読んで，あとの[問1]～[問3]に答えよ。

With the changes in society, schools have increasingly been asked to take on a broader educational role of not only academic instruction, but also instruction in social-emotional and coping skills. This ①<u>call to action</u> has come from the increasing social and emotional needs of students in schools today. In the United States, there are approximately 50 million children and adolescents registered in public schools each year (National Center for Education Statistics, 2005). These students enter school buildings (②) various backgrounds, personal experiences, family factors, and cultural beliefs, which can affect students' learning potential, behavior, and emotional development. (③) a daily basis, schools are asked to help students who display behavioral and emotional difficulties to achieve academically.

In addition to these personal factors that students bring with them when they walk through the school doors, approximately 10% of all youth will be identified as having a mental-health disorder while they are (④) school age (National Institute of Mental Health, 2004). Moreover, approximately 12% to 20% of students under the age of 18 will have a need for mental-health services to address emotional or behavioral difficulties, even if they do not meet the criteria for a formal diagnosis (UCLA Center for Mental Health in Schools, 2006). In large urban schools, up to 50% of students may demonstrate a need for additional support to address emotional, behavioral, and learning needs (Center for Mental Health in Schools, 2003). Mental-health concerns and emotional stressors can affect a child's ability to learn and grow academically (Adelman & Taylor, 1998; 2000). Students who demonstrate emotional or behavioral difficulties in schools often have poorer academic performance and may have an increased number of negative social interactions (Coleman & Vaughn, 2000). Epstein and Cullinan (1994) found that difficulties with emotional and behavioral issues can lead to higher levels of truancy, suspension, tardiness, expulsion, attention-seeking behavior, and poor peer relationships.

Based upon this information, that a significant portion of students entering schools have some level of mental-health needs, teachers, administrators, and staff are required to adapt to the needs of their students in order to provide the education they deserve. The school system has the unique opportunity and potential ability to provide support and services to a large population of students in need, and has access to students who are spending a significant portion of their day in the school building. In addition to providing services to students with significant needs, the school system can also function in a preventing role to reduce factors that could be impeding a student's learning. Providing this type of mental-health service for students allows them to be more available for learning in the classroom, which is the primary goal of education. Intervening early in the lives of children also may reduce the need for mental-health supports later in life. With this type of preventive intervention in place, students are provided the opportunity to learn coping strategies to manage stressful situations and negative emotions that may stunt their emotional and academic development.

〔*COGNITIVE-BEHAVIORAL INTERVENTIONS IN EDUCATIONAL SETTINGS* (2012)　一部編集等あり〕

[問1]　下線部①とほぼ同じ意味を表す語を，次のア～エから1つ選び，その記号を書け。

ア　conclusion　　イ　project　　ウ　urge　　エ　responsibility

[問2]　本文中の(　②　)～(　④　)に入る最も適切な語の組み合わせを，次のア～エから1つ選び，その記号を書け。

ア　②　of　　③　with　　④　on

イ　②　with　　③　on　　④　of

ウ　② on　③ with　④ of
エ　② of　③ on　④ with

[問3]　次の(1)～(4)の英文について，本文の内容と一致するものにはTを，一致しないものにはFをそれぞれ書け。

(1) About 12% to 20% of students at school are encouraged to see a psychiatrist because of their emotional or behavioral difficulties.

(2) It can be said that the students' emotional or behavioral difficulties affect not only their academic performances but how successful they are at socializing.

(3) Because of their architectual characteristics, schools may play an important role in supporting the students showing some difficulties in behavior.

(4) Children provided with the type of preventive intervention mentioned in the article may have more chances to mentally stay fit later in life.

(☆☆☆◎◎◎)

【4】あなたは中学校英語科教員として，ある中学校で第1学年の生徒に英語を教えているとする。次の[問1]，[問2]に答えよ。

[問1]　現行の中学校学習指導要領「外国語」における「第2　各言語の目標及び内容等　英語　2内容　(1)言語活動」に示されている「書くこと」について，第1学年において，どのような到達目標を設定するか。また，設定した目標に生徒が到達したかどうかを把握するために，どのような課題を与えるべきか。英語で書け。

[問2]　[問1]の到達目標を達成するために，「書くこと」について，1年間を通してどのような工夫を行い指導するか。120語以上150語未満の英語で述べよ。なお，語数を記入すること。

(☆☆☆◎◎◎)

【高等学校】

【1】次の英文を読み，あとの[問1]～[問8]に答えよ。

I recently watched my sister perform an act of magic.

We were sitting in a restaurant, trying to have a conversation, but her children, 4-year-old Willow and 7-year-old Luca, would not stop fighting. The arguments－over a fork, or who had more water in a glass－were unrelenting.

Like a magician quieting a group of children by pulling a rabbit out of a hat, my sister reached into her purse and produced two shiny tablets, (①) one to each child. Suddenly, the two were quiet. Eerily so. They sat playing games and watching videos, and we continued with our conversation.

After our meal, as we stuffed the tablets back into their magic storage bag, my sister felt (②).

"I don't want to give them the tablets at the dinner table, but if it keeps them (③) for an hour so we can eat in peace, and more importantly not disturb other people in the restaurant, I often just hand it over," she told me. Then she asked: "Do you think it's bad for them? I do worry that it is setting them up to think it's O.K. to use electronics at the dinner table in the future."

I did not have an answer, and although some people might have opinions, no one has a true scientific understanding of ⓐ<u>[for a generation / hold / raised / the future / might / what]</u> on portable screens.

"We really don't know the full neurological effects of these technologies yet," said Dr. Gary Small, director of the Longevity Center at the University of California, Los Angeles, and author of "iBrain: Surviving the Technological Alteration of the Modern Mind." "Children, like adults, vary quite a lot, and some are more sensitive than others to an abundance of screen time." [A]

But Dr. Small says we do know that the brain is highly sensitive to stimuli, like tablet and smartphone screens, and spending too (④) time with one technology and (⑤) time interacting with people like parents at the dinner table could hinder the development of certain communications skills.

So will a child who plays with crayons at dinner rather than a coloring application on a tablet be a more socialized person?

Ozlem Ayduk, an associate professor in the Relationships and Social Cognition Lab at the University of California, Berkeley, said children sitting at the dinner table with a print book or crayons were not fully engaged with the people around them, either. "There are value-based lessons for children to talk to the people during a meal," she said. "It's not so much about the tablet versus nonelectronics." [B]

Parents who ⓑ[but / choice / hand / have / little / to] over their tablet can at least control what a child does on those devices.

A report published last week by the Millennium Cohort Study, a long-term study group in Britain that has been following 19,000 children born in 2000 and 2001, found that those who watched more than three hours of television or videos a day had a higher chance of conduct problems, emotional symptoms and relationship problems by the time they were 7 than children who did not. The study, of a sample of 11,000 children, found that children who played video games — often age-appropriate games — for the same amount of time did not show any signs of negative behavioral changes by the same age. [C]

Which brings us back to the dinner table with my niece and nephew. While they sat happily staring into those shiny screens, they were not engaged in any type of conversation or staring off into space thinking, as my sister and I did as children when our parents were talking. [D]

"Conversations with each other are the way children learn to have conversations with themselves, and learn how to be alone," said Sherry Turkle, a professor of science, technology and society at the Massachusetts Institute of Technology, and author of the book "Alone Together: Why We Expect More From Technology and Less From Each Other." "Learning about solitude and being alone is the bedrock of early development, and you don't want your kids to miss out on that because you're ⓒpacifying them with a device."

Ms. Turkle has interviewed parents, teenagers and other children about the use of gadgets during early development, and says she fears that children who do not learn real interactions, which often have flaws and imperfections, will come to know ⓓa world in which perfect, shiny screens give them a false sense of intimacy without risk.

And they need to be able to think, independent of a device. "They need to be able to explore their imagination. To be able to gather themselves and know who they are. So someday they can form a relationship with another person without a panic of being alone," she said. "If you don't teach your children to be alone, they'll only know how to be lonely."

〔*International Herald Tribune　April 2, 2013* 一部編集等あり〕

[問1]　本文中の(　①　)，(　③　)に入る最も適切な語の組み合わせを，次の(ア)～(エ)から1つ選び，その記号を書け。

(ア)　①　handing　　③　occupying
(イ)　①　handing　　③　occupied
(ウ)　①　handed　　③　occupying
(エ)　①　handed　　③　occupied

[問2]　本文中の(　②　)に入る最も適切な語句を，次の(ア)～(エ)から1つ選び，その記号を書け。

(ア)　too optimistic　　(イ)　least pessimistic　　(ウ)　slightly guilty
(エ)　fully innocent

[問3]　下線部ⓐ，ⓑについて，[　　]内の語句を本文の流れに合うように正しく並べかえよ。

[問4]　次の英文は，本文中の A ～ D のいずれかに入る。本文の流れから考えて最も適切な場所を選び，その記号を書け。

And that is where the risks are apparent.

[問5]　本文中の(　④　)，(　⑤　)に入る最も適切な語の組み合わせ

を，次の(ア)～(エ)から1つ選び，その記号を書け。

(ア) ④ much ⑤ more

(イ) ④ much ⑤ less

(ウ) ④ long ⑤ short

(エ) ④ little ⑤ much

[問6] 下線部ⓒが表す意味として最も適切なものを，次の(ア)～(エ)から1つ選び，その記号を書け。

(ア) calming (イ) upsetting (ウ) depressing

(エ) annoying

[問7] 下線部ⓓは，どのようなものか。日本語で具体的に書け。

[問8] 本文の内容と一致するものを，次の(ア)～(エ)から1つ選び，その記号を書け。

(ア) Dr. Gary Small says that children are more sensitive than adults to plenty of screen time.

(イ) Ozlem Ayduk states children who play with crayons at dinner are entirely absorbed in the conversation with the people around them.

(ウ) A report by the Millennium Cohort Study found children who played video games more than three hours a day showed signs of negative behavioral changes by the time they were 7.

(エ) According to Ms. Turkle, it is important for children to learn real interactions during early development so they don't develop an incorrect sense of relationships without risk.

(☆☆☆◎◎◎)

【2】次の英文を読み，あとの[問1]～[問9]に答えよ。

Here is a brief episode from a listening class in which intermediate-level learners of English as a second language were asked to (①) at the meaning of unfamiliar words. The group included three students from Japan and two each from Korea and China. (The letters J, K, or C indicate which country the student was from.) As we join their interaction, the teacher is playing an audio-recording (②) the word 'outstripped', (③) as a target for guessing because it was (④) to be in the vocabulary of these listeners. As you read the episode, look for the listening tactics of the students and the teaching tactics of the teacher.

AUDIO	I suppose the third most obvious problem for preventive medicine to tackle in the developing world / is the problem of uncontrolled population growth / there's the danger that food supplies may be outstripped by population increases
T	(*stops cassette*) so + now + + what do you think 'outstripped' means? (*waits for about five seconds*) what do you guess it means?
K1	I don't know + I never hear this before + what does it mean?
T	but that's why I'm asking you to guess! (*laughter*) + + anyone?
K1	we don't know this word + really + + please explain us
J1	you can play it again + once + once more + so we can listen well
T	no + ok what I want you to do now is + everybody write down now what you think 'outstripped' means + I'll give you five seconds to write down your guess and then ten seconds to compare what you have written (*waits for 15 seconds*) right + that's it + time's up + + what do we have?
J1	something like 'less than'
T	ok
J2	'not enough' ? maybe?
T	ok
K1	'beaten'
T	right
C1	I have 'defeated'
K2	I have 'destroyed'

T ok
C2 'exhausted'?
J3 'less than' or 'insufficient'
T brilliant + every one of those guesses is fine
(*author's classroom data 2002*)

What makes an effective listener? ⓐWhen it comes to assessing someone's ability as a listener, we have to bear in mind that listening can take various forms, which make different demands on us as listeners—whether in our own language or another. Michael Rost has suggested there are four main types of listening (Rost 2002: 158): ***appreciative***—for pleasure and relaxation, such as (⑤); ***informational***—to gain knowledge, such as (⑥); ***critical***—to assess the validity or relevance of what is being said; and ***empathic***—to understand someone's feelings, such as (⑦). Of course, those four categories are not hermetically sealed off from each other. [A], in some academic cultures university students are expected to combine informational and critical listening in lectures and seminars, and not simply to accept what they hear, but ⓑ[question / to / to / ready / rather / be] and debate.

In English, two words commonly used to describe a person's ability to listen, 'good' and 'effective', are used in different contexts and with different connotations. When we say someone is a 'good listener', what we have in mind is their competence in empathic listening; on the other hand, the term 'effective listener' is more likely to be used about informational listening. In the literature on second language listening strategies, effectiveness is related in some cases to the listener, in others to the strategy itself, or to the use of the strategy. [B], one of the first studies of second language listening strategies was entitled 'A study of the listening strategies used by skillful and unskillful college French students in aural comprehension tasks' (De Filippis 1980), showing a focus on the learners' skill in using strategies. Another, called 'A preliminary enquiry into the successful and unsuccessful listening strategies of beginning college Japanese students' (Fujita 1984), clearly assumed that it was the (⑧) that were effective or ineffective.

However, any strategy has to be assessed in its context of use: 'Logically, individuals will apply different strategies depending on their personality, cognitive style, *and the task at hand*' (Bacon 1992: 161, my emphasis). The effectiveness of the mental and other actions taken by a listener in pursuit of comprehension always have to be judged in relation to the specific listening activity they are engaged in, and instruction in listening strategies should be about *when* and *how* to use a particular strategy (Vandergrift: 2004). For instance, using cognate words to understand spoken English may work well for a French or Italian learner of English, but (⑨) well for a Thai or Hungarian. Furthermore, it may be (⑩) effective when the French and Italian learners are listening to formal English — where Latin-based vocabulary is (⑪) common than it is in everyday conversation, which tends to feature a higher proportion of shorter words of Germanic origin. In applying listening strategies, (⑫) is everything.

Some 30 years of research into learning strategies in general, and second language listening in particular, ⓒ[build up / us / allowed / have / to] a comprehensive taxonomy of strategies of potential value to the second language learner. In this context we should separate learning strategies (engaged in the cause of development of second language proficiency) from *communication strategies* (which are brought into service to deal with current communication problems). In the listening strategy literature, strategies are conventionally divided into three main categories: *cognitive* — used to make sense of what we hear; *metacognitive* — used to plan, monitor, and evaluate our understanding; and ⑬*socioaffective* — strategies which either involve other people in our efforts to understand, or which we use to encourage ourselves to understand.

〔Lynch, T, 2009. *Teaching second language listening*, Oxford: Oxford University Press　一部編集等あり〕

[問1]　本文中の(　①　)~(　④　)に入る最も適切な語を，次の語群からそれぞれ1つずつ選び，書け。ただし，必要があれば形を変えて書くこと。

[choose / likely / unlikely / guess / contain]

[問2]　下線部ⓐを日本語に直せ。

[問3]　本文中の(　⑤　)~(　⑦　)に入る最も適切な語句を，次の(ア)~(エ)からそれぞれ1つずつ選び，その記号を書け。

(ア)　watching a travel programme

(イ)　listening to music or a joke

(ウ)　when a doctor listens to a patient or when we listen to a friend talking about family problems

(エ)　when we listen to the sales pitch of a used-car dealer or the campaign speech of a political candidate

[問4]　下線部ⓑ，ⓒについて，[　　]内の語句を本文の流れに合うように正しく並べかえよ。

[問5]　本文中の A ， B に共通して入る適切な語句を，次の(ア)~(エ)から1つ選び，その記号を書け。

(ア)　On the contrary　　(イ)　For example　　(ウ)　In contrast

(エ)　In addition

[問6]　本文中の(　⑧　)に入る最も適切な一語を，本文中から抜き出して書け。

[問7]　本文中の(　⑨　)~(　⑪　)に入る最も適切な語の組み合わせを，次の(ア)~(エ)から1つ選び，その記号を書け。

(ア)　⑨　more　　⑩　less　　⑪　less

(イ)　⑨　more　　⑩　less　　⑪　more

(ウ)　⑨　less　　⑩　more　　⑪　less

(エ)　⑨　less　　⑩　more　　⑪　more

[問8]　本文中の(　⑫　)に入る最も適切な一語を，本文中から抜き出して書け。

[問9]　下線部⑬はどのようなものか，具体的に日本語で説明せよ。

(☆☆☆◎◎◎)

【３】下の(1)～(7)は，与えられた日本文に対して生徒が黒板に書いた英文である。生徒の英文をできるだけ生かすという観点で，正しい英文にするには，どのように直せばよいか。次の例にならって書け。

> (例)　オリンピックは2020年に日本で開催される。
>
> The 2020 Olympics will be taken place in Japan.
> take place

(1)　私は北海道でスキーすることを楽しみにしています。

I'm looking forward to ski in Hokkaido.

(2)　私はその果物が好きになった。

I became to like the fruit.

(3)　その映画はとてもつまらなかったので，私は眠ってしまった。

The movie was so bored that I fell asleep.

(4)　私が駅に着くとすぐに電車が出てしまった。

No sooner I got to the station than the train left.

(5)　明日雨が降れば，野球の試合は中止になります。

Our baseball game will be canceled if it will rain tomorrow.

(6)　もし消防隊員が着くのが少しでも遅れていたら，家は燃えてしまっていただろう。

If the firefighters had not arrived earlier, the house would be burned down.

(7)　どんなに遅くなっても，必ず私に電話をしてください。

No matter how you may be late, be sure to phone me.

(☆☆◎◎◎◎)

【4】現行の高等学校学習指導要領「外国語」における「第2款　各科目　第5　英語表現Ⅰ　2　内容」の項目のひとつに，「発表の仕方や発表のために必要な表現などを学習し，実際に活用すること。」という記述がある。このことについて，次の(1)，(2)の条件に従い，あなたならどのような言語活動を行うか，120語程度の英文にまとめて書け。なお，語数を記入すること。

《条件》

(1)　授業において発表の仕方や発表のために必要な表現などは既に生徒に示されている。

(2)　その表現を実際に活用し，定着させるための日々の言語活動であること。

(☆☆☆◎◎◎◎)

解答・解説

【中高共通】

【1】Part1　No.1　C　No.2　B　No.3　A　No.4　D　No.5　B　No.6　B　Part2　No.1　C　No.2　A　No.3　D　No.4　A　Part3　No.1　229 (natural world heritage) (sites are).

No.2　agriculture, infrastructure, settlements (うち2つ)

No.3　Asia (was).　No.4　(It decreased significantly) in Europe.

No.5　Climate change (did).

〈解説〉スクリプトは公開されていない。選択肢からPart1，Part2ともに平易な放送内容と質問であると想像できるが，日頃からリスニング教材などを活用してnative speaker の英語に慣れておくことが大切である。また，Part3は，記述式の問題であるので，できれば放送前に設問に目を通しておくこと。数字や固有名詞などを聞き逃さないように注意したい。なお，world heritage site「世界遺産」，outstanding universal value「顕著な普遍的価値」, significantly「著しく」, pine beetle outbreak「松くい虫の発生」である。

【中学校】

【1】問1　①　ウ　②　ア　③　エ　④　イ　問2　・空気, 水, 土など自然の存在　・人間や他の動物や植物, 微生物にいたるまでが, 生きるために自然に依存しているという事実　問3　イ
問4　⑦　人間は, 自分で生きているのではなく, 大きな存在によって生かされている。　⑧　科学や技術が, 洪水のように人類を飲み込んでしまってはならない。　問5　isolation　問6　[All you have to do is to develop] within you, …　問7　イ

〈解説〉問1　空欄の前後の文章から, 文意がつながる選択肢を探す。空欄①の直前の文章にwonderful friends in this world, 空欄後の文章にwonderful people thereとある。したがって空欄には「人」に関する選択肢が入ると推測される。ウのI have some in history, too.のsomeの後にはfriendsが省略されていると考えられるのでウが適切である。「歴史上にも, 私には友人がいる」として, 前文の「私はこの世にたくさんの素晴らしい友人を持って幸せだ」と対比させている。　空欄②に続く文章では, 筆者が「自分はもう長く生きられないので, 21世紀を見ることはないが, 君たちは21世紀を見て素晴らしいリーダーになることだろう」と告げている。その段落の最初の文であるから, アのOne thing makes me sad, though.「一つ悲しいことがあるのだが」が正解。fill of the 21st century「21世紀を思う存分」。　空欄③の直後に「私は君たちにこんな質問をしたい」と続くので, 選択肢から質問文を選ぶ。エ「未来という名の街角で君を呼びとめ,『すみませんが, 田中さん。あなたが生きている21世紀はどんな世界ですか。』とたずねることができたらどんなに素敵だろう」が正解。　空欄④を含む第6段落にはイが入り,「もちろん21世紀がどのようなものか, 私が予言することは全くできないが, 私が言えることがある。これが人間の生きていく基本の道だ。それを私は歴史から学んだ」となる。　問2　下線部⑤

を含む文の意味は「未来だけでなく，太古の昔や現在においても，変わらないものがいくつかある」。変わらないものの具体例は，その次の文章のthe existence of Nature以下の部分と，the fact that以下の部分に示されている。　問3　yardstickとは「判断や比較の基準，ものさし」を意味する語である。　問4　⑦　on one's own「一人で，独力で，自分自身で」。　⑧　allow＋名詞(人・もの)＋to～「名詞(人・もの)が～することを許す」。　問5　第15段落では，人間が一人では生きていけないこと，助け合って生きていくべきことが述べられている。よって孤立や分離を意味するisolationが入る。　問6「思いやり」という感情は本能ではなく，獲得するために訓練が必要なのだが，例えば，友人がよろけたときどうするかという話の流れである。「ケガをしたに違いないという(相手を思いやる)感情を，毎回自分の中に持てばよい」が正解。All you have to do is to ～はよく使われる表現。直訳は「あなたがやらないといけないことの全ては～だ」。「～するだけでいい」としばしば訳される。　問7　空欄⑪が入る文の前半部分の意味は「あなたがそのような自分を作れば」。「そのような自分」とは他の人種にも思いやりの感情をもった人間を指す。よってイ「21世紀は，人類が調和の中で生きることのできる時代に必ずやなるだろう」が続くのが適切である。

【2】問1　(1)　イ　(2)　エ　(3)　ウ　(4)　ア　(5)　ア　(6)　ア　(7)　エ　(8)　イ　(9)　ウ　(10)　エ

問2　(1)　記号…ウ　正しい表現…anything　(2)　記号…エ　正しい表現…borrowed　(3)　記号…イ　正しい表現…tell　(4)　記号…ア　正しい表現…much　(5)　記号…ア　正しい表現…excited　(6)　記号…イ　正しい表現…to seeing

〈解説〉問1　(1)　付加疑問文を完成させる問題。否定文の後なので，肯定の疑問形をつける。　(2)　関係代名詞whichが正解。whichは名詞や名詞句ばかりでなく，直前の文全体を先行詞とすることもある。

(3)　仮定法。「もし私が約束を守っていたら，今は幸せになっているだろう」。If節は，過去のことを指すのだから，過去の事実に反する仮定としてhad keptという仮定法過去完了が使われている。それに対して主節の方には，nowがある。現在の事実に反する仮定は仮定法過去で表すので，主節ではwould beという仮定法過去の形が使われる。If節と主節で，表す時が異なっている。　(4)「田中氏は秘書に9月5日(　　)仕事に復帰できないだろうと言った」なので，アのbefore～「～より前に」が入る。なお，within「～以内に」はwithin three weeksのように使い，within September 5thでは「9月5日その日のうちに」というニュアンスになる。　(5)　交通機関の料金を表すのはア。サービスに対する料金はイ，経費はウ，謝礼がエ。なお，通行料はtoll。
(6)　so［such］～that…で「とても～なので…」。問題文のようにa hurryと名詞を伴う場合，suchを使う。　(7)　save「時間，労力，金を省く，節約する」という意味。「もしあなたがもっと読みやすく書けば，私の手間がかからないだろう」。　(8)　What do you say to～？は「あなたは～に対して何と言いますか？」「～はどうですか？」と相手に提案する言い方。toは前置詞である。why not? は，提案などに対して「そうしましょう。いいですよ」と同意する言い方。　(9)　realizeには「～を実現する，達成する」という意味がある。　(10)「私たちは故キング牧師を非常に慕っている」。cherish the memory of ～で「～(故人)を慕う」。Reverend Kingはアメリカの公民権運動指導者マーティン・ルーサー・キング・ジュニア牧師の通称。　問2　(1)「彼女はそのニュースを聞いたとき，悲しくて他に何も言えなかった」。「何も，どんなことも，全く」という否定のニュアンスはanything。　(2)「借りる」はborrow-borrowed-borrowed。「貸す」はlend-lent-lent。
(3)　talkは自動詞なので目的語をとらない。　(4)　比較級を強めるのはmuch。　(5)　人が興奮した状態にあることを表す場合はexcited。
(6)　look forward toのtoは前置詞。よって後ろは名詞(動名詞)にする。

【3】問1　ウ　　問2　イ　　問3　(1)　F　　(2)　T　　(3)　F
(4)　T

〈解説〉問1　call to actionとは「行動への要請，行動喚起」。よってウの「催促，督促」が適切である。　問2　②　様々な背景，個人的経験，家庭的要素，文化的信念という言葉を従えることから，所有を表す前置詞withが正解。　③　on a daily basisで「日常的に，毎日のように」の意味。　④　be＋of＋名詞で形容詞的意味になる用法がある。while they are of school ageで「彼らが学齢期にある間に」。　問3　(1)　本文第2段落第2文では，「約12～20％の生徒が正式な診断の基準に満たないが，メンタルヘルスサービスを受ける必要がある」と述べている。「精神科医にかかるよう勧められている」とは一致しない。　(3)　本文第3段落第2文では，「学校制度には，問題を抱えた生徒たちをサポートする独自の機会がある」と述べている。「学校の建築上の特徴が生徒のサポートに重要な役割を果たす」とは一致しない。(2)，(4)は本文の内容と一致する。

【4】問1　The students can write about themselves in more than three sentences or 15 words. I will let the students write short essays about themselves or their ideas.　問2　I'll try the following things. First, having fun in writing is important for first-year students. I'll choose topics, for example about their favorite things that are popular among the students to help them exchange their ideas with their classmates. They will share their sentences in pairs and become more comfortable expressing them in English. Second, I'll give them opportunities to communicate with foreigners by greeting cards to enhance students' writing motivation. I'll give the students as many authentic opportunities as possible. When they want to use words they haven't learned, I'll teach the students how to consult dictionaries to find the words they want to use, or how to change difficult words into easier ones. Third, I'll make a CAN-DO list, and give positive feedback to the students every unit so they can know how their writing skills are getting better and have more confidence in writing English. (149語)

〈解説〉問1　「書くこと」の到達目標の設定について，公開解答では，

「自分自身のことについて(3文以上または15語以上で)書くこととし，ショートエッセイを課す」としている。他には「行事や旅の思い出を書く」，「葉書やメールを書く」などを目標に掲げて到達度を把握することもできる。読み手を意識して書くことが大切であるので，だれに対して書くのか設定を明確にするとよい。　問2　到達目標の達成について，公開解答では，「1　書くことを楽しめるようなトピックを選ぶこと。　2　実際にやりとりをする機会を与えることで動機づけをすること。　3　CAN-DO listを作成し，生徒に成果をフィードバックすることで自信を持たせること」の3点を挙げている。公開解答のように「第1に～」「第2に～」「第3に～」などの表現を利用すれば，話の展開がわかりやすくなる。書くことに抵抗のある生徒は多いので，アイディアマップを利用して考えを可視化し，書く内容を整理させたり，モデル文を示したり，「使えそうな表現・語彙を提示する」など一連の流れを作ったりすることで，苦手な生徒の負担感を軽減するなどの工夫が考えられる。

【高等学校】

【1】問1　(イ)　　問2　(ウ)　　問3　ⓐ　what the future might hold for a generation raised　　ⓑ　have little choice but to hand　　問4　D
問5　(イ)　　問6　(ア)　　問7　完全な輝かしい画面が，危険のない間違った親近感を与える世界　　問8　(エ)

〈解説〉問1　①　姉が子どもたちにタブレットを手渡したという場面なのでhandingが正しい。　③　they＝occupiedの関係が成立するSVOCの文。意味は「もしそれが彼らを夢中にし続ければ」。if it keeps them occupiedが正解となる。　問2　空欄の次の姉の発言から，食事の席で子どもにタブレットを仕方なく与えていることがわかる。よって(ウ)の「少し罪悪感がある」が正解。　問3　ⓐ　what the future might hold「将来待ち受けているだろうこと」。raised on～「～で育った」。
ⓑ　have little choice but to～「～することを除き選択はない，～するより仕方ない」。butはexcept「～を除いて」の意。　問4　英文は「そ

してそれが危険が明白であるところだ」という意味。第12段落では，「テレビやビデオを1日3時間以上見た子どもは，7歳までに様々な問題を起こすことが多いが，同時間ゲームをした子どもが7歳までに否定的な行動の変化を示す兆候は全くない」とする調査結果を紹介している。かえってそれが危険だと述べるくだりである。　問5　コミュニケーションスキルの発達を妨げると考えられるのは，ある技術に多くの時間を費やすこと，食卓で(言葉による)やりとりする時間がないことである。よって，④はmuch，⑤はlessとなる。　問6　下線部ⓒを含む全文の意味は，「孤独について学ぶことや一人でいることは，幼年期の発達の基礎である。あなたは道具で子どもをなだめているからといって，子どもにそれを逃してほしくはないでしょう」。pacify＝calmである。　問7　a worldを修飾するin which以下を訳す。
問8　第7段落第2文に「画面に接する時間が多いことに，他の人より敏感な者もいる」とある。子どもと大人を比較して述べているのではないので(ア)は誤り。(イ)も第10段落第1文後半の内容「食卓でクレヨンや絵本で遊ぶ子どもも，周りの人と全く関わっていない」と異なる。(ウ)は，第12段落の「問題を起こすのはテレビやビデオを見た子どもでありゲームをした子どもでない」という内容と逆のことを述べている。

【2】問1　①　guess　②　containing　③　chosen　④　unlikely
問2　リスニング力を測るときに心に留めておかなければならないことは，リスニングが様々な形式をとり得るということ，そしてそれゆえ聞き手に求められるものも様々であるということだ。
問3　⑤　(イ)　⑥　(ア)　⑦　(ウ)　問4　ⓑ　rather to be ready to question　ⓒ　have allowed us to build up　問5　(イ)
問6　strategies　問 7　(エ)　問8　context　問9　理解しようと努める中で他者と関わるストラテジー(戦略)や，自分自身を励まして理解しようとするために使用するストラテジー(戦略)
〈解説〉問1　①　guess at「～を推測する」で「なじみのない単語の意味

を推測するよう求められた」の意。　② containingで「outstrippedという語を含む音声再生装置」。　③ chosenで「推測するためのターゲットとして選ばれた」。　④ unlikelyで「これらの聞き手の語彙にはありそうになかったので」。　問2　when it comes to ～で「(話が)～するということになると，～に関していえば」。toは前置詞。bear in mindは「心に留めておく」。　問3　⑤は，appreciative listening「鑑賞的なリスニング」を説明する部分なので(イ)の「音楽やジョークを聞く」が適切である。　⑥ informational listening「情報を得るためのリスニング」は(ア)の「テレビ番組を観る」。　⑦ empathic listening「親身になって聞くこと」なので(ウ)の「医師が患者の訴えを聞く，あるいは友達の家族の問題について話すのを聞く」。　問4　ⓑは，not A but rather B「AではなくむしろB」を含む文。よって「聞いたことを受け入れるためだけでなく，むしろ質問する準備をするために」と並び替える。ⓒは「allow＋人＋to」を使い，「第2言語習得者にとって潜在的に役立つ方策の包括的分類基準を作り上げることを可能にした」とする。　問5　空欄Aの前では，「リスニングの4カテゴリーは，お互い(相容れないよう)密閉されていない」ことを具体的に述べている。同様に空欄Bの前では，「第2言語のリスニングストラテジーに関する文献では，有効性は，聞き手に関係する場合もあるのだが，ストラテジーそのもの，つまりストラテジーの使用に関係する」ことを述べている。ともに，空欄の後では前の文の具体例を提示しているので，空欄に入るのは(イ)「例えば」が正解。　問6　この段落のまとめの文章である。「有効か有効でないかは，ストラテジーである(聞き手ではない)」となる。　問7　空欄⑨の前にbutがあるので，文の前半work wellを否定する表現になればよいからlessが正解。空欄⑩はfurthermore「さらに，そのうえ」で文章が始まり，有効であるフランス人とイタリア人の例を再度提示しているのでmoreが正解。空欄⑪はformal Englishがどういうものかの説明箇所である。文脈から，「formal Englishには日常会話の英語よりもラテン語の語彙が『多く』使われている」と判断できるのでmoreが正解である。　問8　本段落のまとめの文であり，段落の初文any strategy has to be assessed in its context of useをもう一度振り返る文となっている。ここから空欄⑫にはcontextが入ることがわかる。「リスニングストラテジーを利用するときには，状況がすべてである」となる。　問9　下線部⑬に続くハイフン以下の部分が答えである。

【3】(1) I'm looking forward to ski in Hokkaido.
skiing

(2) I became to like the fruit.
began(got / came)

(3) The movie was so bored that I fell asleep.
boring

(4) No sooner I got to the station than the train left.
had I got

(5) Our baseball game will be canceled if it will rain tomorrow.
rains

(6) If the firefighters had not arrived earlier, the house would be burned down.
have been

(7) No matter how you may be late, be sure to phone me.
late you may be

〈解説〉(1)　look forward toのtoは前置詞なので，後ろには名詞(動名詞)を置く。　(2)　becomeは後ろに名詞や形容詞をとり「～になる」。「～するようになる」という意味でbecome to doは不可。　(3)　boredは人が退屈した状態を表す。　(4)　I had no sooner got to the station than the train left.も同意であるが，No soonerを文頭に置くと倒置が起きNo sooner had I got to…となる。　(5)　時や条件を表す副詞節中では未来のことであっても「実際にあること」と考えるから，現在形で表す。　(6)　仮定法過去完了。よって主節は助動詞の過去形＋have＋過去分詞。　(7)　「どんなに遅くなっても」はNo matter how late＝However late。

【4】At the beginning of each class, I will use 10 minutes for students to practice making presentations. First, I will divide them into groups of four and have them decide the order in which they speak. Second, writing down the topic on the board, I will give them a minute for the speaker to prepare for the speech and for the listeners to think about possible questions. They are expected to speak clearly with enough eye contact. After a minute of speaking, the listeners ask questions and make comments for a minute. I will time the activity with a stopwatch. They will take turns for 10 minutes. In this way, students can get used to using the expressions and speaking in public. (122語)

〈解説〉高等学校学習指導要領解説「外国語編」「第2章　第5節　英語表現I　2　内容　(2)　ウ」には，「発表に当たっては，原稿を書いてそれを読むだけではなく，アウトラインや大切なポイントを書いたメモに基づいて発表したり，何も見ないで発表したりといった，様々な発表の仕方を指導することが大切である。また，内容を単に暗記するのではなく，内容を理解し，聴衆と目を合わせながら発表できるようにすることも必要である」とある。これらの内容を踏まえて模範解答は，スピーチ活動をするにあたり，その場でトピックを与え，考えをまとめる時間を1分に限定すること，アイコンタクトを十分すること，聞き手には質問やコメントをさせることで，インターアクションの時間を設けることなどを盛り込んだ内容となっている。最終的なゴールを生徒に提示し，10分の帯活動の継続が生きるようにしなければならない。なお，学習指導要領は英語版と同解説も含めて必ず熟読しておくこと。

2017年度　実施問題

【中高共通】

[1]はリスニングテストです。放送の指示に従ってください。

【1】放送を聞いて，[Part1]～[Part3]の各問に答えよ。

[Part 1]

No. 1

(A) Today.

(B) Tomorrow.

(C) The day after tomorrow.

(D) Next Monday.

No. 2

(A) See the tennis match.

(B) Finish her assignment.

(C) Go to Kinokuni Tennis Park.

(D) Buy two tickets for the tennis match.

No. 3

(A) Restaurant.

(B) Plaza Hotel.

(C) Hospital.

(D) Convenience store.

No. 4

(A) Fishing.

(B) Hiking.

(C) Rafting.

(D) Swimming.

No. 5

(A) Sandwiches.

(B)　Hot dogs.

(C)　Pancakes.

(D)　Chicken soup.

No. 6

(A)　Join the party.

(B)　Marry Kevin.

(C)　Decide to have a party.

(D)　Propose to Kevin.

[Part 2]

No. 1　This conversation takes p1ace...

(A)　at a station.

(B)　at a hotel.

(C)　at a restaurant.

(D)　at a ticket counter.

No. 2　The woman wants to...

(A)　use the Wi-Fi.

(B)　have the user ID.

(C)　use a hotel computer.

(D)　have the password.

No. 3　The woman decided to go to...

(A)　an opera.

(B)　a classical concert.

(C)　a musical.

(D)　a rock concert.

No. 4　The woman ordered scrambled eggs, toast, ham, ...

(A)　chicken salad and coffee.

(B)　tuna salad and coffee.

(C)　chicken salad and hot chocolate.

(D)　tuna salad and tea.

[Part 3]

No. 1　How many people are there in the world who go hungry?

No. 2　Why is it important for Japan to use the resources carefully?

No. 3　What kinds of industrial products are banned from being dumped? Give two examples.

No. 4　What is the only way to deal with plastic bags and wrapping materials?

No. 5　What percentage of our garbage can be reduced when reusable shopping bags are used?

(☆☆☆◎◎◎)

【中学校】

【1】次の英文を読んで，あとの[問1]～[問7]に答えよ。

There are few insects that people respectfully call by an ①honorific. I am referring to the way Japanese people call silkworms *okaiko-sama*. Bestowing the honorific shows the degree of awe people have in the way the worms produce glossy silk thread. Silk has long been admired as a source of riches.

Raw silk used to be a major export item for Japan. However, with the emergence of synthetic fibers, ②production declined. About 50 years ago, there used to be 800,000 silkworm farmers in Japan. Now, there are (　③　) than 3,000. ④In fact, the silkworm industry appears to be hanging by a thread. Recently, (　⑤　), silkworms have begun to attract renewed attention.

Cocoons that are the source of silk are made from protein that physiologically agrees with the human body. It is also believed to prevent bacteria and mold breeding and helps to prevent damage by ultraviolet rays. As a natural material, it has great potential health benefits. Already, cosmetics products that use silk protein are on the market.

Japan is also active in analyzing genetic information of the silkworm. Last month, Japanese scientists announced they had deciphered 80% of the silkworm genome, a world first. I am told the information will lead to the development of medicines and agricultural chemicals. ⑥The silkworm [role / is / the / leading / playing] in the vanguard of insect technology.

【 Silkworms have been used by humans for thousands of years and we can't find them in the natural environment in Japan any longer. Unlike honeybees, which also have lived very closely with humans, silkworms cannot find food for themselves or escape any longer. Silkworms don't do any harm to humans. It takes special skill to produce silk, and the silkworm is a gentle insect that makes it a research subject without any faults. 】

They hatch, become larvae and repeatedly shed their skin before they produce thread to wrap themselves up. ⑦Silkworms not only [also / of life / teach us / contribute / the mystery / but] to the advancement of life science.

〔*VOX POPULI, VOX DEI* (2004)　一部編集等あり〕

[問1]　下線部①の語を，中学校第3学年の生徒が理解できるように平易な英語を用いて30語以内で説明せよ。

[問2]　下線部②の理由を日本語で書け。

[問3]　文中の(　③　)，(　⑤　)に入る最も適切な語を，次のア～エから1つずつ選び，その記号を書け。

ア　much　　イ　moreover　　ウ　fewer　　エ　though

[問4]　下線部④を日本語に直せ。

[問5]　下線部⑥，⑦の[　　]内の語(句)をそれぞれ正しく並べかえよ。

[問6]　次の英文は，文中の【　　】の部分を，ほぼ同じ内容になるように書き換えたものである。次の(　ア　)～(　オ　)に入る最も適切な語(句)を語群より選び，その語(句)を書け。

Silkworms have been used by humans for thousands of years and are (　ア　) found in their natural habitat in Japan. Unlike honeybees, which also have a long history of (　イ　) with humans, silkworms have lost their (　ウ　) to feed themselves or escape. They pose no (　エ　) to humans. It takes special skill to produce silk, and the silkworm is a gentle insect and we regard it as an (　オ　) research subject.

〔語群〕

coexisting　no longer　ideal　risk　easy
ability　no more　unless　profit　able

[問7]　本文のタイトルとして最も適切なものを次のア～ウから1つ選び，その記号を書け。

ア　Silkworms in the limelight again as a Japanese export item
イ　Thank silkworms for health benefit they offer
ウ　The Japanese growth thanks to silkworms and honeybees

(☆☆☆◎◎◎)

【2】次の[問1]，[問2]に答えよ。

[問1]　次の(1)～(10)について，(　　)に入る最も適切な語または語句を，ア～エからそれぞれ1つずつ選び，その記号を書け。

(1)　You'll have to get up (　　) tomorrow morning.
ア　early　イ　fast　ウ　soon　エ　at once

(2)　That's the (　　) fish I've ever had.
ア　good　イ　better　ウ　best　エ　much better

(3)　I cannot believe that you didn't even know when World War Ⅱ (　　) out.
ア　break　イ　breaks　ウ　broke　エ　broken

(4)　He could not help (　　) when he heard the news.
ア　laugh　イ　laughing　ウ　laughed　エ　to laugh

(5)　Mary can play the violin, not to (　　) the piano.
ア　say　イ　talk　ウ　speak　エ　mention

(6)　Japan (　　) the policy of a consumption tax in 1989.
ア　adapted　イ　added　ウ　adhered　エ　adopted

(7)　It was (　　) of the staff of the shop to bring the child a candy and a glass of tea on such a hot day.
ア　considerable　イ　considerate　ウ　considered
エ　considering

(8)　Last year I made (　　) with many people in Australia.

　ア　frineds　　イ　goods　　ウ　contacts　　エ　intimates

(9)　Yumi (　　) her brother to help her with her homework.

　ア　let　　イ　made　　ウ　had　　エ　got

(10)　Garbage was carefully saved and fed (　　) the pig.

　ア　to　　イ　at　　ウ　with　　エ　of

[問2]　下の英文は，「夏休み」というタイトルで生徒が書いた英作文である。生徒の英文をできるだけ生かすという観点で，正しい英文にするには，どのように直せばよいか。次の例にならって書け。

(例)　I <u>am like</u> apples. 　　　　like

I went to Shiga during the summer vacation with my family. My grandmother's house standing near Lake Biwa. In August 6th we saw fireworks. They were very beautiful in the sky.

I wanted getting a present for my friend. So I went to a shop. Many kinds of key chains were sold there. I bought that. The next day I went to swimming. After that we had dinner at a Japanese restaurant. I forgot my cap there.

(☆☆☆◎◎◎)

【3】次の英文を読んで，あとの[問1]～[問5]に答えよ。

A number of personality characteristics have been proposed as likely to affect second language learning, but it has not been easy to confirm in empirical studies. As with other research investigating the effects of individual characteristics on second language learning, studies of a similar personality trait produce different results. For example, it is often argued that an ①<u>extroverted</u> person is well suited to language learning but research does not always support this conclusion. Although some studies have found that success in language learning is correlated with learners' scores on questionnaires measuring characteristics associated with extroversion such as assertiveness and adventurousness, others have found that many successful language learners would not get high scores on measures of extroversion. Lily Wong Fillmore (1979) observed that, in certain learning situations, the quiet observant learner may have greater success.

Another aspect of personality that has been studied is inhibition. It has been suggested that inhibition discourages risk-taking, which is necessary for progress in language learning. This is often considered to be a particular problem for adolescents, who are more self-conscious than younger learners. In a series of studies in the 1970s, Alexander Guiora and his colleagues (1972) found support for the claim that inhibition is a negative force, at least for second language pronunciation performance. One study involved an analysis of the effects of small doses of alcohol, known for its ability to reduce inhibition, on pronunciation. Study participants who drank small amounts of alcohol did better on pronunciation tests than those who did not drink any. While results such as these are interesting, they may have more to do with performance than with learning. We may also note, in passing, that when larger doses of alcohol were administered, pronunciation rapidly deteriorated!

Learner anxiety — feelings of worry, nervousness, and stress that many students experience when learning a second language — has been extensively investigated. For a long time, researchers thought of anxiety as a permanent feature of a learner's personality. In fact, the majority of language anxiety scales like the Foreign Language Classroom Anxiety Scale (Horwitz, Horwitz, and Cope 1986) measure anxiety in this way. So, for example, students are assumed to be 'anxious' if they 'strongly agree' with statements such as 'I become nervous when I have to speak in the second language classroom'. However, such questionnaire responses do not take account of the possibility that anxiety can be temporary and context-specific.

A

Peter MacIntyre(1995) argues that 'because nervous students are focused on both the task at hand and their reactions to it ... [they] will not learn as quickly as relaxed students'.

Of course, it has also been argued that not all anxiety is bad and that a certain amount of tension can have a positive effect and even facilitate learning. Experiencing anxiety before a test or an oral presentation can provide the right combination of motivation and focus to succeed. Because anxiety is often considered to be a negative term, some researchers have chosen to use other terms they consider to be more neutral. In a study of young adults learning French in an intensive summer programme, Guy Spielmann and Mary Radnofsky (2001) used the term 'tension'. They found that tension, as experienced by the learners in their study, was perceived as both beneficial and detrimental and that it was also related to the learners' social interactions inside and outside the classroom. 〔　②　〕

A learner's willingness to communicate (WTC) has also been related to anxiety. We have all experienced occasions when we tried to avoid communicating in a second language. WTC may change with the number of people present, the topic of conversation, the formality of the circumstances, and even with whether we feel tired or energetic at a given moment. 〔　③　〕

This is consistent with research carried out by Richard Clément, Peter MacIntyre, and their colleagues, who argue that learners who willingly communicate in a wide range of conversational interactions are able to do so because of their communicative confidence. In a series of studies they have shown that communicative confidence is shaped by two variables: how relaxed L2 learners are and how competent (or incompetent) they feel about their L2 ability. These factors are directly influenced by previous contacts with L2 speakers and are considered to be the main contributors to communicative confidence (Clément, Baker, and MacIntyre 2003). 〔 ④ 〕

Several other personality characteristics such as self-esteem, empathy, dominance, talkativeness, and responsiveness have also been studied. The research does not show a clearly-defined relationship between one personality trait and second language acquisition.

〔Patsy M. Lightbown & Nina Spada(2013). *How Languages are Learned.* Oxford University Press 一部編集等あり〕

[問1] 下線部①の語と置き換えても文意が変わらないものは次のア～エのどれか。その記号を書け。

ア popular　イ intellectual　ウ successful　エ outgoing

[問2] 次のア～ウの文は文中の［ A ］に入っていたものである。本文の流れに合うように並べかえて入れるとどのような順序になるか，記号を書け。

ア Whatever the context, anxiety can interfere with the learning process.

イ Other researchers investigating learner anxiety in second language classrooms see anxiety as dynamic and dependent on particular situations and circumstances.

ウ This permits distinctions to be made between for example, feeling anxious when giving an oral presentation in front of the whole class but not when interacting with peers in group work.

[問3] 次の英文は，文中の〔 ② 〕～〔 ④ 〕のどこに入るか。最も適切な場所の番号を書け。

A colleague in Canada, who works in the area of second language learning and speaks several languages, recently confessed that he avoided the corner store in his neighbourhood because the proprietor always spoke

French to him. He recognized the proprietor's efforts to help him improve his skills in this new language, and was grateful for it, but, as he told us with embarrassment, it was just easier to go to the store where he could use English.

[問4]　次のア～エのうち，willingness to communicate(WTC)との関連が文中で述べられていないものを1つ選び，その記号を書け。

ア　content of the conversation

イ　the research on personality

ウ　physical condition

エ　formality of the situation

[問5]　次の(1)～(4)の英文について，本文の内容と一致するものにはTを，一致しないものにはFをそれぞれ書け。

(1)　When we teach adolescents, we should be aware that their inhibition may discourage them to take some risks while making performances in language learning.

(2)　All learners who are nervous and always worrying will learn as quickly as relaxed students because anxiety is a permanent feature of leaners' personality.

(3)　Guy Spielman and Marry Radnofsky found tension can be beneficial when the learners interact only inside the classroom.

(4)　No research has succeeded in finding a clear relationship between one personality trait and second language learning.

(☆☆☆◎◎◎)

【4】あなたは中学校英語科教員として，ある中学校で第2学年の生徒に英語を教えているとする。

あなたは教科書等を活用して語彙や文法の指導を十分に行っており，生徒の定期テスト(リスニング問題・筆記問題)の結果は満足できるものである。

しかし，スピーキングテストを実施してみると，「話す力」が定着していないということがわかった。そこであなたは生徒に「話す力」を身に付けさせるために，「即興で話す力」が必要であると考えた。

今後，その生徒たちに「即興で話す力」を身に付けさせるために，授業において，どのような工夫を行うか。具体的な活動を含めて，120語以上150語未満の英語で述べよ。なお，語数を記入すること。

(☆☆☆☆◎◎◎)

【高等学校】

【1】次の英文を読み，[問1]～[問9]に答えよ。

Humans have been screwing with their body clocks — and getting less sleep — ever since the Wizard of Menlo Park had his very bright idea. Indeed, our classic eight-hour-night only dates back to the invention of the light bulb in the late 1800s. Historians believe that before the dawn of electric lighting most people got plenty of sleep, and practiced what they call "(①) sleep," snoozing for several hours in the first part of the night, when darkness fell, then waking in the middle of the night for a few hours of eating, drinking, praying and chatting with friends, before ducking back under the covers again until morning. The arrival of electricity, argues sleep historian A. Roger Ekirch, led to (②) bedtimes and (③) hours of sleep overall.

We're still waging a war on sleep, and ⓐwe are still winning. Researchers at the University of Chicago recently studied our sleep patterns over time and concluded that we now sleep between one and two hours less than we did 60 years ago. In the 1970s, most Americans slept about 7.1 hours per night: Now the ⓑmean sleep duration has plunged to 6.1 hours.

So where's all this sleep gone to? And why are we losing it?

Modern technology is certainly a large part of the problem. Smartphones, tablets and computer screens all emit a bluish light; great for saving power, but also just right for disrupting our body clocks. "The lights on these electronic devices are colored like enriched moonlight," says Charles Czeisler, the director of Harvard Medical School's Division of Sleep Medicine. These blue lights suppress the production of ⓒmelatonin, the hormone that controls the body's day-night cycle. So reading in bed with a backlit device, he says, makes it harder to fall asleep and makes you more tired the next day.

Shifting all the blame for our sleep problems onto blue light, (④), might be disingenuous. The bigger problem might be that we've created and now live in a world where stimulation doesn't stop when the sun goes down — thanks, Tom! — and it's making us all addicts. Research shows that ⓓ[our / check / time / we / every / email], Twitter feed or Facebook timeline and find a new piece of information, we get a shot of dopamine — a chemical our brains release to simulate pleasure. "We eventually associate texts, Twitter [and] Facebook with the promise of instant ⓔgratification," says Kathy Gill, an expert in human-computer interaction at the University of Washington. The temptation to get that quick dopamine shot can be ignored through willpower, says Gill, but willpower's at an all-time low when we haven't gotten enough sleep. Hence the cycle of sitting up in bed, listlessly refreshing our email even when it's way past our bedtime and we really should put our computers and phones down. And our head on a pillow.

〔*NEWSWEEK 26 01/30/2015*〕

[問1]　本文中の(①)に入る最も適切な語を，次の(ア)～(エ)から1つ選び，その記号を書け。

(ア)　sustained　(イ)　segmented　(ウ)　unbroken

(エ)　uninterrupted

[問2]　本文中の(②)，(③)に入る最も適切な語の組み合わせを，次の(ア)～(エ)から1つ選び，その記号を書け。

(ア)　② earlier　③ longer　(イ)　② earlier　③ less

(ウ)　② later　③ more　(エ)　② later　③ fewer

[問3]　下線部ⓐが表す意味として最も適切なものを，次の(ア)～(エ)から1つ選び，その記号を書け。

(ア)　we have a sound sleep

(イ)　we have a light sleep

(ウ)　our sleep is getting shorter

(エ)　our sleep is getting longer

[問4]　下線部ⓑと同じ意味を含む英文を，次の(ア)～(エ)から1つ選び，その記号を書け。

(ア)　I want to know the <u>mean</u> annual rainfall here.

(イ)　He plays a <u>mean</u> trombone.

(ウ)　I feel <u>mean</u> in wet weather.

(エ)　That's what I <u>mean</u>.

[問5]　下線部ⓒは，どのようなものか。日本語で具体的に書け。

[問6]　本文中の(　④　)に入る最も適切な語または語句を，次の(ア)～(エ)から1つ選び，その記号を書け。

(ア)　consequently　　(イ)　for instance　　(ウ)　however

(エ)　meanwhile

[問7]　下線部ⓓについて，[　　]内の語を本文の流れに合うように正しく並べかえよ。

[問8]　下線部ⓔが表す意味として最も適切なものを，次の(ア)～(エ)から1つ選び，その記号を書け。

(ア)　pleasure　　(イ)　willpower　　(ウ)　rejection　　(エ)　addict

[問9]　本文の内容と一致するものを，次の(ア)～(エ)から1つ選び，その記号を書け。

(ア)　A bluish light of electronic devices is good for our body clocks.

(イ)　When we read with some backlit devices at night, we have difficulty in sleeping.

(ウ)　The sun controls our body clocks in modern society.

(エ)　We get a very good sleep thanks to the quick dopamine shot.

(☆☆☆◎◎◎)

【2】次の英文を読み，[問1]～[問12]に答えよ。

ⓐ<u>The idea of teachers' acceptance of the cultural differences that exist in ELT*[1] is central to any serious discussion about attempting to reduce</u>

language anxiety in the classroom. While this principle may seem fundamental, it has been proven, in my experience, a difficult concept for some teachers to embrace. That is, teachers may have ethnocentric ideas about what rudeness is, and how students should behave in the classroom. It is thus advisable for teachers to consider the possibility such as apparent aloofness, avoidance, and introversion in learners' behavior may be due to anxiety. Teachers' negative reactions to this type of behavior most likely only serve to exacerbate their learners' anxiety.

In efforts to encourage speaking in EFL*2 classes in Japan, teachers would be well advised to consider what situations their learners are inclined to speak in and why and how these situations are different from those in the West. Japanese learners are reluctant to talk in situations where they will stand out in front of their peers. The notion that language learning can only take place with (①) students volunteering individually is merely a reflection of Western ethnocentrism. Nevertheless, many students will expect their English classes taught by foreigners to be (②), and some will, in fact, welcome the new experience. (③), as Anderson (1993) suggests, too different too soon may alienate students. A better approach seems to be a combination of techniques that draw on the dynamics of the Japanese classroom, with strategies that promote a Western style of interaction. Group-work activities have proven to be especially effective in getting my students to speak more (see Cutrone 2002).

In addition, EFL teachers in Japan should be careful not to show (④) when learners are reluctant to speak, as this will only exacerbate the problem by adding to the learners' apprehension. In Japan, where there is evidence that people may be quieter than other cultures by nature (Zimbardo 1977), there is always the danger of Western EFL teachers ⓑ[their / be / to / students / pressuring] more outspoken. In my opinion, teachers would be well served in extending their own (⑤) of silence when interacting with learners, as this may encourage learners to speak more.

In further efforts to make the learning environment less stressful, teachers should attempt to move away from the (⑥) domain commonly found in conventional classrooms in Japan, and aim for a more (⑦) domain commonly associated with family, friends, and co-workers. In calling for this approach, Williams (1994) asserts that in intimate situations, Japanese people appear more relaxed because they are released from cultural and institutional restraints and thus in intimate classrooms learners are free to explore the target language and feel more comfortable speaking in front of others. ⓒ One of the ways teachers can create intimacy between students is to choose topics relating to learners' personal experiences and backgrounds and have learners share this information in group activities. ⓓ Williams (1994) argues that (ア) (イ) students know about each other and have in common, (ア) (イ) comfortable they are likely to be. Similarly, teachers showing a personal interest in their students' lives from time to time can also help in creating an intimate classroom. Stevick (1980) calls this the *removal of the teacher's mask,* and some of the strategies his research suggests include being friendly with students, engaging them in conversations, mixing in small talk from time to time, and speaking to them on a one to one basis more often.

Another way for teachers to create intimacy in the language classroom is to move away from the evaluation paradigm, which includes less positive evaluation as well as negative evaluation. According to Stevick (1980), ⓔ[causes / is / stress / it / the evaluative environment / that], not the content. In a review of research on feedback, Williams and Burden (1997) report that students really need to feel that the teacher has a genuine interest in them as people, and not merely in evaluating the L2*3 they produce. Thus, the challenging part for teachers seems to be [A]. One of the ways teachers can move further away from the evaluation paradigm in language classrooms is by (⑧) their use of error correction. While students may say on a conscious level that they would like to be corrected strictly, their anxious reactions indicate (⑨). In my experience, overt error correction often inhibits students from expressing themselves freely and can lead to high levels of anxiety. Seemingly, teachers would be well served in taking less obtrusive methods in their error correction practices and waiting until a certain level of trust has been established between themselves and the student.

There are some other ways teachers can help reduce language anxiety in the classroom. First, they can employ activity types that cause lower levels of anxiety (such as pair work) and gradually introduce activity types that cause higher levels of anxiety (such as speech giving). (⑩), teachers can help students to better cope with anxiety-provoking situations themselves: Horwitz et al. (1986) suggest techniques such as giving advice on effective language learning strategies, journal keeping, and behavioral contracting (a simple positive-reinforcement tool that is widely used by teachers to change student behavior). Finally, relaxation exercises such as yoga, meditation, and biofeedback have also been suggested as ways to allay students' anxiety (Doyon 2000).

The problem of learners' language anxiety remains one of the greatest obstacles teachers have to overcome in language classrooms. [B] In Japan, this problem often stems from, and results in, cultural misunderstandings. [C] I hope to have shed some light on this complex phenomenon, which teachers can only deal with successfully if they are properly informed. [D] Nonetheless, there is much we do not yet know about language anxiety (particularly about its relationship with other factors such as motivation, personality, and self-confidence), so more research in this area would be particularly fruitful. [E]

ELT*[1] : English Language Teaching

EFL*2 : English as a foreign language

L2*3 : second language

〔*Pino Cutrone. 2009. Overcoming Japanese EFL Learners' Fear of Speaking. University of Reading LANGUAGE STUDIES WORKING PAPERS, Vol. 1, 59-61.*〕

[問1]　下線部ⓐを日本語に直せ。

[問2]　本文中の(　①　)，(　②　)に入る最も適切な語の組み合わせを，次の(ア)～(エ)から1つ選び，その記号を書け。

(ア)　①　positive　　②　similar

(イ)　①　aggressive　　②　different

(ウ)　①　passive　　②　distinct

(エ)　①　defensive　　②　new

[問3]　本文中の(　③　)，(　⑩　)に入る最も適切な語を，次の(ア)～(エ)からそれぞれ1つずつ選び，その記号を書け。

(ア)　However　　(イ)　Namely　　(ウ)　Therefore

(エ)　Moreover

[問4]　本文中の(　④　)，(　⑤　)に入る最も適切な語の組み合わせを，次の(ア)～(エ)から1つ選び，その記号を書け。

(ア)　④　annoyance　　⑤　tolerance

(イ)　④　irritation　　⑤　intolerance

(ウ)　④　patience　　⑤　sufferance

(エ)　④　calmness　　⑤　acceptance

[問5]　下線部ⓑ，ⓔについて，[　　]内の語または語句を本文の流れに合うように正しく並べかえよ。

[問6]　本文中の(　⑥　)，(　⑦　)に入る最も適切な語の組み合わせを，次の(ア)～(エ)から1つ選び，その記号を書け。

(ア)　⑥　relaxing　　⑦　close

(イ)　⑥　friendly　　⑦　ritual

(ウ)　⑥　ritual　　⑦　intimate

(エ)　⑥　traditional　　⑦　formal

[問7]　下線部ⓒがさす内容を日本語で具体的に書け。

[問8]　下線部ⓓについて，文意が通じるように(ア)，(イ)に入る最も適切な語をそれぞれ書け。

[問9]　本文中の［ A ］に入る最も適切なものを，次の(ア)～(エ)から1つ選び，その記号を書け。

(ア)　having students realize the importance of being evaluated in the classroom

(イ)　having students feel good about themselves without feeling as if they were being evaluated

(ウ)　having students evaluate the L2 they produce by themselves

(エ)　having students feel interested in the L2, not in being evaluated

[問10]　本文中の(　⑧　)，(　⑨　)に入る最も適切な英語の組み合わせを，次の(ア)～(エ)から1つ選び，その記号を書け。

(ア)　⑧　clearly asserting　　⑨　similarly

(イ)　⑧　clearly asserting　　⑨　otherwise

(ウ)　⑧　carefully controlling　　⑨　similarly

(エ)　⑧　carefully controlling　　⑨　otherwise

[問11]　次の英文は，本文中の［ B ］～［ E ］のいずれかに入る。本文の流れから考えて最も適切な場所を選び，その記号を書け。

The research to date has contributed to our understanding of language anxiety, and provides useful insights to teachers as they consider classroom methods and practices.

[問12]　本文の内容と一致するものを，次の(ア)～(エ)から1つ選び，その記号を書け。

(ア)　Strategies that promote a Western style of interaction are best to have students speak more in EFL classes in Japan.

(イ)　Teachers should avoid showing an interest in their students' lives to create an intimate classroom.

(ウ)　Error correction can keep students from expressing themselves freely in the language classroom.

(エ) It is effective for teachers to make use of only activity types that cause lower levels of anxiety to reduce language anxiety.

(☆☆☆◎◎◎)

【3】下の(1)～(7)は，与えられた日本文に対して生徒が黒板に書いた英文である。生徒の英文をできるだけ生かすという観点で，正しい英文にするには，どのように直せばよいか。次の例にならって書け。

> (例) 国体は2016年に岩手県で開催される。
>
> The National Sports Festival will be taken place in Iwate Prefecture in 2016.
> (be taken place → take place)

(1) 彼は足を組んで椅子に座った。

He sat in a chair with his legs crossing.

(2) 彼は先日腕時計を紛失したので，それを買う必要があった。

He lost his watch the other day, so he needed to buy it.

(3) もし彼がアドバイスしてくれなかったら，彼女は今頃成功していないだろう。

If he did not advise her, she would not be successful now.

(4) その猫は子どもたちに世話をされていた。

The cat was taken care by the children.

(5) 彼は携帯電話を盗まれた。

He was stolen his mobile phone.

(6) トルコと和歌山の友情を感じることができる串本を訪れたい。

I want to visit Kushimoto, which I can feel the friendship between Turkey and Wakayama.

(7) 彼女は私の肩に手を置き，すべて大丈夫だよと言った。

She lay her hand on my shoulder and said everything would be all right.

(☆☆☆◎◎◎)

【4】現行の学習指導要領「英語表現Ⅰ」における「内容」の項目のひとつに，「与えられた話題について，即興で話す。」という記述がある。このことについて，あなたは授業でどのような言語活動を行うか。120語程度の英文でまとめなさい。なお，語数を記入すること。

(☆☆☆☆◎◎◎)

解答・解説

【中高共通】

【1】Part1　No.1　C　No.2　B　No.3　A　No.4　C　No.5　D　No.6　A　Part2　No.1　B　No.2　A　No.3　C　No.4　B　Part3　No.1　There are more than eight hundred million people (in the world).　No.2　Because Japan (actually) relies on other countries for resources (such as food, metal and energy).

No.3　Refrigerators and washing machines. (TVs, microwavesも可)

No.4　It is to burn them.　No.5　Seven percent of our garbage can be reduced.

〈解説〉文章の内容は日常会話レベルだが，単に選択肢を選ぶだけでなく記述で解答する問題もあり，事前にnative speakerの話すスピードに慣れておくことが必要である。毎日5分でもいいので英語を聞く訓練をしておきたい。ラジオやテレビ番組を英語で視聴したり，好きな英語の曲を聴いたり映画を見たりするだけでも練習になる。試験の際は，聞き取りづらい問題があってもあまりこだわり過ぎず，次の問題に集中し聞き逃しのないようにする。本問のように質問や解答の選択肢が問題用紙に示されている場合は，放送が始まる前にひととおり目を通しておきたい。

【中学校】

【1】問1　It is the word we use when we talk about someone or something great. For example, I put “san” or “sama” at the end of someone’s name. (27語)　　問2　合成繊維が登場したから。　　問3　③　ウ　　⑤　エ　問4　実際に，養蚕産業は風前のともしびのように見える。

問5　⑥　The silkworm [is playing the leading role] in the vanguard of insect technology.　　⑦　Silkworms not only [teach us the mystery of life but also contribute] to the advancement of life science.　　問6　ア　no longer　　イ　coexisting　　ウ　ability　　エ　risk　　オ　ideal　(7)　イ

〈解説〉問1　honorificは「敬語，敬称」という意味の名詞。もしもこの単語の意味が分からなかったとしても，1文目について例示された2文目の文章をヒントに解答したい。そこには人々が虫に敬称をつけて呼ぶ例として，日本人が蚕を「おかいこさま」と呼ぶことが挙げられている。　問2　②では「生産が減少した」といっている。理由はその直前の句に原因・理由を表す前置詞withを伴って書かれているので，この部分を訳せばよい。　問3　③　日本における養蚕産業の衰退を数字で説明した段落である。③の前の文章では「およそ50年前，日本には80万の養蚕農家が存在した」とその隆盛ぶりを伝えており，それと対比させる形で「今は～」と続くので，「(3000軒)より少ない」とするfewerが適当である。　⑤　養蚕産業の衰退を説明した文の後に「養蚕産業が最近新たに注目されるようになった」と反対の内容が続くので，逆説の接続詞thoughでつなぐのがよい。　問4　In fact「実際に」という熟語で始まるSVCの第2文型である。主語(S)がthe silkworm industry，動詞(V)はappears (to be)，状態を表す補語(C)はhanging by a threadで，Cの部分を直訳すると「糸でぶら下がっている状態」，つまり「非常に危ない，風前のともしび」となる。　問5　⑥　与えられた語句の中からplay the role「役割を担う」という熟語を見つけることができる。動詞がplayingと進行形になっていることからその前にbe動詞isがくると予測でき，残るleadingは名詞roleの前に置く。　⑦　not only A, but also Bの構文である。teach (us)とcontributeを同格の動詞として構文のAとB にあてはめ，残りのthe mysteryとof lifeをteach (us)の補語として配置する。並べかえ部分の後の文章はcontributeを修飾するのがふさわしいため，同格である動詞の順番はteach (us)が先でcontributeが後となる。この構文全文の意味は「かいこは生命の神秘を私たちに教えるだけでなく，生命科学の発展に貢献する」となる。

問6　(ア)には【　】内1文目のwe can't find them [⋯] any longer，(イ)は2文目の[⋯]honeybees,[⋯]have lived very closely with humans，(ウ)はsilkworms cannot find food for themselves or escape any longer，(エ)は3文目のSilkworms don't do any harm，そして(オ)は4文目の最後のwithout any faultsと近い意味の単語をそれぞれ選択肢から選べばよい。

(7)　アは，第2段落最後に「かいこは再び注目をあび始めた」という記述がある程度で，全体の主旨とまではいえない。ウは本題とは関係がない。

【2】問1　(1)　ア　(2)　ウ　(3)　ウ　(4)　イ　(5)　エ
(6)　エ　(7)　イ　(8)　ア　(9)　エ　(10)　ア

問2　I went to Shiga during the summer vacation with my family. My grandmother's house standing near Lake Biwa. In August 6th we saw
is / stands　On
fireworks. They were very beautiful in the sky.

I wanted getting a present for my friend. So I went to a shop. Many kinds
to get
of key chains were sold there. I bought that. The next day I went
one
to swimming. After that we had dinner at a Japanese restaurant. I forgot my
swimming　left
cap there.

〈解説〉問1　(1)「早起きする」はget up early。　(2)　後ろについてfishを説明する現在完了形の節I've ever hadがあることから，最上級bestが予想される。　(3)　World War II は第二次世界大戦のこと。過去のことを表しているので動詞breakは過去形brokeとなる。 (4) cannot help ～ingで「～することをやめられない」という意味の熟語である。そのため進行形のlaughingが答えとなる。 (5) not to mention…はwithout mentioning…と同意で「…は言うまでもなく」という意味。
(6) policy「政策」を採用するのはadopt。アのadaptは「適合させる」という意味になるので注意したい。 (7) 店員の対応についてof considerate「思いやりのある」とほめている内容の文章。人の性質・特徴を表すときには[of＋名詞]の形容詞句を使う。アconsiderableは「かなりの」という意味。まぎらわしいので注意すること。
(8)「～と友人になる」はmake friends with～。 (9)「人に～をさせる(してもらう)」はget＋O(人)＋to doとなる。 (10)「ゴミは豚に餌として与えられた」という意味で受動態の文章。そのため前置詞はtoとなる。withを伴う場合は能動態になるべきなので注意したい。
問2 文法的な誤りは，以下A～Fの6か所ある。まず A. 2文目「建物などが建っている」という場合，進行形は使わないので，standingをisあるいはstandsに直す。 B. 3文目の文頭前置詞Inについて，時間を表す前置詞にはat，on，inの3つがあり，特定の日付を表す場合はonを使う。inはもっと広い単位の時間(月や週など)，atはピンポイントの時間や瞬間(at 0:00など)に使う。 C. 第2段落1文目，動詞wantedの後ろはto不定詞になるべき。 D. 4文目thatは前文の「たくさんの種類のキーホルダー」のうち一つを指す指示語として不適切。不定代名詞のoneが妥当。 E. 5文目went to swimmingはwent swimmingが正しい用法。 F. 7文目，forgotだと「帽子の記憶をなくした」という意味になる。忘れ物の場合は，置いてきてしまったというニュアンスでleftを使う。

【3】問1 エ 問2 イ→ウ→ア 問3 ③ 問4 イ
問5 (1) T (2) F (3) F (4) T
〈解説〉問1 extroverted personは「外向型の人」という意味であり，その単語と意味が大きく変わらないものはエのoutgoingである。

問2　Aの前の段落では，学習者の第2外国語に対する不安が言語習得にどのように影響するかという研究について説明されている。その続きとなる段落を選択肢の3つの文章で完成させればよい。アは「前後関係がどうであれ，不安は学習過程に影響しうる」と結論を述べているので，末尾にくることがわかる。また，ウは「これは，例えば…」と，前文を受けて例示をしている文章なので，この3文の流れは，イで提起した話題についてウで例を示し，アで締めくくる形だとわかる。
問3　いつもフランス語で話しかけてくる店主を避けるフランス語学習者の例を挙げている。学習中の第2外国語で話すことを避けたいと思う学習者の気持ちが書かれているのは，③の前の部分である。
問4　WTC(コミュニケーションへの意欲)に変化を与えるであろうものとして，本文中でthe number of people present, the topic of conversation, the formality of the circumstances, and even with whether we feel tired or energetic at a given momentが挙げられている。アはこの中のthe topic of conversation，ウはwe feel tired or energetic (at a given moment)，エはthe formality of the circumstancesの言い換えである。　問5　(1)　第2段落に述べられている。　(2)　第3段落最後の文のwill not learn as quickly as relaxed studentsと一致しない。　(3)　only inside the classroomの部分が，第4段落最後の文のinside and outside the classroomと一致しない。
(4)　最後の1文の内容と一致する。

【4】I'll give the students more chances to make impromptu speech and have a chat with their partners. For example, I'll give the students "today's topic" every lesson, and have them talk about it for a few minutes in pairs. In the activity, they are to talk with new partners every lesson. If the students can't find the right words, I'll encourage them to try to express themselves using familiar words and phrases. I'll also encourage them to keep up their conversations by using gestures.

Topics have to be interesting for the students, and should be relevant to what they have learned in class. I'll carefully choose topics, which get students interested in their partners through the chat. When they accomplish the activity mentioned above, I'm sure they'll feel confident and happy. As a model, I'll try to speak English as much as possible. (146語)

〈解説〉英作文では，起承転結を意識し，求められた答えを語数制限内で記入する。この問題では，生徒に「即興で話す力」を身に付けさせるために，具体的に何をするかということが文章の中心となる。模範解答では，今日のtopicについてペアで話し合いをさせることについて詳細に述べている。文章の内容はもちろん大切だが，「どのような工夫を行うか」という課題に対し，説得力のある文章を正しい文法で書くことが重要だ。文末は，それまでの話の流れを受けてできるだけ前向きな文章でまとめる。テーマや字数制限を決めて事前に練習し，英作文に慣れておくとよい。

【高等学校】

【1】問1　(イ)　問2　(エ)　問3　(ウ)　問4　(ア)　問5　体の昼夜のサイクルを制御するホルモン。　問6　(ウ)　問7　every time we check our email　問8　(ア)　問9　(イ)

〈解説〉問1　“(　①　) sleep”はその直後に書かれている，夜の初め頃に数時間うたた寝し，真夜中に起きて2～3時間ほど活動し，再び朝まで眠るスタイルのことである。そのため，(イ)のsegmented(区分された)という単語が適切である。　問2　電気の発明のおかげで睡眠スタイルがどのように変わったかという文章の穴埋め問題。寝る時間は「遅く」なり，睡眠時間は「短く」なっているので(エ)を選ぶことができる。　問3　ここまでの文章で人類の睡眠時間が徐々に短くなってきていることが述べられており，「我々はいまだに睡眠と戦っている，そして我々はいまだに勝ち続けている」といっているので，ⓐは睡眠時間が短くなることを指す。　問4　ⓑのmeanは「平均の」という意味の形容詞。そのため，同じ意味で使っているのは「平均年間降水量」の(ア)である。　問5　名詞と名詞を「, (コンマ)」でつないだmelatonin, the hormoneという形は同格を表す構文で，the hormone以下がmelatoninを説明しているので，この部分を訳せばよい。
問6　④を含む文の前の段落4文目に「ブルーライトがメラトニンの生産を抑える」とあり，それを受けて「睡眠問題のすべての責めをブルーライトに負わせるのは不誠実であろう」と続いているので，逆説の接続詞howeverが適切。　問7　[　　]内の語の中で，主語となるのはwe，動詞はcheck，目的語はemailである。これをevery time「～するときはいつも」の後におくことで「私たちがメールチェックをするときはいつも…」という文章が成立する。残ったourは名詞emailの前におく。　問8　ⓔ　gratificationは「満足させること，満足感」という意味。この単語の意味を知らなくても，SNSは私たちに喜びを与えドーパミンを生み出すと前文で書かれていることからも意味を推測できる。
問9　(ア)は第4段落4文目に「ブルーライトは身体の昼夜のサイクルをコントロールするホルモンの分泌を抑える」とあるので誤り。(イ)は第4段落最後の文の内容と一致する。(ウ)は本文には書かれていない。(エ)は本文の第5段落3文目に「ドーパミンは脳が快感を刺激するために出すホルモン」とあるので誤り。

【2】問1　英語教育に存在する文化の違いを教師が受け入れるという考えは，教室で言語への不安を減らそうとするどんな真剣な議論においても，その中核をなすものである。　問2　(イ)　問3　③　(ア)　⑩　(エ)　問4　(ア)　問5　ⓑ　pressuring their students to be　ⓔ　it is the evaluative environment that causes stress　問6　(ウ)
問7　学習者の個人的経験や背景に関連のある話題を選び，グループ活動でこの情報を学習者に共有させること。　問8　(ア)　the　(イ)　more　問9　(イ)　問10　(エ)　問11　D　問12　(ウ)
〈解説〉問1　ⓐを適切に訳すには文型をまずおさえたい。主語はThe idea of teachers' acceptance of the cultural differences that exist in ELTまで。動詞はisで，それ以降は補語となる第2文型の文章である。枠組みが見えたらそれぞれの修飾部分に注意して訳す。be central to～は熟語で意味は「～の中核をなす」。　問2　前後の日本語訳はそれぞれ①「語学学習は，個々が自発的に行動する…な生徒がいてのみ起こりうるという考えは西欧の自国中心主義の反映にすぎない」，②「外国人教師のクラスでは日本人教師とは…教えてもらいたいと思っている」である。
問3　③は前文の「外国人教師の授業に対して，生徒たちは何か違った授業を期待する」という内容を受けて，「違い過ぎたり，性急過ぎたりすると，生徒を(かえって)疎外してしまう」と言っているので，逆説の接続詞howeverが適切。⑩では，「教師は生徒たちが教室で言語に対する不安を少なくする手助けをすること」，そして「自分たちからそれに立ち向かうようにするべきだ」と述べていることから「そのうえ，さらに」という意味のmoreoverが適切である。　問4　④を含む文は，日本のEFL教師に対し，学習者が話すのを嫌がるときにこういう態度を見せてはいけないといっている。また，生徒がもっと話しやすくなるために教師には⑤が必要だといっている。
問5　ⓑ　there is always the danger of Western EFL teachers「西洋のEFL教師たちには常に恐れがある」といい，恐れの内容をⓑ以下で説明している。pressuringという現在分詞のあとに目的語their studentsがきて「生徒たちにプレッシャーをかけること」という意味となる。不定詞to doは形容詞節more outspokenの前に入れて，pressuring their studentsの後に続く。　ⓔ　単語群を見てみるとit，is，thatがあることから強調構文であると推測できる。また，ⓔの部分の後に否定的な意味でnot the contentとあることから，it isの後にはcontentと反対の意味を持つ語が入り，it is the evaluative environment(評価的状況だ) that ～ not the content(内容ではなく)と言う大枠が推測できる。　問6　日本人の学習者がどうすればより英語を話そうとするか学習の環境づくりの工夫について述べている文章の穴埋めである。⑥には次の文のcultural and institutionalが対応しており，⑦にはintimate situationsが対応しているので，それぞれritual，intimateが入る。　問7　ⓒのOne「(方法の)一つ」はto choose以下に書かれているので，この部分を訳せばよい。
問8　Williamsが論じた内容は，前半が「お互いに共通点があることを知る」後半が「安心することができる」といっているので，「～すればするほど，…である」(the more～, the more…)という熟語が入ると考えられる。　問9　この部分までの話の流れで，生徒が「評価されている」と感じることが第2言語の学習の妨げになると述べられていた。それを踏まえた上で選択肢を見てみると，(ア)と(ウ)は明らかに文意にそぐわず，(エ)「学生に，評価にではなく第2言語に興味があると感じさせること」よりも(イ)「生徒たちが評価されていると感じないように，彼らを気分良くさせること」が適切である。　問10　⑧に注目すると，(ア)，(イ)にはassert「断言する」，(ウ)，(エにはcontrol「統制する」の語が使われており，(ウ)，(エ)が適切だと考えられる。⑨を含む文章には文頭にwhile(一方)があり,「厳しく直してほしいと言う一方で，生徒たちの不安な反応は…示している」となるので，⑨にはotherwise「違ったふうに」が入る。　問11　挿入する英文では,「研究が第2言語に対する学習者の不安への理解を深め，教師たちが指導法や授業を考えるヒントとなった」といっている。「それにも関わらず私たちには知らないことがまだたくさんある」と始まるDの前に入れると意味がつながる。　問12　(ア)「EFLのクラスで西洋式のやり方を進めることが，生徒たちに英語を話させる最上の方法だ」は第2～3段落の主旨と一致しない。(イ)「教師は生徒の生活に興味を示すことを避けるべき」は第4段落1文目の内容と異なる。(エ)「言語の不安を減らすために活発な生徒だけを利用するのが教師にとって効果的」は，本文で述べられている内容と一致しない。(ウ)は，第5段落7文目error correctionからfreelyまでの内容と一致する。inhibit(s)～from…を選択肢ではkeep～from…に言い換えている。

【3】(1)　He sat in a chair with his legs crossing.
crossed

(2)　He lost his watch the other day, so he needed to buy it.
one

(3)　If he did not advise her, she would not be successful now.
had not advised

(4)　The cat was taken care by the children.
care of

(5) He was stolen his mobile phone.
He had his mobile phone stolen.

(6) I want to visit Kushimoto, which I can feel the friendship between
where
Turkey and Wakayama.

(7) She lay her hand on my shoulder and said everything would be all right.
laid

〈解説〉(1) with＋名詞＋過去分詞で「～されている状態で」という意味になる。この場合は「彼の足が組まれた状態で」というニュアンスで，過去分詞crossedを使う。訂正前はwith＋名詞＋現在分詞の形になっており，動作をずっとし続けている状態(running，shiningなど)に使われる。 (2) itは特定代名詞なので，この話の中に出てくる特定の腕時計，つまり「なくした腕時計」のことを意味してしまう。たくさんある腕時計の中の一つを買う場合には，不定代名詞のoneを使う。
(3) 過去の事実の反対の仮想を話す場合は，仮定法過去完了の否定文を使いIf＋主語＋had not＋過去分詞～となる。 (4) 「世話をする」は熟語でtake care of～である。 (5) He was stolenとすると，彼自身が盗まれたことになってしまう。使役動詞have(この問題では時制が過去なのでhad)を使い，his mobile phoneがstolenの主語となるよう配置する。
(6) 串本という地名が先行詞となるため，場所を表す関係副詞whereが適切。 (7) and以下の動詞がsaidと過去形になっているので，時制を統一してlayも過去形にする。

【4】The activity I will do is “topic box.” I will make a small box named “topic box” and put a lot of topics in it. The topics should be the ones which are familiar to the students. Students have to pick out a topic from the box and have to talk about it for 30 seconds.

Students make groups of four. They make a speech to the students in each group, not to the whole class. This will make them more relaxed. The students in each group make some comments or questions after the speaker finishes talking. In this way, more students can have opportunities to speak English.

I believe this activity will develop students' speaking ability to speak promptly. (120語)

〈解説〉　英作文では，起承転結を意識し，求められた答えを語数制限内で記入する。模範解答では，topic boxという箱の中から引いた話題について，4人のグループの中で30秒間スピーチをするという活動について書いている。グループ活動やペア活動などは友人同士で話すことで気軽に英語を使うことができるし，ゲーム感覚で参加できるように工夫するのも一つの方法である。それに慣れれば，毎回誰か一人が3分間スピーチをするようスケジュールを事前に組み，クラスの前で発表する機会を作るなど活動のレベルアップを図りたい。文章の内容はもちろん大切だが，説得力のある文章を正しい文法で書くことが重要である。文末は，それまでの話の流れを受けてできるだけ前向きな文章でまとめる。テーマや字数制限を決めて事前に練習し，英作文に慣れておくとよい。

2016年度　実施問題

【中高共通】

[1]はリスニングテストです。放送の指示に従ってください。

【1】放送を聞いて，[Part 1]～[Part 3]の各問に答えよ。

[Part 1]

No. 1

(A)　To India.

(B)　To a photo shop.

(C)　To the new port.

(D)　To the airport in an hour.

No. 2

(A)　The Thai restaurant.

(B)　The Chinese restaurant.

(C)　The Korean restaurant.

(D)　The Indian restaurant.

No. 3

(A)　Track 12.

(B)　Track 13.

(C)　Track 20.

(D)　Track 30.

No. 4

(A)　He grew up in Egypt.

(B)　He studied it in college.

(C)　He learned it from his father.

(D)　He learned it by traveling around Egypt.

No. 5

(A)　At 9:30.

(B)　At 10:00.

(C)　At 4:30.

(D)　At 5:00.

No. 6

(A)　By taxi.

(B)　By limousine bus.

(C)　By subway.

(D)　By car.

[Part 2]

No. 1　Every day the man watches TV for...

(A)　less than 30 minutes.

(B)　about 30 minutes.

(C)　about 1 hour.

(D)　more than 2 hours.

No. 2　The man mainly watches TV...

(A)　in the morning.

(B)　around midday.

(C)　in the evening and at night.

(D)　in the morning and at night.

No. 3　On the new channel, the man would like to see...

(A)　local news focusing on the community.

(B)　shows like travel programs.

(C)　documentaries and local news programs.

(D)　travel programs and children's programs.

No. 4　The man would advise the new channel to...

(A)　spend more money on drama and to improve the sound quality.

(B)　train their broadcasters to higher standards and to talk more to customers.

(C)　improve the sound quality and to talk more to customers.

(D) broadcast interviews with famous people and to talk more to customers.

[Part 3]

No. 1 What is the usage of natural resources essential for?

No. 2 According to the speaker, how is the fresh water used for our daily life? Give two examples.

No. 3 How much virtual water does a Japanese person consume a day?

No. 4 What will happen to the freshwater resources if people use them without care?

No. 5 Why should Japanese people protect the world's water?

(☆☆☆◎◎◎)

【中学校】

【1】次の[問1]～[問3]に答えよ。

[問1] 次の(1)～(10)について，(　　)に入る最も適切な語または語句を，ア～エからそれぞれ1つずつ選び，その記号を書け。

(1) His composition is (　　) than yours.

ア bad　イ more bad　ウ worst　エ worse

(2) Would you mind (　　) the window?

ア open　イ to open　ウ opening　エ opened

(3) I will not go to the party (　　) Tom goes with me.

ア unless　イ as long as　ウ not until　エ till such time

(4) When she was a young girl, she used to wish she (　　) a princess.

ア became　イ be　ウ is　エ were

(5) The teacher said that two parallel lines never (　　) each other.

ア crossing　イ cross　ウ crossed　エ was crossed

(6) I bought this pen (　　) two thousand yen.

ア for　イ at　ウ by　エ on

(7) (　　) from a distance, it looked like a human face.

ア Seeing　イ Seen　ウ To see　エ Saw

(8)　She told me about the event as if she (　　) it, with her own eyes.

ア　see　　イ　has seen　　ウ　sees　　エ　had seen

(9)　Our ALT (　　) in Japan for five years next year.

ア　will have lived　　イ　will live　　ウ　have lived

エ　lives

(10)　When a big typhoon hit the island, the whole village was (　　) by the flood.

ア　submitted　　イ　subscribed　　ウ　submerged

エ　subordinated

[問2]　次の英文は，「私の夢」というタイトルで生徒が書いた英作文である。下線部①～⑥のうち正しいものには○を書き，誤りのあるものは正しく直せ。

I want to improve my ①<u>ability on speaking</u> English most of all. There are three ②<u>reasons of this</u>. First, I have wanted to be a good English speaker since I became a junior high school student. The second reason is that if I can speak English well, I ③<u>will can</u> get a good job when I graduate from college. The most important reason is that with good ④<u>speaking</u> English I will have chances to be ⑤<u>sent to abroad</u> to work. It is my dream to work in a foreign country, especially the United States, so to make my dream ⑥<u>come true</u>, I have to communicate in English.

[問3]　次の英文を読んで，あとの(1)～(3)に答えよ。

Koya-san is one of the most sacred sites in Wakayama. There are many places to see. I can highly recommend *Okuno-in*.

Okuno-in is found on the eastern fringe of the mountain-top surrounded by ancient Japanese cedars. From the entrance at First Bridge (*Ichino-hashi*), over Middle Bridge (*Nakano-hashi*) and on to Kobo Daishi's tomb runs a road approximately two kilometers long. *Okuno-in* is framed by the three mountains of Koya (*Koya Sanzan*), Mani, Yoryu and Tenjiku, and, dimly lit even during the day, an aura hangs in the air around the countless tombs found among the cedar trees. Through the ages, the faithful have gathered here; the center of enlightenment for all Japan.

① 【supported / what / for / *Okuno-in* / has / 1,200 years】 is the belief that even now Kobo Daishi is alive on the mountain, providing succor to the needy. Kobo Daishi underwent his "transition" on the 21st of March 835, a day that he bad prophesied some time earlier. This was not achieving nirvana, but entering a living state of perpetual Samadhi (meditative concentration). People ② 【spiritual / achieve / connection / wanting / to / a / with / Kukai】 in this meditative state have, from olden times, came to *Okuno-in* to lay ashes to rest and for memorial (③). The *Okuno-in* Sando is both the approach route to Kobo Daishi's mausoleum, and at the same time, a path of remembrance for the famous and obscure of history ④lay to rest in these sacred precincts in graves that number, some say 100,000, others 200,000.

〔ANCIENT ROAD TO KUMANO & KOYA (2007)　一部付記等あり〕

(1)　下線部①，②の【　　】内の語句を正しく並べかえよ。ただし，文頭の語も小文字にしている。

(2)　(　③　)に入る最も適切な語を，次のア～エから1つ選び，その記号を書け。

ア　guarantees　　イ　repairs　　ウ　services　　エ　securities

(3)　下線部④の語を，適切な形に直して書け。

(☆☆☆◎◎◎)

【2】次の英文を読んで，あとの[問1]～[問8]に答えよ。

Having considered how similarly-aged children share certain characteristics (Piaget) and how the social environment, in particular social interaction with parents and teachers, can make a difference in terms of offering unique, enriching experiences (Vygotsky), I shall now explore the issue of uniqueness.

Teachers and parents often notice that individual children enjoy different activities.

[　　　あ　　　]

When assessing children's intelligence, many psychologists have argued for the need to take such differences in individuals into account. Howard Gardner, an American psychologist, in a publication entitled ①<u>*Frames of Mind: Theory of Multiple Intelligences*</u> (1983) suggested that intelligence had no unitary character, rather, it manifested itself in many different ways in different children. He refers to these multiple intelligences as 'frames of mind'. The types of intelligences are linguistic, logico-mathematical, musical, spatial, bodily/kinaesthetic, interpersonal, intrapersonal, and natural. New ideas and new practical interpretations with regard to the types of basic intelligences are constantly developing and Table 1.2 merely summarizes the main features of each type of intelligence.

According to Gardner's framework, in the example about working with stories, the first group of children would be described as showing particular strengths in the areas of musical and bodily/kinaesthetic intelligences while the second group exhibit linguistic and spatial intelligences. Teachers who are aware of this framework can ensure that their teaching is meaningful to all children with any one or any (　②　) of these intelligences.

Linguistic	Sensitivity to the sound, rhythm, and meaning of words and the different functions of language
Logico-mathematical	Sensitivity to and capacity to detect logical and numerical patterns, ability to handle long chains of logical reasoning
Musical	Ability to produce or appreciate pitch, rhythm, or melody and aesthetic-sounding tones, understanding of the forms of musical expressiveness
Spatial	Ability to perceive the visual/spatial world accurately, to perform transformations on those perceptions, and to recreate aspects of visual experience in the absence of relevant stimuli
Bodily/kinaesthetic	Ability to use the body skillfully for expressive as well as goal oriented purposes, ability to handle objects skillfully
Interpersonal	Ability to detect and respond appropriately to the moods, temperaments, motivations, and intentions of others
Intrapersonal	Ability to discriminate complex inner feelings and to use them to guide one's behavior, knowledge of one's own strengths, weaknesses, desires, and intelligences
Naturalist	Ability to recognize and classify varieties of animals, minerals, and plants

Table 1.2: *Gardner's Multiple Intelligences. Adapted from L. Berk*: Child Development, *Allyn and Bacon* 2005.

These descriptions of intelligences can be related to another term commonly used in the educational literature, i.e. 'learning styles'. Styles can describe personality types such as more careful and reflective children as opposed to impulsive and more interactive children. Other styles, related to personality features, describe cognitive categories such as ③<u>analytic</u> or global learners. Analytic learners are those with an attention to detail and global learners are those who are more holistic in their approach. Finally, some styles describe perceptual differences. Some children prefer listening to new input while others need lots of visual stimulus. Yet others are (④), which means that they like to feel and touch things and move their body in expressive ways to aid their learning and communication.

⑤It is important for teachers to take into account that all children have stronger and weaker aspects of their multiple intelligences and preferred learning styles. Some of the early preferences and styles might change with time but there will always be a variety of learners in every class. Therefore teachers need to incorporate a variety of activities into second and foreign language classrooms to ensure that everybody's preferences are catered for at least some of the time. For example, when new rhymes or songs are introduced in an English class, it is a good idea to present them using a variety of techniques. [　⑥　]. This will cater for learners with an auditory preference. [　⑦　]. This activity will cater for visual learners. Finally, [　⑧　], too. This will cater for kinaesthetic learners. Incorporating various 'senses' also makes learning memorable and fun. Once aware of having to cater for different intelligences, teachers can make their lessons more accessible to all children.

〔Annamaria Pinter (2006). *Teaching Young Language Learners.* Oxford University Press.　一部編集等あり〕

[問1]　下線部①の中では，intelligenceはどのように定義されているか。日本語で書け。

[問2]　文中の[　あ　]に入る適切な英文になるように，次のア～ウの各文を正しく並べかえ，順番を記号で書け。

ア　At the same time, they may show very little interest in writing, drawing, or coloring.

イ　Other children might get embarrassed if asked to join in with singing and dancing but enjoy writing or drawing based on the story.

ウ　For example, if we take working with stories, children who are musical often enjoy singing and dancing and expressing themselves through drama and ballet.

[問3]　文中の(　②　)に，次のように定義される英語1語を書け。

two or more things joined or mixed together to form a single unit

[問4]　下線部③analyticの対義語を，次のア～エから選び，その記号を書け。

ア　synthetic　　イ　realistic　　ウ　sympathetic　　エ　romantic

[問5]　文中の(　④　)に入る最も適切なものを，次のア～エから選び，その記号を書け。

ア　intrapersonal　　イ　bodily/kinaesthetic　　ウ　linguistic

エ　spatial

[問6]　下線部⑤を日本語に直せ。

[問7]　文中の[　⑥　]～[　⑧　]に入る最も適切なものを，次のア～ウから1つずつ選び，その記号を書け。ただし，文頭の語も小文字にしている。

ア　children can watch the teacher miming the actions and join with the words and actions

イ　children can also look at the text of the song or the rhyme in the book or look at the illustrations

ウ　children can listen to the teacher or the tape saying or singing the rhyme or the song

[問8]　次の文は，本文を要約したものである。次の(　①　)～(　④　)に入る最も適切な語を，あとのア～オから1つずつ選び，その記号を書け。ただし，各語はそれぞれ1度しか用いないこととする。

Children within the same age groups may show similar characteristics but at the same time they are also very different as individuals with their strengths and (　①　) as learners. While teachers can benefit from familiarizing themselves with the universal aspects of children's development, it is also important that this is balanced out with focus on the individual child. Teachers will have to use their best judgement in deciding about the most (　②　) materials and techniques to fit their learners of different ages in different (　③　). By incorporating variety into everyday practice, teachers of children can make their lessons full of (　④　) for all learner types and intelligences.

ア　contexts　　イ　preferences　　ウ　stimulation
エ　suitable　　オ　unique

(☆☆☆◎◎◎)

【3】次の[問]を読み，下の[問1]，[問2]に答えよ。

> [問]“What is your favorite sport?”に対する返答を，理由や説明を含めて，3文以上の英語で書きなさい。ただし，語数は全部で20語以上とし，符号は語数に含まないものとする。

[問1]　この[問]の解答例として，中学校卒業時の生徒に期待する英文を書け。

[問2]　次の図と文は，上の[問]に対する中学3年生の解答の結果と分析である。この結果を踏まえてあなたなら，中学3年生の生徒にどのような指導を行うか。学習指導要領に示された言語活動の「書くこと」の項目を踏まえ，下の書き出しに続けて，120語以上の英語で具体的に書け。

According to the language activities for writing in Course of Study,

【結果】　(調査人数700人)

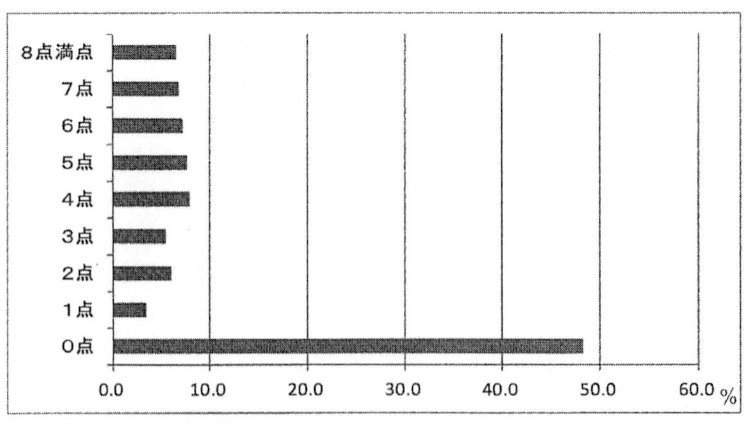

【分析】
「英語で積極的にコミュニケーションを図り，自分の考えを自由に表現しようとする態度は見られたが，指定された条件に従い，与えられたテーマについて的確に表現する力には，生徒の間に大きな差がみられた。」

(☆☆☆◎◎◎)

【高等学校】

【1】次の英文を読み，あとの[問1]～[問9]に答えよ。

Of all the calamities that have befallen Kouhei, age 18, in the past month—the March 11 earthquake that devastated his home in Futaba Town, the radiation seeping from the quake-and-tsunami-damaged Fukushima Daiichi nuclear power plant next door, the fleeing from shelter to shelter with nothing more than the clothes on his back—it is the smallest of privations that elicits emotion. [A] In March, Kouhei graduated from high school in Futaba. [B] Describing his family's plight, Kouhei answers questions in a brave monotone, assuming the ⓐmantle of the eldest of five siblings, the man in the house now that his father is in the hospital. [C] It is only the lack of a proper graduation in this ritual-based nation that finally makes him crack. [D] "Graduation ceremonies are for sending us out into the world as adults, " he says, blinking hard as he waits in line for free clothing at an evacuation center in Saitama Prefecture, north of Tokyo. "But for me, I cannot start my future yet. I don't know what I will do."

As Japan has floundered for two decades since its economic bubble burst—a post-industrial. high-tech society that had resigned itself to a slow, inexorable decline after the boom years of the 1980s—its young people have languished. The over-indulged and underemployed cohort has given rise to a dictionary's worth of sociological neologisms: *freeters*, young Japanese who choose part-time, dead-end, low-paid work instead of striving for more fulfilling careers; *hikikomori*, anxious youth who [E];herbivores, grazing, passive young men who care more about their looks than their careers; and parasite singles, young adults who, even if they have good jobs, live at home to avoid paying rent and rely on their parents for food and laundry so they can use their disposable income for frivolous purchases.

But as their nation tries to cope with the ⓑ[has / disaster / seen / never / world / the / natural / ever / costliest], one that has left tens of thousands dead or missing and some 360, 000 homeless, the country's coddled youth are rising to meet a new era's challenges. In unprecedented numbers, young Japanese have volunteered to help earthquake victims, bringing time, money and in some cases social-networking expertise that can reunite missing family members and coordinate aid efforts.

At the Saitama Super Arena, where recent graduate Kouhei is sheltering, crowds [F] are here today for another reason. By 9:30 a.m., the emergency center has reached its maximum [G] , most [H]. An additional 1,500 waiting for a chance to help will have to come back tomorrow. Masayuki, 18, is one [I]. He is holding a sign that says "60s." His friend is holding another that says "WOMEN." Together they form a duo that is organizing evacuee women in the 60-to-69 age bracket to go for their baths. "Some people say that young Japanese don't have a good spirit," says Masayuki. stamping his feet in the frigid weather. "But when it comes down to it, we want to help, not just with money but with real (①)."

It's standard history that [J]. "Often it takes a huge crisis to make a society change," says Toshihiko Hayashi, an economics professor at Doshisha University, who has studied the legacies of natural disasters. "For Japan, even two lost decades after the bubble burst were not enough to fundamentally change the country's economic and political systems. But this crisis is different. It could be the catalyst that finally changes Japan."

Whether that momentum will carry through in the months and years needed to rebuild Tohoku is (②) clear. Nevertheless, encouraging signs are emerging even from the most ruined places. Keita just graduated from the middle school in Kesennuma, a town largely torn up by the tsunami. After the 15-year-old's apartment building was damaged by the tidal wave and later consumed by flames, he and his family evacuated to the middle school, which was turned into an emergency shelter. To fill his free time, Keita has volunteered at the school, helping to clean floors made dirty by evacuees. "When we do something, we forget," says the rosy-cheeked, broad-shouldered boy.

And if you're young, even in Kesennuma, there are things to look forward to. On this sunny day, as puffy clouds drifted through a brilliant blue sky, Keita and two friends took off for another school, where the results of the high school examination they had taken before the earthquake were posted. All three, it turned out, had made the grade for their high school of choice. ⓒ<u>Head butts, high fives and much whooping ensued</u>. For a moment, life on Tohoku's wounded coast was bright with hopes and dreams for the future.

〔*TIME Asia* (April 4. 2011)　一部編集等あり〕

[問1]　次の文は，本文中の[　A　]～[　D　]のいずれかに入る。本文の流れから考えてどこが最も適切か，その記号を書け。

But there was no commencement ceremony.

[問2]　下線部ⓐが表す意味として最も適切なものを，次の(ア)～(エ)から1つ選び，その記号を書け。

(ア)　a medical condition in which a person feels very sad and anxioius

(イ)　an important role or responsibillity that passes from one person to another

(ウ)　a loose piece of clothing without sleeves, worn over other clothes

(エ)　a feeling of sadness that lasts for a long time and cannot be explained

[問3]　***hikikomori***の説明となるように，[　E　]に入る英語を書け。

[問4]　下線部ⓑについて，[　　]内の語を本文の流れに合うように正しく並べかえよ。ただし，不要な語が1語含まれている。

[問5]　本文中の[　F　]～[　I　]に入る英語を，それぞれ次の(ア)～

(エ)から1つずつ選び，その記号を書け。

(ア)　of 500 volunteers

(イ)　of the lucky ones who scored a volunteer spot

(ウ)　of local teens who usually come for rock concerts

(エ)　of whom are young

[問6]　本文中の(　①　)に入る最も適切な語を，次の(ア)～(エ)から1つ選び，その記号を書け。

(ア)　donation　　(イ)　work　　(ウ)　wages　　(エ)　property

[問7] 文脈から考えて，[　J　]に入る最も適切な英語を，次の(ア)～(エ)から1つ選び，その記号を書け。

(ア)　the unexpected can't change social attitudes dramatically

(イ)　the unexpected can turn social attitudes upside down

(ウ)　the unexpected can't help people change their personal priorities

(エ)　the unexpected can happen if we have lost hope

[問8]　本文中の(　②　)に入る最も適切な語または語句を，次の(ア)～(エ)から1つ選び，その記号を書け。

(ア)　nearly　　(イ)　at least　　(ウ)　far from　　(エ)　more or less

[問9]　下線部ⓒについて，Keita and two fiendsがそのようにした理由を日本語で簡潔に書け。

(☆☆☆☆◎◎◎◎◎)

【2】次の英文を読み，あとの[問1]～[問13]に答えよ。

Teachers are the keys to improving students' communication skills, especially when students are engaged in tasks. Through working on tasks, students are effectively challenged, which results in enhancement of their English language skills. Vygotsky (1978) affirms the importance of Zone of Proximal Development (ZPD), which is defined as "the distance between the actual development level as determined by independent problem solving and ⓐthe level of potential development as determined through problem solving under adult guidance or in collaboration with more capable peers." Teachers know their students' present levels, set appropriate goals, provide tasks that bring out students' abilities with assistance of mentors, advanced peers, or ⓑ<u>themselves</u>, and evaluate outcomes through these tasks.

(①), it is highly recommended to teach students how to communicate with others in English in varied contexts. Thus, setting tasks for conversations in authentic situations in a classroom is valuable. Some recommended activities are role play, group discussion, and interviews. In role play, students have opportunities to speak as different characters. This motivates them to be engaged in communication. They can also practice discourse and strategic competence, such as what words to stress, where to pause, how to make eye contact, and what gestures to use. This activity is useful since it can be similar to situations outside of the classroom (Crookall & Oxford, 1990). In group discussion, students are asked to express their opinions on a certain topic. In this process, they need to research the subject and support their argument (Green, Christopher, & Lam, 2002). They also need to interact with others in English. Another suggested activity to facilitate students' communicative abilities is interviewing. Topics and interviewees may vary, (②) on purposes for practices. Students may be engaged in developing interview questions, rehearsing, and interacting with interviewees. The students have opportunities to exchange dialogues in meaningful ways. These pedagogical activities (③) in this section assist students' communicative competence.

Not ⓒ [<u>authentic / for / tasks / effective / only / are</u>] students, but integrated tasks are also important. Since language education is no longer viewed as separating reading, writing, speaking, and listening from the point of the balanced literacy, students are encouraged to learn more effectively with tasks including diverse language skills. Individual communication skills should not be taught in isolation. Students benefit from combined tasks as these foster their communication skills as well as other elements in integrated language arts literacy events.

Another argument is the significance of teacher training. Lamie's (2000) study with high school English teachers in Japan revealed (④) opportunities of professional development. In order for the teachers to equip effective pedagogy for communicative competence within the framework of the MEXT guidelines, it is (⑤) to deepen knowledge on methodologies and master useful instruction. Hiramatsu (2005) calls for more opportunities, such as seminars and workshops, for the teachers to reflect on their instruction and develop knowledge and professional and effective *CLT approaches.

Many students learn English in the Japanese setting, which does not allow them to be exposed to an English-speaking world in their daily lives. The way they think, behave, and communicate is heavily influenced by their Japanese education, which can result in some specific difficulties. (⑥), in the Japanese culture, people value harmony with others and have respect for the elderly. When teachers ask students to demonstrate their communicative performance, students hesitate to break the silence of an entire classroom. There is a Japanese saying. 'Silence is gold'; silence is valuable in the Japanese culture. Out of respect for peers, oral performance in front of the class requires an enormous effort by the students to overcome ⓓthis conflict.

Additionally, respecting older people is a traditional principle in the Japanese culture. Students' veneration for teachers implies keeping quiet, (⑦) looking up to teachers in another culture—the United States, for example—does not necessarily mean remaining silent. In Japanese schools, students bow to their teachers at the beginning and end of each class to show their respect. By living in such a culture and learning other subjects with this concept, it is (⑧) for Japanese students to adapt themselves to (⑨) conversational interactions, especially when they only happen in English class.

[A]

In other words, Japanese people as listeners infer speakers' real intentions with a limited amount of oral utterance or their non-verbal behaviors. The Japanese word, *ishindenshin*, thought transference or tacit understanding, demonstrates this unique communication style. Conversation in the Japanese language is conducted with this format. People guess and interpret what speakers mean "based not only on [B] but also on [C] " (Takanashi, 2004). In the Japanese culture, in which cooperation with others, respectful behavior, and implicit communication are highly considered as virtues, English teachers experience difficulty with cultivating their students' conversational skills in English and encouraging them to use English in the classroom. In this context, teachers need to [D]. Understanding cultural differences and teaching these elements will help students learn English from a wider perspective (Ike, 1995).

* CLT : Communicative Language Teaching

〔Yuko Iwai.(2009) Toward Communicative Competence in the Japanese Context:The Challenges Facing Japanese English Teachers.THE JOURNAL OF ASIA TEFLVol.6.No.2　一部編集等あり〕

[問1]　下線部ⓐはどのようなレベルであるか，日本語で具体的に書け。

[問2]　下線部ⓑは何をさすか。本文中の英語1語を書け。

[問3]　本文中の(　①　)，(　⑥　)に入る最も適切な語または語句を，次の(ア)～(エ)からそれぞれ1つずつ選び，その記号を書け。

(ア)　For example　(イ)　However　(ウ)　As a result

(エ)　Moreover

[問4]　本文中の(　②　)，(　③　)に入る最も適切な語の組み合わせを，次の(ア)～(エ)から1つ選び，その記号を書け。

(ア)　②　leaned　③　expressing

(イ)　②　counting　③　stating

(ウ)　②　depending　③　described

(エ)　②　relied　③　mentioned

[問5]　下線部ⓒについて，[　　]内の語を本文の流れに合うように正しく並べかえよ。

[問6]　本文中の(　④　)，(　⑤　)に入る最も適切な語の組み合わせを，次の(ア)～(エ)から1つ選び，その記号を書け。

(ア)　④　enough　　⑤　unsuitable
(イ)　④　insufficient　　⑤　advisable
(ウ)　④　few　　⑤　sensitive
(エ)　④　countless　　⑤　passable

[問7]　下線部ⓓの内容を日本語で具体的に書け。

[問8]　本文中の(　⑦　)に入る最も適切な語を，次の(ア)～(エ)から1つ選び，その記号を書け。

(ア)　besides　　(イ)　while　　(ウ)　nevertheless
(エ)　therefore

[問9]　本文中の(　⑧　)，(　⑨　)に入る最も適切な語の組み合わせを，次の(ア)～(エ)から1つ選び，その記号を書け。

(ア)　⑧　challenging　　⑨　active
(イ)　⑧　easy　　⑨　active
(ウ)　⑧　difficult　　⑨　inactive
(エ)　⑧　boring　　⑨　inactive

[問10]　本文中の[　A　]に，意味の通った文章となるように次の(ア)～(ウ)の文を並べかえて入れると，どのような順番になるか。その記号を書け。

(ア)　Opposed to this framework, Hall explains that the Western culture is based on the low context.

(イ)　Another aspect of Japanese culture is that people interact with one another in the high context.

(ウ)　Hall compares the former as “one in which most of the information is either in the physical context or internalized in the person” to the latter as the one in which “mass of the information is veasted in the explicit code.”

[問11]　本文中の[　B　]，[　C　]に入る最も適切な英語の組み合わせを，次の(ア)～(エ)から1つ選び，その記号を書け。

(ア)　B　what has been understood　　C　what has been written
(イ)　B　what has been understood　　C　what has not been understood

(ウ)　B　what has been said　　　　C　what has been written

(エ)　B　what has been said　　　　C　what has not been said

[問12]　本文中の[　D　]に入る最も適切な英語を，次の(ア)～(エ)から1つ選び，その記号を書け。

(ア)　separate four languages skills instead of integrating them

(イ)　have students interact with one another in the low context

(ウ)　foster students' cultural awareness along with their languages skills

(エ)　keep students from paying attention to cultural aspects

[問13]　本文の内容と一致するものを，次の(ア)～(エ)から1つ選び，その記号を書け。

(ア)　Role play is not effective for students to acquire communicative skills because they speak as diverse characters.

(イ)　A classroom is an ideal place for students to learn English, because they have only limited chances to communicate with others.

(ウ)　The Japanese communication style makes it almost impossible for Japanese students to learn Engish.

(エ)　Understanding the Japanese cultural characteristics and encouraging students to practice orally in realistic settings will help students improve their English.

(☆☆☆☆◎◎◎◎)

【3】下の(1)～(7)は，与えられた日本文に対して生徒が黒板に書いた英文である。生徒の英文をできるだけ生かすという観点で，正しい英文にするには，どのように直せばよいか。次の例にならって書け。

(例)　国体は2015年に和歌山県で開催される。

The National Sports Festival will <u>be taken place</u> in Wakayama Prefecture in 2015.
take place

(1)　彼は私を雪の中で40分間待たせた。

He kept me waited in the snow forty minutes.

(2)　和歌山を訪れる観光客の数が増えている。

The number of tourists who come to Wakyama have been increasing.

(3)　そこに行くもっとも簡単な方法は飛行機だ。

The most easiest way to get there is by airplane.

(4)　以前は仕事のあとに飲みに行ったものだが，今は行かない。

I was used to going drinking after work.

(5)　彼女は若いころ教師であったことを誇りにしている。

She is proud of being a teacher when she was young.

(6)　メンバーのうち5人は時間どおりに来たのだが，それ以外の人達は遅れた。

Five of the members came on time, but others were late.

(7)　あなたのご都合がよければ，新宮におこしください。

If you are convenient, please visit Shingu.

(☆☆☆☆◎◎◎◎)

【4】次の文は，高等学校学習指導要領解説　外国語編・英語編(平成22年5月)における「第3章　英語に関する各科目に共通する内容等」の一部である。

英語に関する各科目の「特質」は，言語に関する技能そのものの習得を目的としていることである。しかし，このような技能の習得のために必要となる，英語を使用する機会は，我が国の生徒の日常生活において非常に限られている。これらのことを踏まえれば，英語に関する各科目の授業においては，訳読や和文英訳，文法指導が中心とならないよう留意し，生徒が英語に触れるとともに，<u>英語でコミュニケーションを行う機会を充実することが必要である</u>。

下線部の趣旨を踏まえた授業をするために，あなたはどのような工夫をするか。120語程度の英文でまとめなさい。また，語数を記入すること。

(☆☆☆◎◎◎◎◎)

解答・解説

【中高共通】

【1】Part1　No. 1　B　No. 2　D　No. 3　D　No. 4　C　No. 5　B　No. 6　C　Part2　No. 1　C　No. 2　D　No. 3　A　No. 4　C　Part3　No. 1　It is essential not only for survival but also for a better life.　No. 2　We satisfy our thirst and cook food. (wash clothes, bathe, flush toilets)　(2つ書けていれば良い。)　No. 3　A Japanese person consumes 1,460 liters of virtual water in a day.　No. 4　They will decline.　No. 5　Because it is one of the fundamental resources for human survival.

〈解説〉リスニングテストでは，放送の前にあらかじめ選択肢に目を通しておくだけで心の余裕ができる。問題に答えるために必要な部分に集中したいが，聞き取りにくい単語が出てきても焦らないこと。焦るあまりそれ以降の部分で聞き漏らしがあってはならない。

【中学校】

【1】問1　(1)　エ　(2)　ウ　(3)　ア　(4)　エ　(5)　イ　(6)　ア　(7)　イ　(8)　エ　(9)　ア　(10)　ウ

問2　①　ability to speak　②　reasons for this　③　will be able to　④　spoken　⑤　sent abroad　⑥　○　問3　(1)　①　What has supported *Okuno-in* for 1,200 years　②　wanting to achieve a spiritual connection with Kukai　(2)　ウ　(3)　laid

〈解説〉問1　(1)　badの比較級はworse，最上級はworstとなる。goodがbetter，bestとなることも合わせて確認しておこう。　(2)　Would/ Do you mind ～ing?で，「～してくれませんか」と相手にお願いをする文になる。wouldで始まるほうがより丁寧な言い方。　(3)「トムが一緒に行ってくれない限り」とすべき部分であるが，すでにI will notと否定文から始まっているので，not untilと重複してnotを使うのは不適切。「～しない限り」の意味のunlessを使うのがふさわしい。　(4)　現実に起こりえない仮定を表す際には，wasの代わりにwereを使う。If I were you「私があなたの立場だったら」などの表現も関連して覚えておこう。　(5)　不変の法則は必ず現在形で表す。The earth goes around the sun.「地球は太陽の周りを回っている」などもよく出題される。
(6)　forは値段を表すことができる前置詞。　(7)　現在分詞にするか過去分詞にするかは，本体部分の主語の視点に立って考えるとよい。ここでのit「それ」は「見る」という動作の主語ではなく「見られる」と動作を受ける立場にあるので，seenが適切。　(8)「彼女は自分の目で見たかのように出来事を語ってくれた」という文。「自分の目で見た」は「語った」よりも過去に起こったことなので，had＋動詞の過去分詞形を使って大過去表現にする。　(9)「来年で日本に5年住んだことになる」という未来完了の表現なので，will have＋動詞の過去分詞形を使うのが適切。　(10)　単純な語彙力を問う問題。正答のウのsubmergeは「沈下する」の意味。submit「提出する」，subscribe「加入する」，subordinate「指揮下に置く」。　問2　①　abilityは必ずto不定詞を伴う。　②　reason for ～で「～の理由」となる。　③　willとcanのような助動詞を2つ続けて使うことはできないので，後の助動詞をbe able toに変更しなければならない。　④「上手に英語を話すことができれば」という文脈であるが，Englishは「話される」立場にあるのでspeakingではなくspokenと受身形にすべき。　⑤　abroadは「海外へ」という際には前置詞を伴わず，単独で「海外へ」の意味を表すことができる。homeなどの単語も同様。　⑥　make＋目的語＋動詞の原形で「(目的語)を～させる」の意味。　問3　(1)　①　この部分は文の中で主語の役割をする部分である。選択肢を見ると，hasとsupportedはペアで使って現在完了形を作ることがわかるだろう。すると，for 1,200 yearsがこの現在完了の動作の期間を表すことがわかる。後は残りのwhatと*Okuno-in*をどう使うかであるが，whatを最初に持ってくることでwhat *Okuno-in* has supported「奥の院が支持してきたもの」という表現を作ることができる。　②　come to *Okuno-in*という動詞が後に続いているので，この部分も文全体の中で主語の役割をする節である。したがって，Peopleの後にはachieveではなくwantingを続けることで，wanting以下全体がPeopleを修飾して「～したい人々」という表現にしなければならない。「空海と霊的なつながりを得たいと思っている(人々)」の意味。　(2)　lay ashes to rest「遺灰を納める」と並列されているので，memorial services「記念の集い」が適切。servicesは「サービス」の他に，「軍での働き」「奉仕」「宗教的な儀式」などの意味がある。　(3)　難しい単語が含まれているが，文全体の意味を大体捉えていれば解ける問題。ここでは奥の院参道が敷かれた目的を述べているので，laid to ～「～のために敷かれた」と過去分詞形で「奥の院参道」を修飾する形にするのが正解。なお，obscureはここでは「世に知られていない」の意味。sacred precinct「(寺などの)境内」。

【2】問1　知能とは単一の特長をもつものではなく，むしろ，様々な子どもたちに様々な特長として現れるもの。　問2　ウ→ア→イ　問3　combination　問4　ア　問5　イ　問6　すべての子どもたちは多重知能に長所と短所をもっているので，好みの学習方法があるということを考慮することは，教師にとって重要である。
問7　⑥　ウ　⑦　イ　⑧　ア　問8　①　イ　②　エ　③　ア　④　ウ

〈解説〉問1　下線部①は本の題名であるが，その内容として述べられているsuggested that以下の部分を日本語に訳せばよい。　問2　第2段落は，子ども個人個人で異なる活動を好むものである，という文から始まる。アは「同時に，彼らは書くこと，お絵かきや色塗りにはほとんど興味を示さないかもしれない」，イは「他の子は，歌や踊りに加わるように言われると恥ずかしがるかもしれないが，その一方でお話に基づいて文を書くことや絵を描くことを喜ぶかもしれない」，ウは「たとえば，ある物語に基づいた活動をすることを考えてみると，音楽的才能のある子どもは歌や踊りが好きで，劇やバレエを通じて自分を表現しようとすることが多い」という内容。「子どもたちはそれぞれ異なる活動を楽しむ」という内容を受けて，ウの「たとえば～」が最初にくる。次は「同時に，～」という並列の関係で始まるア，最後にイとなる。　問3 「2つ以上の物が組み合わさって1つの単位になっている構成」ということで，本文を見ると空欄②には「組み合わせ」という意味の単語を入れるのがふさわしいことがわかる。
問4　直後の文でAnalytic learners are those with an attention to detailと書かれていることがヒントになる。analytic「分析的」に対するのはsynthetic「統合的」。　問5　空欄④の直後に，「物に触って感触を得ることで学習する」と書かれていることがヒント。　問6　it is 形容詞 for 人 to ～で「～することは(人)にとって(形容詞)である」というのが基本的な構造。stronger and weaker aspects of their multiple intelligencesとpreferred learning stylesは並列の関係になっている。　問7　アは「子どもたちは先生がしている身振りを見て，言葉や身振りでそれに加わることができる」，イは「子どもたちは歌詞や本に書かれている歌の韻を踏んでいる部分を見たり，絵を見ることもできる」，ウは「子どもたちは歌ったり韻を読んでいる先生またはテープの音声を聞くことができる」という内容。各空欄の直後に続いているThis will cater for …の内容に合わせてそれぞれを当てはめる。auditory「聴覚の」，visual「視覚の」，kinaesthetic「運動感覚の」。　問8　①　「学習者としての強みや(　①　)」なので，「強み」と並列できるのはpreferences「興味関心」しかない。　②　ここにはmaterialsを修飾する形容詞が入るが，この後にto fit their learners …と「学習者それぞれに適した教材を選ぶ」旨が記されているので，suitableが適切とわかる。　③　learners of different ages in different (　③　)「異なる(　③　)における異なる年齢の学習者」なので，contexts「背景，文脈」を入れるのが適切。ここでのcontextはbackgroundやcultureの類義語として使われている。
④　空欄前の部分がfull ofと前置詞で終わっているので，空欄には名詞が入る。full of stimulation「刺激にあふれた」の意。

【3】問1　My favorite sport is tennis. I'm a member of the tennis club. I've played tennis for three years. I enjoy playing it with my friends.

問2　(According to the language activities for writing in Course of Study,) teachers should focus on writing students' thoughts and feelings with regard to issues like what they have experienced in everyday situations. In order to allow students to express themselves in English, we can provide them opportunities to write about their experiences, but that alone is not sufficient. We should teach how to write. Now, I will explain one brain storming technique called "fish-born framework", to help my students write English essays. First, I give them a topic and introduce "webbing." It will help them to expand their thoughts. Then they frame the paragraphs logically using fish-born framework. By thinking again and again about what they really want to write, they can be successful in their essay writing. No matter how many opportunities are given to the students, they cannot write their essays appropriately without knowledge of how to choose topics and how to organize the paragraphs.　(146語)

〈解説〉問1　中学校で習う程度の単語や構文を使用して，文法的な間違いのないように作文すればよい。あまり難しい表現を使わないように注意。　問2「指定された条件に従い，与えられたテーマについて的確に表現する力」を伸ばすにはどうすればよいかを考える。いろいろなアイディアから取捨選択し，適切な段落構成をして作文していく力，ともいえるだろう。解答する際には，最初に日本語でどういった構成にしていくかを計画するとよい。「第一に」，「第二に」，「結論として」などの表現を用いて論の展開をわかりやすくするとポイントが高くなるだろう。

【高等学校】

【1】問1　B　　問2　(イ)　　問3　have completely withdrawn from society, even locking themselves in their bedrooms for years at a time

問4　costliest natural disaster the world has ever seen　　問5　F　(ウ)

G (ア)　H (エ)　I (イ)　問6 (イ)　問7 (イ)
問8 (ウ)　問9 地震が起こる前に受験していた高等学校の入試結果が発表され，進学が決まったから。

〈解説〉問1 commencementには「開始」以外に「学位授与式」という意味もある。「しかし学位授与式はなかった」という文なので，「3月にKouheiは双葉町の高校を卒業した」という1文の直後の空欄Bに入れるのが適切。卒業したけれども学位授与式がなく，将来に向かっての一歩を踏み出すことができない心境に置かれているのである。
問2「5人兄弟の長兄としてのⓐ, 父が入院している中で一家の大黒柱」という文脈から，mantleは「受け継がれる重要な役目，責任」という予測がつく。　問3 「不安を抱えて(E)する若者」ということで，空欄Eに入れるのは「家にとどまっている」「社会から断絶している」などの表現がふさわしい。　問4 「これまでで最も甚大な被害を伴う自然災害」ということで，costliest natural disaster everという並べ替えをすることができるが，残りの選択肢を見るとeverとneverを一緒に使うことができないことがわかってくる。そこで，「世界がこれまでに目にした中で最も甚大な被害を伴う自然災害」costliest natural disaster the world has ever seenという表現を作るのが正しいとわかる。実際にすでに起こった災害について話しているので，the world has never seen「一度も目にした事がない」とするのは間違い。
問5 F「[F]である群集は今日は別の理由でここに集まっている」なので，「普段ロックコンサートを聴きにくる地域の若者」が正解。G「午前9時半までには，この緊急センターはその最大[G]に達していた」なので，「500人のボランティア」が正解。　H「その500人のうちほとんどは[H]」なので，「若者」を入れる。　I「18歳であるMasayukiは[I]の一人である」なので，「ボランティアの空きを手に入れたラッキーな者」を入れる。GとIが混乱してしまいそうだが，Gの直後に「さらに1500人が」という記述があることを考えると，Gには「500人」という具体的な数字を入れるのが自然。　問6 「単にお金ではなく実際の(①)」なので，(イ)のwork「作業」を入れるのが適切。donation「寄付」，wages「賃金」property「財産」。

問7 「(J)というのは歴史の定石である」で，その直後には「大きな災害がない限り社会を変えるのは難しい」という発言がある。したがって「予期しないできごとが社会の姿勢を完全に変えることができる」という意味の(イ)が正解。 問8 「この動力が東北再建に必要な何か月，何年といった期間継続するかどうかは(②)」という文脈。直後には「しかしながら，最も被害が大きかった地域からも，希望を持てるような兆候が現れ始めている」とあるので，空欄②に入るのは「明確というには程遠い」という表現が適切。 問9 「おでこを合わせる仕草，ハイタッチや口笛，歓声」という動作について言及している部分。直前の部分を読むと，「震災前に受けた高校入試の結果が3人とも合格だった」ことが書かれている。

【2】問1 大人の指導や，より高い能力をもつ仲間と協力すれば，問題解決できる潜在的なレベル 問2 teachers 問3 ① (エ) ⑥ (ア) 問4 (ウ) 問5 only are authentic tasks effective for 問6 (イ) 問7 「沈黙」が尊ばれる文化の中で育った生徒が，クラスの前で口頭演習をする際に感じる大きな心理的負担 問8 (イ) 問9 (ア) 問10 (イ)→(ア)→(ウ) 問11 (エ) 問12 (ウ) 問13 (エ)

〈解説〉問1 下線部ⓐは「潜在的な上達のレベル」という意味であるが，直後にその説明として「大人の指導の下で，または自分よりも能力のある同級生との共同作業による問題解決の中で見出される」と書かれている。 問2 下線部ⓑを含む文の主語はteachersなので，「彼ら自身」はteachersを指す。 問3 ① 段落同士の関係性を知るには，各段落の最初の一文を読んでいけばよい。第1段落が「生徒のコミュニケーション技術を伸ばす鍵は教師にある」と言っているのに対して，第2段落は「様々な状況下での英語でのコミュニケーションを生徒に教えることは非常に推奨されている」と始まっている。したがって，空欄①には追加的な視点を示すことで論点を強調するMoreoverが入る。

⑥　空欄⑥の直前には「行動やコミュニケーションの方式は，彼らが受けてきた日本式教育に非常に影響を受けており，これが特定の問題を引き起す場合がある」と書かれてあり，直後には「日本文化では協調を重んじ，敬老の精神が大切にされている。教師がコミュニケーションの演習をするように指示すると，生徒は沈黙を破るのに抵抗を示す」と書かれているので，空欄⑥で始まる文は「特定の問題」の例を示す働きをしているものと判断できる。　問4　②　depending on「～によって」という表現。lean on「～にもたれかかる」，count on「～を信頼して頼る」，rely on「～を頼る」。　③　describedまたはmentionedを入れることで，「このセクションで説明した教育手法」という意味になる。　問5　not only A but (also) B「AであるだけではなくB」という表現を知っていれば，簡単に解くことができるだろう。ここでAに名詞ではなく節が入る場合には，主語と動詞の位置を入れ替えるというルールがある。文法書に戻って再度確認しておこう。
問6　④　enough「十分な」，insufficient「不十分な」，few「ほとんどない，ごく少数の」，countless「数え切れないほどたくさんの」という意味。ここでは，「教師にもっと多くの研修機会を与えなければならない」という文脈なので，insufficientを入れるのが適切。　⑤「～のためには，手法に関する知識を深めて，使用効果の高い指示方法を身につけることが(　⑤　)」という文脈なので，advisable「望ましい」が適切。unsuitable「適していない」，sensitive「敏感な」，passable「まずまずの」。　問7　指示語の指す内容は，通常その直前の部分に書かれている。ここでは，「沈黙は金なり，とされる日本文化の中でクラス全員の前で口頭発表をすること」で，文化と授業の要求の間でconflictが起こる，とされているのである。　問8「先生に敬意を示すことは，すなわち沈黙を守ることである。(　⑦　)アメリカのような他の文化では，先生を尊敬するということは，必ずしも静かにしていることを意味するものではない」という文。whileには「～の間」以外に「その一方で」という意味もある。　問9「授業の最初と最後に先生に対してお辞儀をすることで礼節を示さなければならないような文

化では，生徒が(　⑨　)の学び方に適応することは比較的(　⑧　)である。ましてや，こういった学びが英語の授業でしか実践されていないならなおさらである」という文脈。英語の授業ではコミュニケーション演習などactive「能動的な」学びが推奨されているが，日本文化の下ではそういったスタイルに適応するのはchallenging「難しい」，という組み合わせを選ぶ。　問10　(ア)の「このフレームワークに反して」，(イ)の「日本文化のもう1つの側面は」，(ウ)の「ホールは前者を…」という指示語がヒントになる。それぞれの指示語が指す内容がその直前にくるように並べ替えをする。　問11　「以心伝心」の説明として，「“(　B　)だけに頼るのではなく(　C　)にも基づいて”，話者の言っていることを理解する」という表現。　問12　「日本文化の中では，英語教師は，生徒の会話能力を育てて教室で実際にその能力を使わせるのに苦労する。こういった状況下では，英語教師は(　D　)しなければならない。文化的な差異を理解しこれらの要素を教えることで，生徒はより広い視点から英語を学ぶことができるようになる」という文脈。したがって，(ウ)の「生徒の言語的な能力とともに，文化的理解を深める」が適切。　問13　(ア)は「ロールプレイは様々な登場人物に扮してコミュニケーションをするので，コミュニケーション技術の上達には効果的ではない」，(イ)は「教室では生徒同士で話す機会が限られているので，英語を学ぶのに理想的である」，(ウ)は「日本式のコミュニケーションを経験した日本人の生徒達にとっては，英語を学ぶことはほとんど不可能である」で，それぞれ本文と一致しない。

【3】(1)　He kept me waited in the snow for forty minutes.
waiting

(2)　The number of tourists who come to Wakayama have been increasing.
has

(3)　The most easiest way to get there is by airplane.
easiest

(4)　I was used to going drinking after work.
used to go

(5)　She is proud of being a teacher when she was young.
having been

(6)　Five of the members came on time, but others were late.
the others

(7)　If you are convenient (for you), please visit Shingu.
it is

〈解説〉(1)　keep＋人＋waitingで「(人)を待たせる」という表現。この時，(人)は「待っている」という状態に保たれ続けるので，waitingを使うのが正しい。　(2)　the number of ～「～の数」が主語なので，動詞は主語が単数の場合に準じなければならない。　(3)　mostと形容詞の最上級easiestは併用することができない。　(4)　I was used to ～ingでは，「～することに慣れていた」という表現になってしまう。「昔は～したものだ」はbe動詞なしのI used to ～で表す。　(5)「若い頃教師であった」は過去のできごとなので，beingではなくhaving beenと過去のできごとを表す形にしなければならない。　(6)　ここでは漠然と「他の人々」を言っているのではなく「特定のグループの中の他の人々」を指しているので，the othersと特定する形にしなければならない。
(7)　you are convenientだと「あなたが便利なら」という意味になってしまう。「(～にとって)都合がよい」はit is convenient (for ～)。

【４】What is important in English class is to learn through communication. I will give students many opportunities to use English in class with activities such as pair work, oral introduction, discussion, presentations and speeches. Each activity must be interesting and active. For example, pair work is a good way to have students communicate in English actively. In the lesson about the subjunctive mood, I will have them ask each other what they would do if they were millionaires. I will encourage them to give some reasons to each other, too. They will enjoy exchanging their ideas with each other. It is important to provide students with good activities. They make English class lively and enable students to develop fluency in English.　(121語)

〈解説〉高等学校学習指導要領解説　外国語編・英語編(平成22年5月)の

「第1部　外国語編　第3章　英語に関する各科目に共通する内容等」では，「教師は，生徒がコミュニケーションを積極的に行おうとする態度を損なわないよう配慮しつつ，意味が伝わらないおそれがあるものは正しく言い換えるといった指導を行うことが考えられる。一方，文字で行うコミュニケーションでは，正確さや適切さが一層重要となる。このため，生徒が書いた英語に誤りや曖昧さがあった場合は，それを正確で適切なものとするよう，文法や語彙を運用する能力を高めながら，きめ細かな指導を行うことが考えられる」としている。このことを踏まえ，コミュニケーションの機会を与えるためにはどのような授業をすればよいかを英語で作文すればよい。英語で小論文を書く際には最初に導入文，最後に結論文を書くことを忘れないように。また，For exampleやFirst，Secondなどの表現を使って書くとまとまりやすく，得点も高くなるだろう。

2015年度　実施問題

【中高共通】

[1]はリスニングテストです。放送の指示に従ってください。

【１】放送を聞いて，[Part 1]～[Part 3]の各問に答えよ。

[Part 1]

No.1

(A)　An expansion of a hospital.

(B)　An annex of a hotel.

(C)　A new post office.

(D)　An old apartment building.

No.2

(A)　She isn't a good speaker of it.

(B)　She can speak it very well.

(C)　She can speak it better than German.

(D)　French is the only language she can speak.

No.3

(A)　She has to pick up Mike's friend.

(B)　Mike will return in a few minutes.

(C)　She will help the man with preparing his presentation.

(D)　It will take too long to prepare the presentation.

No.4

(A)　They are going to play outside.

(B)　They are going to exercise individually.

(C)　They are going to train themselves hard as usual.

(D)　They are going to exercise more than usual next week.

No.5

(A)　She has nothing to do with the bribe.

(B) She is guilty of taking a bribe.

(C) She was taken in by some clients.

(D) She did offer a bribe to some clients.

No.6

(A) Someone got hurt.

(B) Someone took his stuff.

(C) He lost his job.

(D) He had to cheer up his friend.

No.7

(A) He'll go to the park.

(B) He'll go to the hospital.

(C) He'll go to his uncle's house.

(D) He'll go to his aunt's house.

No.8

(A) A lazy man.

(B) An introverted man.

(C) A motivated man.

(D) A methodical man.

No.9

(A) It's terrific.

(B) It's unpleasant.

(C) It's terrible.

(D) It's very bad.

[Part 2]

No.1 Why does the woman use a digital voice recorder ?

(A) Because it can record her voice.

(B) Because it helps her to make good notes.

(C) Because it is difficult for her to attend the lecture.

(D) Because it saves hours of time.

No.2　How does the man read ?

(A)　He tries to grasp the gist of the book first.

(B)　He reads as carefully as possible first.

(C)　He highlights the unknown words.

(D)　He tries to understand every single word.

No.3　What does the man think about the lecture on the French Revolution ?

(A)　He thinks it's boring.

(B)　He thinks it's interesting.

(C)　He thinks it's strange.

(D)　He thinks it's challenging.

No.4　What does the woman have to write about ?

(A)　The zoo.

(B)　History.

(C)　Animal behavior.

(D)　Animal language.

[Part 3]

No.1　How many species of mammals have become extinct since European settlement of Australia ?

No.2　Why were some species saved only on offshore islands ?

No.3　Give one example of an extreme natural condition that might cause catastrophic results for wild animals in Australia.

No.4　What happens to wild animals when natural habitats are divided or isolated by the pressures of human activities ?

No.5　What is the best way to preserve the habitats of the native animals ?

(☆☆☆◎◎◎)

【中学校】

【1】次の英文を読んで，あとの[問1]～[問6]に答えよ。

In the story told by the Roman poet Ovid, Pygmalion is a sculptor who falls in love with a statue he has created. George Bernard Shaw borrowed the theme for his play *Pygmalion* – later (　a　) into the musical *My Fair Lady* – in which Professor Henry Higgins makes over the Cockney flower girl Eliza Doolittle, becoming besotted with her even as he teaches her how to speak proper English ("The rain in Spain stays mainly in the plain...")

Psychologists, too, have (　b　) up the motif, researching what they call the "Pygmalion effect". The finding, as social psychologist Robert Rosenthal puts it, is "that <u>①【 of / another / what / expects / one person 】</u> can come to serve as a self-fulfilling prophecy." Rosenthal and his coauthor Lenore Jacobson <u>②coined</u> the term to describe the striking results of an experiment they (　c　) out in a California school in 1965. Students took a test that was said to be able to identify <u>③ "growth spurters,"</u> or those who were poised to make strides academically. Teachers were given the names of pupils <u>④【 bloom / about / who / to / were 】</u> intellectually – and sure enough, these students showed a significantly greater gain in performance over their classmates when tested again at the end of the year.

But here's the thing: the "spurters" were actually chosen at random. The only difference between them and their peers, Rosenthal writes, "was in the mind of the teacher." And yet the expectations (　d　) in the mind of the teacher – or the parent, or the manager, or the coach – can make an enormous difference. Research conducted since Rosenthal and Jacobson's original study has determined that <u>⑤【 all / the Pygmalion effect / applies / kinds/ to / settings / of 】</u>, from sports teams to the military to the corporate workplace.

Just how do (　e　) expectations promote greater achievement ? It's not some magical act of inspiration. Rather, Rosenthal and others have found that higher expectations lead teachers (or other authority figures) to act differently in regard to the learner, in four very specific ways:

1　They create a warmer "socioemotional climate" for the learners they regard as high-potential, often conveying this warmth through non-verbal signals: a nod, an encouraging smile, a touch on the shoulder.

2　They teach more material, and more difficult material, to learners they see as especially promising.

3　They give up-and-coming learners more opportunities to contribute, including additional time to respond to questions.

4　<u>⑥They offer their "special" learners feedback on performance that is more detailed and more personalized – not just a generic "Good job."</u>

It can be difficult to deliberately change our expectations of others. But we can consciously change our behavior. By adopting the set of behaviors above, we'll be acting like our kids, our students or our employees have great potential – potential that they'll more than likely live up to.

[問1]　文中の(　a　)～(　e　)に入る最も適切な語を，次の(ア)～(カ)から1つずつ選び，その記号を書け。ただし，各語はそれぞれ1度しか用いないこととする。

(ア)　picked　　(イ)　turned　　(ウ)　carried　　(エ)　held

(オ)　elevated　　(カ)　proved

[問2]　下線部①，④，⑤の【　　】内の語句を正しく並べかえよ。ただし，【　　】内のみを書くこと。

[問3]　下線部②と同じ意味を表す語を，次の(ア)～(エ)から1つ選び，その記号を書け。

(ア)　invented　　(イ)　violated　　(ウ)　completed

(エ)　finalized

[問4]　下線部③の内容を日本語で具体的に書け。

[問5]　次の質問に英語で答えよ。

According to Rosenthal, why did the students who were chosen at random promote great achievement ?

[問6]　下線部⑥を外国語の教科指導の場面として考えるとき，どのような指導が考えられるか。80字程度の日本語で具体的に書け。

(☆☆☆◎◎◎)

【2】次の英文を読んで，あとの[問1]～[問6]に答えよ。

The communicative approach in language teaching(CLT) starts from a theory of language as communication. The goal of language teaching is to develop what Hymes(1972) referred to as "communicative competence." Hymes coined this term ①【 a / contrast / view / order / communicative / to / in 】 of language as a rebuttal to Chomsky's theory of competence. Chomsky believed that children are born with an inherited ability to learn any human language and produce grammatically correct sentences. Hymes held that such a view of linguistic theory was sterile, that linguistic theory needed to be seen as a part of a more general theory incorporating communication and culture. Hymes's theory of communicative competence was a definition of what a speaker needs to understand to communicate in the target language.

A related analysis of communicative competence is found in Canale and Swain(1980), in which four dimensions of communicative competence are identified: grammatical competence, sociolinguistic competence, discourse competence, and strategic competence. Grammatical competence refers to what Chomsky calls linguistic competence and what Hymes intends by what is "formally possible." It is the domain of grammatical and lexical capacity. Sociolinguistic competence refers to an understanding of the social context in which communication takes place, including role relationships, the shared information of the participants, and the communicative purpose for their interaction. Discourse competence refers to the interpretation of individual message elements in terms of their interconnectedness and of how meaning is represented in relationship to the entire discourse or text. ② Strategic competence refers to a person's ability to keep communication going when there is a communication breakdown or to enhance the effectiveness of the communication.

Savignon(1983) describes the relation of the four components of communicative competence as in the inverted pyramidical diagram shown below.

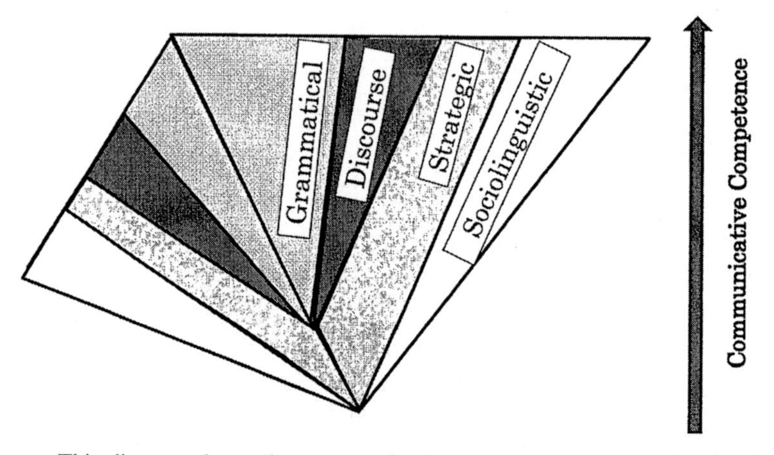

This diagram shows that communicative competence can consist of only (a) competence and (b) competence before learners acquire (c) competence. Even gestures or facial expression without language can convey messages when both the producer and the receiver intend to interpret it. There is no particular order to teach four components and when learners increase one component, it would affect the other components, then communicative competence as a whole would increase. None of ③ them is less important than the others.

Savignon(1983) discusses techniques and classroom management procedures associated with a number of CLT classroom procedures (e.g., group activities, language games, role plays), but ④【 these / nor / activities / neither / the ways 】 in which they are used are exclusive to CLT classrooms. Finocchiaro and Brumfit offer a lesson outline for teaching the function "making a suggestion" for learners in the beginning level of a secondary school program that suggests that CLT procedures are evolutionary rather than revolutionary:

1 【 A 】
2 Oral practice of each utterance of the dialog segment to be presented that day
3 Questions and answers based on the dialog topic(s) and situation itself
4 Questions and answers related to the students' personal experiences
5 【 B 】
6 Learner discovery of generalizations or rules underlying the functional expression or structure
7 Oral recognition, interpretative activities
8 【 C 】
9 Copying of the dialogs or modules if they are not in the class text
10 Sampling of the written homework assignment
11 Evaluation of learning

Such procedures is found in many "orthodox" CLT texts. Although each unit has an ostensibly functional focus, new teaching points are introduced with dialogues, followed by controlled practice of the main grammatical patterns. The teaching points are then contextualized through situational practice. This serves as an introduction to a freer practice activity, such as a role play or improvisation.

[問1] 下線部①，④の【　　】内の語句を正しく並べかえよ。ただし，【　　】内のみを書くこと。

[問2] 下線部②を日本語で簡潔に説明せよ。また，下線部②に関して，学習者が使うストラテジーの1つに"pause fillers"というものがある。それはどのようなものか，具体的な表現を2つ，それぞれ英語2語以上で書け。

[問3]　文中の(　a　)～(　c　)に入る語の組み合わせとして，最も適切なものを，次の(ア)～(エ)から1つ選び，その記号を書け。

(ア)　(　a　)　discourse　　(　b　)　grammatical
　　(　c　)　sociolinguistic

(イ)　(　a　)　grammatical　　(　b　)　strategic
　　(　c　)　discourse

(ウ)　(　a　)　sociolinguistic　　(　b　)　discourse
　　(　c　)　strategic

(エ)　(　a　)　sociolinguistic　　(　b　)　strategic
　　(　c　)　grammatical

[問4]　下線部③は何を指すか。本文中から抜き出して英語2語で書け。

[問5]　文中の【　A　】～【　C　】に入る最も適切な活動を，次の(ア)～(ウ)からそれぞれ1つずつ選び，記号で書け。

(ア)　Study one of the basic communicative expressions in the dialog or one of the structures which exemplify the function

(イ)　Presentation of a brief dialog or several mini-dialogs, preceded by a motivation and a discussion of the function and situation – people, roles, setting, topic, and the informality or formality of the language which the function and situation demand

(ウ)　Oral production activities – proceeding from guided to freer communication activities

[問6]　本文によれば，ChomskyとHymesは言語の能力について，それぞれどのように考えているか。その違いがわかるように日本語で簡潔に述べよ。

(☆☆☆☆◎◎◎)

【3】ある中学校の第2学年の英語科の授業で4月にインタビューテストを行った。次の表は，そのテストから明らかになった生徒の実態と学年末の学習到達目標である。この目標を達成するために，あなたは年間を通じ，授業でどのような工夫をして指導をするか。具体的な指導例

も含めて120語以上170語以下の英語で書け。また，語数を記入すること。

生徒の実態	学習到達目標
・単語や句による発話が多いが，限られた種類の単文であれば文で発話できる。 ・会話が続かず，途中で沈黙してしまうことが多い。	質問に対して理由をつけて答えたり，会話を継続・発展させるために，自らも相手に質問をしたりするなど，尋ねられたこと以上の情報を加えて話すことができる。

(☆☆☆◎◎◎)

【高等学校】

【1】次の英文を読み，あとの[問1]～[問7]に答えよ。

An increasing number of people are absorbed so much in playing games, chatting and surfing online that the habit is (①) them problems in their daily lives. Internet addiction should be (②) as a social problem (③) both children and adults. Families, educators and the central and local governments should take measures to combat the problem, including education, advice and counseling for people who have developed Internet addictions.

[A]

This number should be taken seriously.

ⓐThe survey asked students to say yes or no to eight questions. Among the questions were the following: (1) Do you feel that you have to gradually increase the hours of using the Internet to gain satisfaction?; (2) Have you tried but failed to shorten your hours online or completely stop using the Internet?; and (3) Did you ever risk damaging important personal relationships due to your Internet habits? The panel of the Health, Labor and Welfare Ministry concluded that 7,952 students or 8.1 percent who said yes to five or more questions had an unhealthy dependence on the Internet.

ⓑSymptoms of Internet addiction include the following: Skipping meals while surfing online; feeling uneasy if a mobile phone is not at hand all the time; staying up all night and sleeping in the daytime; withdrawing from society; failing to concentrate on studies or work; and becoming sick due to malnutrition. It is important for people to understand that Internet addiction can have serious consequences, including damage to important personal relationships, including family ties.

Special attention must be paid to online games in which Internet users form a virtual team and attack the enemy. If the team wins, team members praise each other and gain a sense of accomplishment, which serves to deepen their addictions. Regardless of whether the team wins or loses, it becomes difficult for team members to quit the team and the game because they fear that doing so would invite criticism from other team members. In both cases, [　④　]. Among children it is becoming popular to chat in a group using a free Internet service. They often sit up all night chatting online, and fear that quitting the chat session will lead to ⓒostracism.

It is important for both parents and teachers to teach students healthy Internet habits. Parents can talk with their children and limit the hours they can play online games. They can also take steps such as prohibiting their children's use of mobile phones at night and installing filters to block access to harmful Internet sites. Teachers should instruct students on how to use the Internet in beneficial ways to further their education and how to avoid developing an online addiction.

It is also important for people – whether adults or children – to realize that ⓓ[virtual online relations/ important and fruitful / more / real-world relationships / much / than / are]. Internet addicts should try to reduce their dependency by having digital detox days and spending more time with friends and family members.

[問1] 本文中の(①)~(③)に入る最も適切な語の組み合わせを，次の(ア)~(エ)から1つ選び，その記号を書け。

(ア) ① causing ② viewing ③ involved
(イ) ① causing ② viewed ③ involving
(ウ) ① caused ② viewed ③ involving
(エ) ① caused ② viewing ③ involved

[問2] 本文中の[A]に，意味の通った文章となるように次の(ア)~(ウ)の文を並べかえて入れると，どのような順番になるか。その記号を書け。

(ア) If the 8.1 percent figure is applied to the total number of students in junior and senior high schools, an estimated 518,000 of them are Internet addicts.

(イ) For the first time ever, a panel of the Health, Labor and Welfare Ministry has carried out surveys covering nearly 100,000 junior high and senior high school students and found out that 8.1 percent of them were addicted to the Internet.

(ウ) The panel distributed questionnaires to some 140,000 students through junior high and senior high schools in Tokyo, Hokkaido and Japan's 45 prefectures and about 98,000 students responded.

[問3] 下線部ⓐの結果，どのようなことが結論づけられたか。日本語で説明せよ。

[問4] 下線部ⓑについて，その例として本文中であげられているもののうち，4つを日本語で答えよ。

[問5] [④]に入る最も適切な文を，次の(ア)~(エ)から1つ選び，その記号を書け。

(ア) people are bound by virtual human relationships

(イ)　people are allowed to quit their jobs or leave school

(ウ)　people are given courage to deal with real problems

(エ)　people are abandoned by their families or friends

[問6]　下線部ⓒが表す意味として最も適切なものを，次の(ア)~(エ)から1つ選び，その記号を書け。

(ア)　the state of being dependent on others

(イ)　the state of being rescued from danger

(ウ)　the state of not being able to sleep

(エ)　the state of not being included in a group

[問7]　下線部ⓓについて，[　　]内の語または語句を本文の流れに合うように正しく並べかえよ。

(☆☆☆◎◎◎)

【2】次の英文を読み，[問1]~[問12]に答えよ。

One image for teaching English as a second or foreign language (ESL/EFL) is that of a tapestry. The tapestry is woven from many strands, such as the characteristics of the teacher, the learner, the setting, and the relevant languages. For the instructional ⓐloom to produce a large, strong, beautiful, colorful tapestry, all of these strands must be interwoven in positive ways. (　①　), the instructor's teaching style must address the learning style of the learner, the learner must be motivated, and the setting must provide resources and values that strongly support the teaching of the language. (　②　), if the strands are not woven together effectively, the instructional loom is likely to produce something small, weak, ragged, and pale – not recognizable as a tapestry at all.

In addition to ⓑthe four strands mentioned above, other important strands exist in the tapestry. In a practical sense, one of the most crucial of these strands consists of the four primary skills of listening, reading, speaking, and writing. This strand also includes associated or related skills such as knowledge of vocabulary, pronunciation, and usage. The skill strand of the tapestry leads to optimal ESL/EFL communication when ⓒthe skills are interwoven during instruction. This is known as the integrated-skill approach. [A]

If this weaving together does not occur, the strand consists merely of discrete, segregated skills – (③) that do not touch, support, or interact with each other. This is sometimes known as the segregated-skill approach. Another title for this mode of instruction is the language-based approach, because the language itself is the focus of instruction (language for language's sake). In this approach, ⓓ[is / for / on / not / learning / the emphasis] authentic communication.

Skill segregation is reflected in traditional ESL/EFL programs that offer classes focusing on segregated language skills. [④] Perhaps teachers and administrators think it is logistically easier to present courses on writing divorced from speaking, or on listening isolated from reading. They may believe that it is instructionally impossible to concentrate on more than one skill at a time. [B]

Even if it were possible to fully develop one or two skills in the absence of all the others, such an approach would not ensure adequate preparation for later success in academic communication, career-related language use, or everyday interaction in the language. An extreme example is the grammar-translation method, which teaches students to analyze grammar and to translate (usually in writing) from one language to another. This method restricts language learning to a very narrow, noncommunicative range that does not prepare students enough for ⓔsuch success. [C]

In contrast to segregated-skill instruction, there are some forms of instruction that are clearly oriented toward integrating the skills. Among them is task-based instruction. In task-based instruction, students participate in communicative tasks in English. Tasks are defined as activities that can stand alone as fundamental units and that require comprehending, producing, manipulating, or interacting in authentic language while attention is principally paid to (⑤) rather than (⑥). In task-based instruction, basic pair work and group work are often used to increase student interaction and collaboration. For instance, students work together to write and edit a class newspaper, develop a television commercial, enact scenes from a play, or take part in other joint tasks.

The integrated-skill approach, as contrasted with the purely segregated approach, exposes English language learners to authentic language and challenges them to interact naturally in the language. Learners rapidly gain a true picture of the richness and complexity of the English language as employed for communication. (⑦), this approach stresses that English is not just an object of academic interest nor merely a key to passing an examination; (⑧), English becomes a real means of interaction and sharing among people. This approach allows teachers to track students' progress in multiple skills at the same time. Integrating the language skills also promotes the learning of real content, not just the dissection of language forms. [D]

With careful reflection and planning, any teacher can integrate the language skills and strengthen the tapestry of language teaching and learning. When the tapestry is woven well, learners can use English effectively for (⑨).

[問1] 下線部ⓐの表す意味として最も適切なものを，次の(ア)～(エ)から1つ選び，その記号を書け。

(ア) a real means of interaction

(イ) an approach to teaching a native tongue

(ウ) a device invented for making strands stronger

(エ) a machine used for weaving thread into cloth

[問2] 本文中の(①)，(②)に入る最も適切な語または語句を，次の(ア)～(エ)からそれぞれ1つずつ選び，その記号を書け。

(ア) For example　　(イ) At last　　(ウ) However

(エ) As a result

[問3] 下線部ⓑは何をさすか。本文中から抜き出して英語で書け。

[問4]　下線部ⓒについて，本文中に書かれている具体例をすべて日本語で答えよ。

[問5]　本文中の(　③　)に入る最も適切なものを，次の(ア)~(エ)から1つ選び，その記号を書け。

(ア)　strong threads　　(イ)　parallel threads　　(ウ)　crossing threads

(エ)　long threads

[問6]　下線部ⓓについて，[　　]内の語または語句を本文の流れに合うように正しく並べかえよ。

[問7]　本文中の[　④　]に入る最も適切な文を，次の(ア)~(エ)から1つ選び，その記号を書け。

(ア)　When do they offer such classes?

(イ)　To whom do they offer such classes?

(ウ)　How do they offer such classes?

(エ)　Why do they offer such classes?

[問8]　下線部ⓔについて，本文中に書かれている具体的内容を日本語ですべて書け。

[問9]　本文中の(　⑤　)，(　⑥　)に入る最も適切な語の組み合わせを，次の(ア)~(エ)から1つ選び，その記号を書け。

(ア)　⑤　listening　　⑥　speaking

(イ)　⑤　speaking　　⑥　listening

(ウ)　⑤　meaning　　⑥　form

(エ)　⑤　form　　⑥　meaning

[問10]　本文中の(　⑦　)，(　⑧　)に入る最も適切な語の組み合わせを，次の(ア)~(エ)から1つ選び，その記号を書け。

(ア)　⑦　Instead　　⑧　moreover

(イ)　⑦　Moreover　　⑧　instead

(ウ)　⑦　Moreover　　⑧　first

(エ)　⑦　First　　⑧　moreover

[問11]　次の文は，本文中の[　A　]~[　D　]のいずれかに入る。本文の流れから考えてどこが最も適切か，その記号を書け。

Finally, the integrated-skill approach can be highly motivating to students of all ages and backgrounds.

[問12]　本文の要旨を踏まえ，本文中の(　⑨　)に入る適切な英語1語を書け。

(☆☆☆◎◎◎)

【3】下の(1)～(7)は，与えられた日本文に対して生徒が黒板に書いた英文である。生徒の英文をできるだけ生かすという観点で，どのように直せばよいか。次の例にならって書け。

(例)　国体は2015年に和歌山県で開催される。

The National Sports Festival will <u>be taken place</u> in Wakayama Prefecture in 2015.
take place

(1)　土曜日まで和歌山にいるから，金曜日に君と一緒に高野山に行きたいなあ。

I'll be staying in Wakayama by Saturday, so I would like to go to Koyasan with you on Friday.

(2)　その女性は少し気分が悪かったので，ソファーに横たわった。

The lady felt a little unwell, so she lied down on the sofa.

(3)　出てきた生徒たちの心配そうな顔つきから判断すると，それは彼らにとって難しい試験だったに違いない。

Judging by worried looks on the students' faces as they came out, it must be a difficult exam for them.

(4)　トムには残念なことに，映画館にはあまりにもたくさんの人がいたので，その映画を見ることができなかった。

Unfortunately for Tom, there were too many people in the movie theater that he couldn't see the movie.

(5)　コンピュータが発明されていなければ，世界は今どのようになっているのでしょうか。

What would the world be like now if the computer wasn't invented?

(6)　その3つの解決策の中で，どれが最もうまくいくと思いますか。

Of the three solutions, do you think which will be the most successful?

(7) バスに乗り遅れたので，私たちはかなり遅れてホテルに到着した。

Having missed the bus, we reached the hotel very lately.

(☆☆☆◎◎◎)

【4】次の文は，平成21年3月に告示された高等学校学習指導要領「外国語」に示されている「外国語科」の「目標」(英語版)である。

To develop students' communication abilities such as accurately understanding and appropriately conveying information, ideas, etc., deepening their understanding of language and culture, and fostering a positive attitude toward communication through foreign languages.

下線部の趣旨を踏まえた授業をするために，あなたはどのようなことに留意するか，120語程度の英文でまとめなさい。また，語数を記入すること。

(☆☆☆◎◎◎)

解答・解説

【中高共通】

【1】[Part 1]　No.1　(B)　No.2　(A)　No.3　(C)　No.4　(D)　No.5　(B)　No.6　(C)　No.7　(D)　No.8　(C)　No.9　(A)

[Part 2]　No.1　(B)　No.2　(A)　No.3　(B)　No.4　(D)

[Part 3]　No.1　Nineteen species have.　No.2　Because they were isolated from non-native animals (that had upset the environmental balance).　No.3　Cyclones. / Drought. / Fires. / Global warming.　No.4　They are unable to sustain their life cycles and perish.　No.5　It is to expand and maintain Australia's national parks and other nature reserves.

〈解説〉リスニングテストの対策としては，日頃からCD，TV・ラジオ放送，インターネット上の音声ファイルなどを通して，native speakerの話すスピードに少しでも慣れておくことが肝心である。訓練を積み重ねて，落ち着いて本番に臨むようにしたい。また，基本的な文法・構文をマスターしておくこと，英文のreadingにおいてひとまず文法のことを考えずに頭から読み下してその意味を全体的にとる練習を重ねておくことも，リスニングには極めて有効である。実戦に際しては，何よりも会話が行われている状況を把握するように努めること。そのために，一字一句の微妙な音に左右されないようにすることが大切である。聞き取れない時は，その前後関係から判断して，文全体の意味をとるように心がけ，会話の全体的な状況を把握することが求められる。会話の中では，例えばI've got to ～，You've ～のような短縮語が多用されることもあらかじめ頭に入れておくとよい。一語一語を聞き取ろうとするのではなく，一つの意味のまとまりとしてとらえるようにする。本問のように質問や解答の選択肢が問題用紙に示されている場合は，放送が始まる前にひととおり目を通しておくことも，より正確なリスニングの助けになる。

【中学校】

【1】問1　a　(イ)　　b　(ア)　　c　(ウ)　　d　(エ)　　e　(オ)

問2　①　what one person expects of another　　④　who were about to bloom　　⑤　the Pygmalion effect applies to all kinds of settings

問3　(ア)　　問4　成績が伸びるとみられる生徒　　問5　Because higher expectations led teachers to act differently in regard to the learner.

問6　生徒が書いたエッセイ等について評価を行う際に，点数だけでなく，工夫している点や良かった点及び改善すべき点等を詳細に伝えるなど，生徒の実態に応じたコメントを書く。(80字)

〈解説〉問1　a　turn into ～「～に変える」。　b　pick up ～「～を取り上げる」。　c　carry out ～「～を実行する」。　d　hold in the mindで「(感情などを)心に抱く」。　e　elevated「高められた」。過去分詞の形容詞的用法として用いられている。elevated expectationsで「高い期待」。

問2 ① expect of ～「～に期待する」の形を作り，「一人の人が他の人に期待すること」の意味にする。 ④ 下線部は「まさに輝こうとしている(生徒達)」という意味になる。whoは関係代名詞として使われる。be about to ～「まさに～する」。 ⑤ 下線部は「ピグマリオン効果はすべての状況に当てはまる」という意味になる。apply to ～「～に当てはまる」。 問3 動詞としてのcoinは，「貨幣を鋳造する」から「何かを作り出す・生み出す」の意味。 問4 spurt「急成長する」の意味からspurterは「急成長する人」。growthは下線部③の前後から「成績が上がること」の意味を推測する。 問5 第4段落第3文にRosenthalらの知見として，「教師は学習者により高い期待を持ち，他と違った行動をとらせる」旨が述べられている。 問6 通り一遍の評価でなく，個々の生徒の取り組みをどのように評価・還元していくかを考える。以下に別解を示す。学習意欲の維持・向上のために，特別の質問を教師が事前に用意し授業中に答えさせる。家庭学習用により高度な問題集を持たせ定期的に点検したり，英文日記を書かせたりしてみる。(83字)

【2】問1 ① in order to contrast a communicative view ④ neither these activities nor the ways 問2 説明 コミュニケーションに支障が生じたときに，コミュニケーションを維持するための能力，または，コミュニケーションの有効性を高めるための能力 表現 “You know,” “Let’s see.” など 問3 (エ) 問4 four components 問5 A (イ) B (ア) C (ウ) 問6 Chomskyは，人間はもともと頭の中で文法的に正しい文をつくる能力をもっていると考え，Hymesは単に文法的に正しい文をつくるだけでは不十分で，その言語が使われている状況や人間関係をふまえて言語を使えるようにならなければならないと考えた。

〈解説〉問1 ① in order toの連語を組み立て，「伝達の考え方を対照するために」という意味にする。 ④ neither ～ norの構文にして，「この活動もどの方法も～ない」という意味にする。 問2 下線部②は

「戦術的能力」の意味。直後のrefers to …以下に注目する。問題文中の“pause fillers”は会話が成り立たないときなどに使う「間を埋めるもの」のこと。解答例の他には，“Really?”「本当？」や“I see.”「なるほど」などがある。　問3　Sociolinguistic「社会言語学の」，Strategic「戦略上重要な」，Grammatical「文法にかなった」の3つの能力が，図の中でDiscourse「会話」の外側，内側のどちらに示されているかで判断する。問4　下線部③を含む文の意味は「どの1つも他の3つより大切でないものはない(＝どれも等しく大切)」。themは第4段落第3文に示されているfour componentsのこと。　問5　(ア)～(ウ)のそれぞれについて，以下に注目して中学校段階のビギナーレベルでの教え方を考えてみる。
(ア)　the basic communicative expressions「基本的な伝達表現」。
(イ)　Presentation of a brief dialog or several mini-dialogs「簡単な対話かいくつかのミニ対話の提示」。　(ウ)　Oral production activities「口頭での発表活動」。　問6　第1段落第4～5文に，ChomskyとHymesの考え方の違いが述べられている。

【3】First, I will provide the students with an appropriate topic and let them brainstorm about it. The students can broaden their ideas and find out what they want to talk about.

Second, I will introduce some reaction words and fillers such as “Let me see.”, “Really?” and so on, so that the students can avoid an awkward silence and continue their conversation.

Third, I will let the students work in pairs. They will start the conversation using yes-no questions. I will encourage them to add some details or reasons to their answers. Furthermore, I will suggest that they should ask questions starting with Who, What, When, Where, Why and How. Those questions are very effective to extend subjects of conversations.

The students will keep trying these activities through the year with different topics and they will gradually get to know how to utilize what they learned in the class and start talking freely in English. (155 words)

〈解説〉表の「生徒の実態」からは，発話に対する積極性はみられるので，相手に発話をうながし会話を成立させるために，生徒自身がどのように話せばよいかを考えさせる指導を考えていく。以下に別解を示す。I will give class through the following three steps. First, I will let the students notice that their English speaking is not enough to communicate with others, especially with any foreigners. I will encourage them to speak English more boldly and not to pay any attention to grammatical errors. Second, I will advise them to use "and, but, yet, etc." as often as possible. And when they get used to using these words to lengthen their speaking, I recommend some other words like "for example, because, however, etc." to them and encourage them to speak longer and longer. Last, I will let them get used to questions-answers practice by using interrogatives like who, when, where, which, and how. In this step, I am sure they will talk about something private or something detailed by speaking a little long sentences. (139 words)

【高等学校】

【1】問1　(イ)　問2　(イ)→(ウ)→(ア)　問3　8つの質問のうち5つ以上の質問に「はい」と答えた7,952人，すなわち8.1％の生徒が不健全なインターネット依存状態にあるということ。　問4　・ネットサーフィン中は食事を抜く　・常に手元に携帯電話がないと不安を感じる　・一晩中起きていて日中は寝ている　・社会からの引きこもり　・勉強や仕事で集中力を欠く　・栄養失調による発病　のうちから4つ　問5　(ア)　問6　(エ)　問7　real-world relationships are much more important and fruitful than virtual online relations

〈解説〉問1　①　the habit is causing them problemsで「その習慣はいろいろの問題を引き起こしている」。cause「引き起こす」を現在進行形の形にする。　②　Internet addiction should be viewed as a social problemで「インターネット依存状態は社会問題としてみなすべきだ」。view as ～「～とみなす」の意味で，viewを受動態の形にする。　③　involving both children and adultsで「子供も大人も巻き込んで」となり，直前のa

social problemを修飾する。involve「巻き込む」を現在分詞の形容詞的用法(後置)の形にする。　問2　(イ)のFor the first time ever, a panel of the Health, Labor and Welfare Ministry …「厚生労働省の調査団が初めて…」の結果の数字を中心に考えるとよい。続く(ウ)は「調査は日本の中学生・高校生を対象に47都道府県で実施された」こと，そして(ア)は「518,000人の中学生・高校生がインターネット依存状態と推定される」という主旨。　問3　The survey「その調査」の結論は，下線部ⓐを含む段落の最後の一文concluded that以下にまとめられている。
問4　Symptoms of Internet addiction include the followingは「インターネット中毒の兆候には次のようなものがある」。この文の直後に「；」で区切りながら解答例に挙げた6つが例示されている。　問5　空欄④の直前のboth casesとは，オンラインゲームで「勝とうが負けようが」ということ。どちらにしてもvirtualな人間関係に縛られるという意味が続くと考えられるので，(ア)が正解。be bound by ～「～に束縛されている」。　問6　ostracismは「追放，村八分」の意味。この場合，グループに入れないことを表す。　問7　more ～ than …の構文にする。「real-world relationshipsがvirtual online relationsよりはるかに重要で実りが多い」という意味。

【2】問1　(エ)　　問2　①　(ア)　　②　(ウ)　　問3　the characteristics of the teacher, the learner, the setting, and the relevant languages
問4　聞く，読む，話す，書くの主要4技能とそれらに関連した語彙，発音，語法の技能　　問5　(イ)　　問6　the emphasis is not on learning for　　問7　(エ)　　問8　・将来，学問上必要なコミュニケーションができること　　・将来，職業上必要となる言語活用ができること　・将来，日常的な対話ができること　　問9　(ウ)　　問10　(イ)
問11　D　　問12　communication
〈解説〉問1　loom「はた織り機」。「タペストリは多くの糸から編まれる」と第1段第2文に述べられているところから判断する。　問2　①　空欄以下には教授法，学習者，環境など，具体的な例が述べられていることに注意する。 ② 空欄以下はその前の文の内容の逆説を表していることに注目する。 問3 the four strands「4つの糸」の内容は第1段落第2文に述べられている，第二言語または外国語として英語を教えるイメージのたとえの解説を示す。 問4 第2段落第2文後半から第3文に述べられている技能を挙げる。 問5 空欄③の直後のthat 以下の文「互いに触れることも支え合うこともない，混じり合うこともない～」から判断する。parallel「平行の」。 問6 主語になる語をしっかり選ぶことが大切。The emphasis is not on～で「～を重要視しない」の意味。 問7 空欄④直後の一文が「たぶん教師や管理者が～と考えているからだろう」の意味だから，Why で始まる疑問文が正解となる。 問8 such success「このような成功」の内容は，同段落第1文で述べられている。 問9 空欄⑤・⑥を含む文では，task-based instruction「課題活動」にはcomprehending, producing, manipulating, interacting が必要だと述べられている。つまりcommunicative skillが大切であると考えられるので，会話術ではformとmeaningのいずれに注意が向けられなければならないかを考える。 問10 ⑦ 空欄の直後のthis approach は第7段落第1文冒頭のThe integrated-skill approach を指していることを考え，空欄以下の文も引き続きthe integrated-skill approachについて述べられていることから正しい語を判断する。
⑧ 空欄以下の文は第7段落第3文の前半で言っていることよりも，空欄⑧の後の内容の方が重要である，という文脈なので，instead「それよりも」が正解。 問11 the integrated-skill approachについて述べられている段落を探すとよい。 問12 本文の要旨は，communicationの手段としての英語をどうしたら修得できるかということである。

【3】(1) I'll be staying in Wakayama <u>by</u> Saturday, so I would like to go to
until / till
Koyasan with you on Friday. (2) The lady felt a little unwell, so she <u>lied</u>
lay
down on the sofa. (3) Judging by worried looks on the students' faces as they came out, it must <u>be</u> a difficult exam for them. (4) Unfortunately
have been

for Tom, there were too (→ so) many people in the movie theater that he couldn't see the movie.　(5) What would the world be like now if the computer wasn't (→ hadn't been) invented?　(6) Of the three solutions, do you think which (→ which do you think) will be the most successful?　(7) Having missed the bus, we reached the hotel very lately (→ late).

〈解説〉(1) byは「～までに」の意味で「完了」を表す。till / untilは「～まで(ずっと)」の意味で「継続」を表す。　(2) lied は他動詞lie「嘘をつく」の過去形。「ソファーに横たわった」の意味だから自動詞lieを過去形にする。　(3) 「難しい試験だったに違いない」は「過去の推定」を表すからmust＋完了形にする。　(4) 「あまりにもたくさんの人がいたので」からso ～ thatの構文を作る。　(5) 「コンピュータが発明されていなければ」は過去の意味を表すから，仮定法過去完了の形had＋過去分詞の形にする。　(6) do you think は疑問詞の後ろで「挿入句」として使われる。　(7) latelyは「最近」の意味。時間が「遅い」はlate。

【4】I think the primary role of an English teacher is to let students feel that they want to express their ideas. First, I'll prepare materials that stimulate students' interests. The materials should contain such tasks as to need the four language skills of reading, writing, speaking and listening. Then, I'll conduct activities that allow students to practice language they can use in real-world situations. I'll also conduct English classes in English in order to enhance the opportunities for students to be exposed to English. Third, I'll give full support and positive feedback to our students that will help them improve themselves as good English speakers. Lastly, I'll create a warm atmosphere that allows our students to use English freely. (119 words)

〈解説〉下線部は「外国語を通じて，積極的にコミュニケーションを図ろうとする態度を育成する」という意味である。これについて高等学校学習指導要領解説外国語編・英語編(平成21年12月)第1部第1章第2節では,「理解できないことがあっても,推測するなどして聞き続けたり読み続けたりしようとする態度や確認したり繰り返しや説明を求めたりする態度,自分の考えなどを積極的に話したり書いたりしようとする態度などを育成すること」と述べている。これを踏まえて解答を作成したい。以下に別解を示す。First of all, I keep “Never to be thrown into the reading- translation method” in mind. Not to be thrown into this traditional way of teaching, I want to have a chance to ask questions in English as often as I can. The questions include wh-questions (by using interrogatives) and questions which students have to express their views. The former is easy to answer but fosters a positive attitude toward communication through foreign language. And the latter is a little hard to answer but helps convey their own ways of thinking. I'm sure this question-answer method will enhance their communicative ability if I have many chances to do so. (108 words)

2014年度　実施問題

【中学校】

【１】放送を聞いて，[Part 1]～[Part 3]の各問に答えよ。

[Part 1]

No.1

(A) He's a hairdresser.

(B) He's a sports instructor.

(C) He's a swimming coach.

(D) He's a dry cleaner.

No.2

(A) Five fifteen.

(B) Six past ten.

(C) Five fifty.

(D) Ten twenty-six.

No.3

(A) It's exciting to live there.

(B) It's exciting to visit.

(C) She likes the crowds.

(D) She likes the heat.

No.4

(A) A new car.

(B) A new bicycle.

(C) A new child.

(D) A new house.

No.5

(A) For relaxation.

(B) For entertainment.

(C) For information.

(D) For excitement.

No.6

(A) It will be held tomorrow.

(B) It will be held next week.

(C) It was held last term.

(D) It was held recently.

No.7

(A) That he's had a boy.

(B) That his daughter is pregnant.

(C) That his daughter has had a baby.

(D) That he had a granddaughter.

No.8

(A) A professional potter.

(B) A house to rent.

(C) A ring.

(D) A rental DVD.

No.9

She thinks that they have to ...

(A) spend more time on the college premises.

(B) get used to working independently.

(C) work harder than they did in high school.

(D) clarify what needs to be done in high school.

[Part 2]

No.1 What does the briefcase look like?

(A) A heavy box-type with one buckle.

(B) A heavy box-type with two buckles.

(C) A soft leather type with one buckle.

(D) A soft leather type with two buckles.

No.2　Which picture shows the distinguishing features?

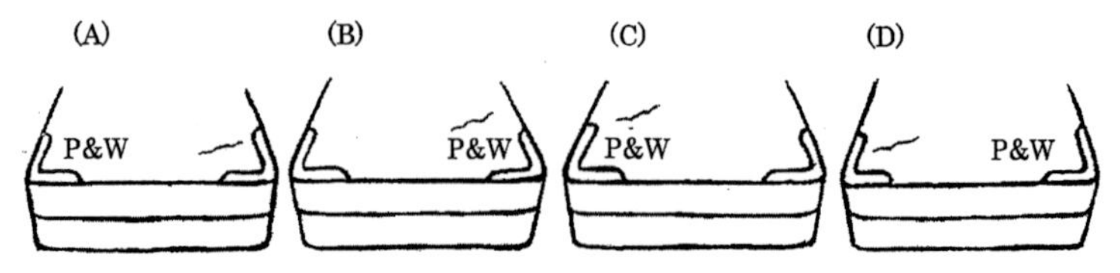

No.3　What did she have inside her briefcase?

(A)　A wallet, pens and a novel.　　(B)　Pens and a novel.

(C)　Papers and a wallet.　　(D)　Papers, pens and a novel.

No.4　What was the situation when she lost her briefcase?

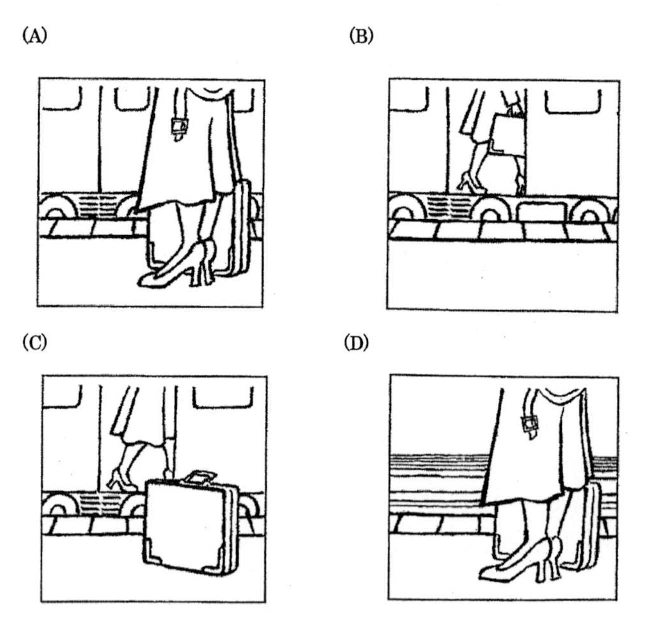

[Part 3]

Questions:

No. 1　How do we feel when we try and are not quickly rewarded?

No. 2　Why does nobody want to sell us anything on a program for change that will take years?

No. 3　Explain "companies' cultures" in other words.

No. 4　Why does Charlie study the cultures of the companies?

No. 5　What does Charlie believe healthy change should be?

(☆☆☆◎◎◎)

【2】次の英文を読んで，あとの[問1]～[問7]に答えよ。

There are always correct answers to problems set for school entrance examinations. But problems can be posed in such a way ①that "There is no correct answer" is the right answer. Why can't a correct answer be (a)? What do you think are the conditions that make the problem unanswerable? This is the kind of arithmetic test being carried out at a primary school in Kobe.

This approach reminds us that we act too hastily in looking for correct answers. We are too (b) about whether our answers are right or not, rather than about the process of solving problems. Instead of taking time to think, we come up with answers quickly. As can be seen from entrance examinations at celebrated private junior high schools, ②【 as / as / many / 20 problems / with 】 given to solve in an hour, students have to produce answers instantly.

From kindergarten to university, every day in the formative years for the brain is (c) in trying to find correct answers. When a person, who has developed a conviction that there are correct answers to all problems, comes up against something to which no right answer exists, he is baffled and does not know what to do. He avoids 【 あ 】 matters and has no interest in them.

"How to" books — like how to associate with others, how to make the most of employes, how to travel abroad, how to win horse race bets, and the fundamentals of golf swings — are (d) up high at bookstores. The clear answers that they give to problems are most probably the reason why they are selling very well. "If you do like this, you are sure to make money." "You are

(e) to improve." "You are going to be liked by others." The stronger the assurance, ③【the attraction / the book / the greater / holds】.

But the reader finds that the book does not live up to its claims of infallibility as soon as he tests it. It often happens that heavy debts incurred after a close reading of a book on how to win at horse race betting without fail 【 い 】 a man his job, and that an amateur golfer, following a club swing theory too faithfully, has to go to a bonesetter.

Why is it that many people read "How to" books, knowing that answers they give are not necessarily correct? Is it a psychology like ④that of a drowning man catching at a straw? Is it a desire to improve oneself incessantly? Is it self-conceit about an ability to make a correct assessment of the answers given for their beneficial applications? Which is the right answer?

Thinking the matter over, we get impatient. ⑤【impatience / in / to / resonse / such】, a book on how to read "How to" books is likely to come out.

[問1]　文中の(a)～(e)に入る最も適切な語を，次の(ア)～(カ)から1つずつ選び，その記号を書け。ただし，各語はそれぞれ1度しか用いないこととする。

(ア) bound　(イ) spent　(ウ) concerned　(エ) declined
(オ) obtained　(カ) piled

[問2]　下線部②，③，⑤の【　】内の語句を正しく並べかえよ。ただし，【　】内のみを書くこと。なお，文頭の語も小文字にしている。

[問3]　下線部①thatと同じ用法のthatを本文中より見つけ，そのthatの直後の2語を書け。

[問4]　文中の【 あ 】に入る最も適切な語を，本文中より抜き出して書け。

[問5]　文中の【 い 】に入る最も適切な語を，次の(ア)～(エ)から1つ選び，その記号で答えよ。

(ア) cost　(イ) get　(ウ) make　(エ) save

[問6]　下線部④thatが指す語を，本文中より抜き出して書け。

[問7]　本文の内容と合うものを，次の(ア)～(エ)から1つ選び，その記号を書け。

(ア)　We never take entrance examinations without being asked a question which has no correct answer.

(イ)　When we look for correct answers to problems in a test, we often take time to think.

(ウ)　It is very difficult for us all to find out what "How to" books tell us isn't always correct.

(エ)　A lot of people who read "How to" books know that such books sometimes tell them wrong answers.

(☆☆☆◎◎◎)

【3】次の英文を読んで，あとの[問1]～[問7]に答えよ。

L1 transfer refers to the influence that the learner's L1 exerts over the acquisition of an L2. This influence is apparent in a number of ways. First, the learner's L1 is one of the sources of error in learner language. This influence is referred to as (　a　) transfer. However, in some cases, the learner's L1 can facilitate L2 acquisition. For example, French learners of English are much less likely to make errors of this kind:

①The man whom I spoke to him is a millionaire.

than are Arabic learners because French does not permit resumptive pronouns (like 'him') in relative clauses whereas Arabic does. This type of effect is known as (　b　) transfer.

L1 transfer can also result in avoidance. For example, Chinese and Japanese learners of English have been found to avoid the use of relative clauses because their languages do not contain (　c　) structures. These learners make fewer errors in relative clauses than Arabic learners of English but only because they rarely use ②them. Finally, L1 transfer may be reflected in the overuse of some forms. For example, some Chinese learners tend to overuse expressions of regret when apologizing in English, in accordance with the norms of their mother tongue.

Theoretical accounts of L1 transfer have undergone considerable revision since the early days of SLA. In the heyday of behaviourism it was believed that errors were largely the result of【 あ 】(another term for negative transfer). That is, the habits of the L1 were supposed to prevent the learner from learning the habits of the L2. In the belief that interference, and thereby learning difficulty, could be predicted by identifying those areas of the target language that were different from the learners' L1, comparisons of the two languages were carried out using (d) analysis. The resulting list of differences was used to make decisions about the content of teaching materials.

As we have already seen, behaviourist theories cannot adequately account for L2 acquisition and they fell out of favour in the early 1970s. This led to two developments. Some theorists, espousing strong mentalist accounts of L2 acquisition, sought to play down the role of the L1. They argued that very few errors were the result of L1 transfer. An analysis of the errors produced by Spanish learners of L2 English, for example, led one pair of researchers to claim that less than 5 percent of the errors were the result of transfer. This minimalist view of L1 transfer, however, has not withstood the test of time.

The second development was to reconceptualize transfer within a (e) framework. This was begun by Larry Selinker. In his formulation of interlanguage theory he identified language transfer as one of the mental processes responsible for fossilization. Subsequently, there has been widespread acknowledgement that learners draw on their L1 in forming interlanguage hypotheses. Learners do not construct rules in a vacuum; rather they work with whatever information is at their disposal. This includes knowledge of their L1. The L1 can be viewed as a kind of 'input from the inside'. According to this view, then, transfer is not 'interference' but a cognitive process.

One of the main objections to a behaviourist account of L1 transfer is that transfer errors do not always occur when they are predicted to occur. That is, differences between the target and (f) languages do not always result in learning difficulty. Whereas a behaviourist theory cannot easily account for this, a cognitive theory, which recognizes that transfer will occur under some conditions but not under others, can do so. SLA has succeeded in identifying some of the cognitive constraints that govern the transfer of L1 knowledge. We will consider two of these constraints; learners' perceptions of what is transferable and their stage of development.

According to Eric Kellerman, learners have perceptions regarding the linguistic features of their own language. They treat some features as potentially【 い 】and others as potentially non-transferable. Broadly speaking, then, learners have a sense of what features in their L1 are in some way basic. They are more prepared to risk transferring such features than they are those they perceive to be unique to their own language. Kellerman found that advanced Dutch learners of English had clear perceptions about which meanings of '*breken*' ('break') were basic in their L1 and which were unique. He also found that they were prepared to translate a sentence like:

Hij brak zijn been. (He broke his leg.)

directly into English, using 'broke' for '*brak*' but were not prepared to give a direct translation of a sentence like:

Het ondergrondse verset werd gebroken. (The underground resistance was broken.)

even though this was, in fact, possible. In other words, the learners【 う 】a basic meaning of '*breken*' but resisted transferring a meaning they perceived as unique.

[問1] 文中の(a)～(f)に入る最も適切な語を，次の(ア)～(キ)から1つずつ選び，その記号を書け。ただし，各語はそれぞれ1度しか用いないこととする。

(ア) native　(イ) unnatural　(ウ) negative
(エ) equivalent　(オ) cognitive　(カ) contrastive
(キ) positive

[問2]　下線部①の英文を，本文の内容を踏まえて，正しい英文に書き直せ。

[問3]　下線部②のthemが指す語句を書け。また，その語句を日本語に訳せ。

[問4]　文中の【　あ　】に入る最も適切な語を，次の(ア)～(エ)から1つ選び，その記号を書け。

(ア)　interference　　(イ)　avoidance　　(ウ)　difference

(エ)　process

[問5]　文中の【　い　】,【　う　】に入る適切な語を，本文の流れから判断し，それぞれ書け。

[問6]　文中のSLAという語を，略さずに英語で書け。

[問7]　本文の内容と合うものを，次の(ア)～(エ)から1つ選び，その記号を書け。

(ア)　Chinese and Japanese learners of English tend to use relative clauses because Japanese and Chinese languages don't have such structures.

(イ)　Larry Selinker insisted that the habits of the mother tongue were supposed to prevent the learner from learning the ones of the second language.

(ウ)　A behaviourist theory can clearly explain the reason why transfer errors do not always occur when they are predicted to.

(エ)　Eric Kellerman claimed that advanced second language learners had a sense to perceive if some features of their L1 are transferable.

(☆☆☆◎◎◎)

【4】現行の学習指導要領では，小学校外国語活動において，外国語の音声や基本的な表現に慣れ親しませることが目標の1つとなっている。高等学校では，授業を実際のコミュニケーションの場面とするため，授業は英語で行うことを基本とすること，と明示されている。

これを受けて，中学校においても，英語で授業を行うことが望ましいと考えられる。

このことについて，次の[問1]，[問2]に答えよ。

[問1]　英語で授業を行うことで，どのようなことが問題となると考えるか。30語以上の英語で書け。

[問2]　[問1]の問題を克服するために，あなたは中学校の英語教師として，どのようなことに工夫して指導するか。具体的な指導例も含めて130語以上の英語で書け。

(☆☆☆☆◎◎◎◎)

【高等学校】

【1】次の英文を読み，あとの[問1]～[問8]に答えよ。

In Japan, roughly 700,000 individuals are in a state of hikikomori, according to government figures released in July 2010. Their average age is 31. The oldest among them, known as the "first-generation hikikomori," are now in their 40s, having isolated themselves from almost all human contact for more than 20 years. Then there are the borderline cases, the 1.55 million people the government finds are (①) on the verge of shutting themselves up in their rooms.

It is remarkable how little it can take to push a person over the brink. School is usually — not — always where it starts. Often — not always — there is bullying. Kato-san (all names in this story followed by "san" are pseudonyms) was not bullied at all. [A] He was doing well in high school, and he was looking forward to studying social welfare at university, when an unspecified illness waylaid him. He recovered physically but remained shaken mentally. He gave up on university, sought part-time work and panicked when his job-hunting led nowhere. At 20, he retreated into his room. He's 30 now.

Yamada-san, (②), was bullied seriously. He dropped out of high school, but later managed to graduate from a correspondence high school. His father was relieved; the problem seemed solved. His father was abroad at the time and by his own admission little involved with his family. The boy, (③)

with unspecified technical skills, spent six months job-hunting, applying to some 30 companies. To no avail. No doors opened. Dismayed he sank into total withdrawal. Like Kato, he's 30 now, looking back on 10 years of life in his room. [　B　]

A magazine's reporter encountered Kato at an unexpected place — in Miyako, Iwate Prefecture, one of the areas hardest hit by the March 11 earthquake. Having left his room at last, Kato participated in an NGO rehabilitation program which, partly for therapeutic reasons, partly in response to an urgent need, sent him and six other hikikomori sufferers to the disaster zone as volunteers. They spent three days wallowing in mud, wilting in heat, and clearing rubble. Exhaustion, Kato learned, is a good cure for insomnia. He was able ⓐ[with, without, closed, eyes, to, his, rest] sleeping pills.

But three days are only three days. "To be honest, it didn't change me," he says. Back in an NGO dorm, he collapsed physically. His insomnia returned. [　C　] However, "ⓑI learned, I think, that while an individual is weak alone, two together can start to get things done, and three and four people pooling their strength can really accomplish something."

Yamada's father disclosed something about the isolation (　④　) in society at large. No one knew about his son's condition — "neither my colleagues at work, nor anyone in the neighborhood." It was a deep, dark, humiliating secret, kept for decades. "My generation" — he's 62 — "doesn't bring private problems to the workplace." Or anywhere else. [　D　]

His wife also kept her son's condition secret. But, ⓒat the end of her rope, she broke the silence at last. She confided in a friend, who knew somebody in a similar situation, who referred the family to an NPO. The NPO's staff — to Yamada senior's astonishment — proved helpful and competent. "I didn't seriously think an outsider could help us with a problem we couldn't solve ourselves, within the family," he says. Yamada junior is far from "cured," but at least he's in consultation with the NPO people — his first human contact outside the family in a decade. For him, as for Kato, there seems to be hope.

Not everyone fits into society. Dropping out, or falling by the wayside, has numerous causes and many manifestations.

We often hear of ⓓtwo extreme forms — homelessness and hikikomori, a withdrawal from all social activities into the security of one's own room, usually in one's parents' home. The former is characteristic of the West, the latter more typically Asian.

Japan is a "hikikomori superpower," says psychologist Tamaki Saito. So is South Korea. The two countries have much in common. Both have Confucian roots that nurture strong family ties. In the more self-consciously individualistic societies, led by the United States, people who fall through the cracks are apt to end up alone on the street. In Japan, for better or worse, there's usually the family to fall back on.

Not always. Experts look ahead with dread to what is being called "ⓔthe 2030 problem." That's the year the hikikomori "first generation" starts to turn 65. They will be left without any money, because their parents will just pass away by that time. Sixty-five is no time of life to start learning the ropes of a cold, unsympathetic and increasingly complex outside world.

[問1] 本文中の(①), (②)に入る最も適切な語句を，次の(ア)～(エ)からそれぞれ1つずつ選び，その記号を書け。

(ア) on the other hand (イ) in the same way

(ウ) more or less (エ) less and less

[問2] 本文中の(③), (④)に入る最も適切な語の組み合わせを，次の(ア)～(エ)から1つ選び，その記号を書け。

(ア) ③ equipped ④ prevailed

(イ) ③ equipping ④ prevailed

(ウ) ③ equipped ④ prevailing

(エ) ③ equipping ④ prevailing

[問3] 下線部ⓐについて，[ ]内の語を本文の流れに合うように正しく並べかえよ。

[問4]　下線部ⓑについて，「私が学んだ」内容を日本語で説明せよ。

[問5]　下線部ⓒが表す意味として最も適切なものを，次の(ア)～(エ)から1つ選び，その記号を書け。

(ア)　having no patience or energy left to cope with the situation

(イ)　having no private reasons for being involved in the situation

(ウ)　having much motivation to improve the situation

(エ)　having necessary skills to overcome the situation

[問6]　次の文は下線部ⓓについて説明したものである。本文の内容に沿って，(　ア　)～(　エ　)にそれぞれ適する日本語を記入せよ。

2つの極端な形態とは，(　ア　)と(　イ　)である。前者は，アメリカのようなより自我の強い，(　ウ　)的な欧米諸国の社会に特徴的に見られるものであり，後者は日本や韓国のような強い(　エ　)が存在するアジア諸国に典型的に見られるものである。

[問7]　下線部ⓔの内容について日本語で説明せよ。

[問8]　次の英文は，本文中の[　A　]～[　D　]のいずれかに入る。文脈から考えて最も適切なものを選び，その記号を書け。

It's a kind of unwritten law.

(☆☆☆◎◎◎◎)

【2】次の英文を読み，[問1]～[問10]に答えよ。

Since the formal release of the new Course of Study (hereinafter, COS) for Japan's primary and secondary schools by the Ministry of Education, Culture, Sports, Science and Technology (MEXT) in 2008 and 2009, there has been some discussion of the potential impact these reforms could have at the secondary school level on the teaching of writing and the development of academic literacy more generally. Kensaku Yoshida (Sophia University) points out that while the new COS contains highly ambitious expectations for English academic proficiency, including debate, presentations and discussion, these standards may only be attainable if the academic skills are developed across various courses. Since the COS now mandates the use of ⓐ<u>these skills</u>

not only in English, but in Japanese subjects as well, Yoshida suggests that the academic skills developed in Japanese could transfer to English, helping to (①) the burden of learning these skills in English classes. But since the new reforms ⓑ[are, be, implemented, to, yet] across the curriculum and there is currently no empirical evidence of this type of skill transfer in this particular learning context, it would be overly (②) at this point to expect any significant changes in students' academic abilities anytime in the near future. Until there is evidence of a large scale implementation of this directive across the curriculum and a transfer of skills from the L1 to the L2 in this context, we believe it is best for teachers to be (③) when adjusting their assumptions about the types of academic skills their students possess.

In a discussion of the implications of the new COS for the teaching of writing, Paul Kei Matsuda (Arizona State University) applauds MEXT's move to eliminate a separate course for English writing and integrate this course with the skills of speaking, listening and reading. But he also points out that ⓒthis move is not sufficient to bring about more effective writing instruction and even suggests that the change could present "(④)". Writing instruction could after all continue to be neglected in an integrated skills curriculum just as easily as it could in a separate course focusing on sentence-level grammar, a situation that would seriously undermine MEXT's directive for integrated skills instruction and academic proficiency. In order to avoid this, Matsuda argues that it is necessary for English teachers to "become aware of the complexity of writing and develop various strategies for teaching writing at various stages of students' language development".

One key aspect of the new COS is the recommendation that the (⑤) skills of writing and speaking be integrated with receptive skills of reading and listening. [A] This move toward an integration of skills is certainly welcome. [B] A well-developed integrated skills course more accurately reflects the way language is used in authentic communicative contexts. [C] Therefore it could provide more varied and meaningful opportunities for language input and output. [D] It is possible when developing tasks aimed at integrating skills that the boundaries between spoken and written forms of communication become blurred, resulting in a fusion, rather than an integration of skills. (⑥) we have sometimes observed well-intentioned efforts to integrate paragraph writing with a presentation by having students first write a paragraph and then memorize it for the purpose of presenting it to their classmates. ⓓSuch a task neglects the distinct features of written and spoken texts and how considerations of purpose and audience affect the way these two genres are realized. It is important (⑦) when integrating spoken and written skills that teachers do not lose sight of the distinct social, cognitive and linguistic features of these two very different modes of communication.

[問1] 下線部ⓐについて，本文中に書かれている具体例をすべて日本語で答えよ。

[問2] 本文中の(①)に入る最も適切な語を，次の(ア)～(エ)から1つ選び，その記号を書け。

(ア) understand　(イ) ease　(ウ) impose　(エ) complicate

[問3] 下線部ⓑについて，[ ]内の語を本文の流れに合うように正しく並べかえよ。

[問4] 本文中の(②)，(③)に入る最も適切な語の組み合わせを，次の(ア)～(エ)から1つ選び，その記号を書け。

(ア) ② optimistic　③ cautious
(イ) ② optimistic　③ incautious
(ウ) ② pessimistic　③ cautious
(エ) ② pessimistic　③ incautious

[問5] 下線部ⓒについて，その内容をわかりやすく日本語で説明せよ。

[問6] 本文中の(④)に入る最も適切な語句を，次の(ア)～(エ)から1つ選び，その記号を書け。

(ア) a single-edged sword　(イ) a double-edged sword
(ウ) a sharp-edged sword　(エ) a miracle-edged sword

[問7]　本文中の(　⑤　)に入る最も適切な語を書け。ただし，アルファベット(p)で始めること。

[問8]　次の英文は，本文中の[　A　]～[　D　]のいずれかに入る。文脈から考えて最も適切なものを選び，その記号を書け。

But with this move toward integration of skills, there is one concern that arises.

[問9]　本文中の(　⑥　)，(　⑦　)に入る最も適切な語または語句を，次の(ア)～(エ)からそれぞれ1つずつ選び，その記号を書け。ただし，下記の語または語句は文頭に来るものも小文字で記している。

(ア)　of course　　(イ)　however　　(ウ)　for example

(エ)　therefore

[問10]　下線部ⓓについて，その内容をわかりやすく日本語で説明せよ。

(☆☆☆◎◎◎)

【3】下の(1)～(7)は，与えられた日本文に対して生徒が黒板に書いた英文である。生徒の英文をできるだけ生かすという観点で，どのように直せばよいか。次の例にならって書け。

(例)　母は私に昼食の用意を手伝うように言った。

My mother <u>said</u> (told) me to help her to prepare for lunch.

(1)　国民体育大会は2015年に和歌山県で開催される。

The National Sports Festival will be taken place in Wakayama Prefecture in 2015.

(2)　母は，私を夜間に外出させてくれない。

My mother doesn't make me go out at night.

(3)　君が着く頃までには，僕はもうそれを終わらせているよ。

By the time you will have arrived, I will have finished it.

(4)　彼は愚かにも彼女が言ったことを信じた。

He was enough foolish to believe what she said.

(5)　バドミントンをするということになると，私たちは誰も彼には勝てない。

When it comes to play badminton, none of us can beat him.

(6) 父の給料は，私の給料よりずっと高い。

My father's salary is much more expensive than mine.

(7) A:「窓を開けてもいいですか。」　B:「どうぞ。」

A: "Do you mind for me to open the window?"　B: "No, not at all."

(☆☆☆◎◎◎)

【４】次の文は，平成21年3月に告示された高等学校学習指導要領「外国語」に示されている「目標」である。

外国語を通じて，言語や文化に対する理解を深め，積極的にコミュニケーションを図ろうとする態度の育成を図り，情報や考えなどを的確に理解したり適切に伝えたりするコミュニケーション能力を養う。

この趣旨を踏まえて，次の英文で書かれた意見に対するあなたの考えを120語程度の英文でまとめなさい。また，語数を記入すること。

English Classes in Japanese Senior High Schools

One of the most important elements necessary to acquire a language is grammar. Not only in terms of the first language, but also for a foreign language, grammar is of primary importance for learners to convey their messages. Thus Japanese high school students should study English at school, mainly focusing on learning grammar. In order to do so, the grammar-translation method is one of the most effective methods and has been widely employed in Japan. This method focuses on the memorization of grammatical features, vocabulary, and direct translations of text in the mother tongue in particular. By translating the target language into the learners' mother tongue, the learners are much quicker to understand the meanings. The medium of instruction should be the mother tongue, which enables teachers to teach grammar and structures more efficiently and effectively.

(☆☆☆☆☆◎◎◎)

解答・解説

【中学校】

【1】Part 1　No. 1　(A)　No. 2　(C)　No. 3　(B)　No. 4　(A)
No. 5　(A)　No. 6　(D)　No. 7　(C)　No. 8　(B)　No. 9　(B)
Part 2　No. 1　(D)　No. 2　(C)　No. 3　(D)　No. 4　(D)
Part 3　No. 1　We actually feel worse than we did before we started.
No. 2　Because no one would buy it.　No. 3　(They are) ways of doing things, and ways of life for the employees.　No. 4　(He studies them) in order to protect their futures.　No. 5　(He believes) it should be a long-term process, whether for a company or the people in it.

〈解説〉リスニング問題の全体的な傾向と留意点は以下の通りである。
Part 1　選択肢に現れるキーワードが問題中でも随所に出現することが予想され，それぞれのキーワードが選択肢に合致するかたちで用いられているかを確認する姿勢でリスニングに挑むとよいであろう。
Part 2　1つの物語を聞いて4つの問いに答える形式である。選択肢のそれぞれにどのような違いがあるのか，文字や絵から瞬時に把握し，ポイントを絞って聞き取れるようにしたい。　Part 3　やや学術的な内容に関するリスニングである。いずれの問いも，内容的に核となる部分を尋ねているものであるようなので，答えにあたるキーワードを確実に聞き取り，簡潔な英語で答えるとよい。

【2】問1　a　(オ)　b　(ウ)　c　(イ)　d　(カ)　e　(ア)
問2　②　with as many as 20 problems　③　the greater the attraction the book holds　⑤　In response to such impatience　問3　there are
問4　unanswerable　問5　(ア)　問6　psychology　問7　(エ)

〈解説〉問1　選択肢は全て動詞で，空欄の前はbe動詞という形(受動態)で統一されているため，単語と前後の本文の意味が分かっているのかを問うているシンプルな問題である。　a　obtained を入れて「正解がなぜ得られないのか」の意になる。　b　be concerned about ～ で「～を心配する」。　c　be spent in ～ で「～に費やされる」。　d　be piled up で「積み上げられる」。　e　be bound to ～ で「～するにちがいない」。
問2　②　as many as「～もの」を組み合わせることができれば，その後ろに数字を並べればよい。　③　the 比較級，the 比較級の問題である。the greater が修飾している the attraction が直後にくる。　⑤　in response to「～に応えて」　問3　①の that は，a way の内容を説明する「～という」を意味する同格節を導いている。これと同じ用法の that は第3段落第2文にある。　問4　空欄の前までの文で，全ての問題に正しい答えがあると信じている人が正しい答えのない問題にぶつかったとき，という内容が述べられているため，【　あ　】mattersは，「正しい答えのない問題」を意味する。　問5【　い　】は heavy debts を主語に，a man と his job を目的語にした文の動詞であることから，cost が選択できる。　問6　名詞の繰り返しを避けるために用いられる that であり，直前の名詞が答えとなる。　問7　第6段落の1文目に，「なぜ多くの人々は(書かれている)答えが正しい必要はないと知りながら『ハウツー』本を読むのか」という問いが投げかけられていることから分かる。

【3】問1　a　(ウ)　b　(キ)　c　(エ)　d　(カ)　e　(オ)
f　(ア)　問2　The man whom I spoke to is a millionaire. 又は The man to whom I spoke is a millionaire.　問3　(語句)　relative clauses　(日本語)　関係詞節(関係詞，関係代名詞も可)　問4　(ア)
問5　い　transferable　う　transferred　(transferedは1点減点)
問6　Second Language Acquisition　問7　(エ)
〈解説〉問1　a　前文で「間違いの原因」とあるので，negative transfer である。　b「フランス人の方が誤りが少ない」のだから，positive transfer である。　c「中国語と日本語には同様の構造がない」という意味なので，equivalent が適切である。　d「二つの言語の比較は(　　)分析をして行われる」という文脈から，contrastive「対比的」が入る。　e　空欄 eに続く箇所に mental processes という言葉が出てくるので，cognitive framework とするのが適切である。　f「目標言語と(　　)言語の違い」なので，native が入る。　問2　後述の文で，フランス語では関係詞節の中では him のような代名詞は許されないと述べられていることから，him のみを省くのが適当である。文法的には whom を除くことも可能であるが，前述の理由より，本問題の解答としては適切ではない。　問3　直前に，relative clauses での誤りが少ないと述べられていることから。　問4　直後の another term for negative transfer「否定的転移の言い換え」から「干渉」が導き出せる。SLAの知識があれば，該当部分よりすぐに判断できる。　問5　直後で対比されているnon-transferableやresisted transferringから，必要な語は容易に導き出せる。　問6　「第2言語習得(論)」の意。　問7　第7段落の3文目にそのような感覚があると述べられ，5文目からはオランダ人の上級英語学習者が具体例として挙げられている。

【4】問1

Junior high school students' English abilities are rather low. Especially in that they have little vocabulary. If English teachers use English so much, many of the students probably won't understand the lessons. I think that's one of the serious problems. (40 words)

問2

In order to solve the problem, I would like to propose three strategies.

First, I would use visual aids, such as pictures, photos and actual objects. When students hear some unfamiliar words, they can easily guess the meanings from visual aids.

Second, I would try to paraphrase complicated sentences into simple ones. For example, I'd say, "a song for children" when I want to talk about a lullaby.

Lastly I would use real experiences when I introduce new grammar items. For example, when I'd introduce past tense to the students, I say two or three

English sentences about what I actually did. In team-teaching, I could introduce sentences with the past tense through conversation with an ALT. Students can guess the meaning of the target sentence from the real conversation.

With those strategies, I can improve students' communicative competence in English lessons through English. (144 words)

〈解説〉英語の授業が明示的な文法指導に傾倒するような「英語について学ぶ」授業になることがないよう，英語が道具(手段)となるような授業を心がけたい。一方で，解答例に挙げられている語彙力の問題だけでなく，英語が苦手な生徒がさらに理解できなくなる，内容が認知レベルの高いものである場合理解が困難になる，といった問題が考えられる。対処法としては，解答例には視覚的な補助，言い換え，TTにおける実際の具体例の提示が挙げられており，その他にも，説明に従事せず，活動(機械的な言語活動と意味重視のコミュニケーション活動)を取り入れることにより繰り返し使って身につけさせる指導スタイルを採ることなども考えられる。

【高等学校】

【1】問1 ① (ウ) ② (ア) 問2 (ウ) 問3 to rest with his eyes closed without 問4 人ひとりは弱いものだが，2人が一緒になれば何かを実行し始めることができる。そして，3～4人がその力を合わせれば，本当に何かを成し遂げることができるということ。

問5 (ア) 問6 ア ホームレス イ ひきこもり ウ 個人主義 エ 家族の絆 問7 2030年は引きこもりの第一世代が65歳にさしかかる年であり，彼らの親が亡くなることで，彼らは経済的基盤を失った状態で取り残されてしまうということ。 問8 D

〈解説〉問1 ① more or less「多かれ少なかれ」 ② 空欄②を含む直前の段落で，学校でまったくいじめを受けていない人の例があげられており，今度はその逆のひどいいじめの例があげられるので，on the other hand が適切である。 問2 現在分詞か過去分詞かを選択する問題である。equip は原形だと「備え付けさせる」の意味がある。surprised などの用法と同様，過去分詞にするのが適当である。
問3　was able to の組み合わせであるため to より始まり，それに続く動詞の原形は rest のみである。with と without の位置は文脈より判断する。　問4　下線部の後ろに続く文を訳せばよい。　問5　何も言わなかった状態から，とうとう沈黙を破ったという内容より導き出すことができる。　問6　下線部のある段落から次の段落まででキーワードを探すことができる。　問7　後述の That's the year 以下に述べられている。　問8　Dを含む段落では，職場に個人的な問題を持ち込まないという暗黙の了解について述べられている。

【2】問1　ディベート，プレゼンテーション，ディスカッション
問2　(イ)　　問3　are yet to be implemented　　問4　(ア)
問5　英作文のための別個の科目を廃止し，この科目を「話すこと」「聞くこと」「読むこと」の技能と統合しようとする文部科学省の動き
問6　(イ)　　問7　productive　　問8　D　　問9　⑥　(ウ)　　⑦　(エ)
問10　生徒に最初にパラグラフを書かせ，次にクラスメートにそれをプレゼンテーションさせるために暗唱させること
〈解説〉問1　英語のアカデミックな能力として直前の文で述べられている。　問2「日本語における学問的技術を向上させることは，英語においてこれらを学ぶことの負担を(　　)にする」ease で「容易にする」。問3　be 動詞があるため，implemented が過去形でなく過去分詞の受動態であることが分かる。そのためこの文の動詞として始めに are があり，yet to の組み合わせに原形の be が続く。　問4　空欄②を含む文の前半で，「この種の技術の転移の実証的な証拠は目下のところない」と述べられていることから，「現時点で生徒の学問的能力における重要な変化を期待するのはあまりに(　　)であろう」の(　　)には optimistic が適切である。それを受けて「教師たちは(　　)であるべき」なので，③には cautious が入る。　問5　直前の1文に，MEXT's move に続く内容で述べられている。　問6　直後の文で述べられている

integrated skills instruction と academic proficiency が double を表している。　問7　空欄直後の writing and speaking という記述から，産出のスキルであることが分かる。　問8　Dの直前では，input と output という両方のスキルを統合することについて述べられているが，Dの後ろからは，話し言葉と書き言葉の境界があいまいになるなど否定的な面について述べられているため，この位置に逆説の接続詞が含まれると考えられる。　問9　⑥　空欄以降で具体例があげられている。
⑦　前述の内容を受けて最後に結論的に著者が意見を述べているので，therefore「それゆえに」が適切である。　問10　直前に述べられているタスクが答えに当たる。

【3】(1)　be taken → take　(2)　make → let　(3)　will have arrived → arrive　(4)　enough foolish → foolish enough　(5)　play → playing　(6)　more expensive → higher　(7)　for me to open → my opening

〈解説〉(1)　take placeはそのもので「行われる」の意味があるため注意が必要である。　(2)　make だと，より強制的な印象になるため，やりたいことをさせてあげる let が適切である。　(3)　条件や時間を表す節の中にあるため，未来のことでも現在形となる。　(4)「十分に～」という意味の enough は常に形容詞の後ろに続く。　(5)　when it comes to の to は前置詞である。　(6)　expensive は「値が張る，高価である」という意味で用いられる。　(7)　mind は to 不定詞ではなく動名詞をとる。

【4】I disagree with the opinion. Of course, it is essential for us to have knowledge of English grammar. But mastering English grammar is not the objective of learning English. The objective is to develop students' communication abilities such as accurately understanding and appropriately conveying information and ideas. In order to achieve this, grammar instruction should be given through effective linkage with language activities without centering instruction on the distinction of terms and usage. It is also important that students should be exposed to as much English as possible in accordance with the students' level of comprehension. Therefore I believe the grammar-translation method, in which the classes are conducted mostly in Japanese, is not an effective way to develop students' communication abilities.

語数［121］

〈解説〉高等学校学習指導要領の，第8節　外国語，第3款　英語に関する各科目に共通する内容等の，3のイで，「文法については，コミュニケーションを支えるものであることを踏まえ，言語活動と効果的に関連付けて指導すること」と示されている。つまり，文法は目的ではなく，手段として指導されなければならない。意味を理解する，伝えたいメッセージを発信するというコミュニカティブな場面において，的確な意味を理解し発信するために必要であるということに留意し，言語活動，あるいはコミュニケーション活動を用いることで文脈のある文法指導を行いたい。

2013年度　実施問題

【中高共通】

【１】放送を聞いて，[Part 1]～[Part 3]の各問に答えよ。

[Part 1]

No.1

(A) Hanging the pictures on the wall.

(B) Taking some photographs of the wall.

(C) Sitting closer to the wall.

(D) Getting the wall painted.

No.2

(A) Making some bread.

(B) Buying some bread.

(C) Eating more bread.

(D) Selling more bread.

No.3

(A) The stereo is cheap.

(B) He's going to try the system.

(C) The stereo's too expensive.

(D) He decided to buy the system.

No.4

(A) He doesn't like to talk about work.

(B) He works very hard at school.

(C) He goes to the same school as the woman.

(D) He agrees with the woman.

No.5

(A) The post office was close by.

(B) He was scared of what was in the package.

(C) He was able to send the package.

(D) The post office was closed when he got there.

No.6

(A) Walk to the mall.

(B) Take a taxi to the mall.

(C) Go to the mall to get on the bus.

(D) Cross the street to wait for the bus.

No.7

(A) The woman cannot get a soda.

(B) He will go downstairs to get the woman a soda.

(C) He does not know where to get a soda.

(D) The woman should go downstairs to get a soda.

No.8

(A) She does not have a car.

(B) She needs a ride.

(C) She is late to class.

(D) She has to go shopping.

No.9

(A) She needs child care that is closer to the university.

(B) She needs someone to take care of her children all the time.

(C) She needs the man to help her more with the children.

(D) She needs to spend more time with the children.

[Part 2]

No.1

(A) To use a neutral option like the English “Ms.”

(B) To use “madame” and “mademoiselle”.

(C) To reduce using “madame” gradually.

(D) To reduce using “mademoiselle” gradually.

No.2

(A) They tend to think beauty is only one aspect of a person's life.

(B) There are more of good-looking people in the world.

(C) They have a better self-image than others.

(D) People resent those who are better-looking than they are.

No. 3

(A) It was 10.6 %.

(B) It was 34.5 %.

(C) It was 47.3 %.

(D) It was 60.3 %.

No. 4

(A) Up to four times every year.

(B) Once every four years.

(C) Four times more often than other snakes.

(D) Once every four months.

[Part 3]

Questions:

No.1 When celebrating New Year's Day, why did the ancient Babylonians force their king to give up his crown and get down on his knees?

No.2 Give two examples of popular New Year's resolutions which Americans make today.

No.3 As a New Year's resolution, what does it mean to stop and smell the flowers?

No.4 As a New Year's resolution, what does it mean not to sweat the small stuff?

No.5 What does the speaker believe New Year's resolutions reflect?

(☆☆☆◎◎◎)

【中学校】

【1】次の英文を読んで，あとの[問1]～[問7]に答えよ。

Suddenly everybody has started talking about trees and plants as a source of strong poison. ①It would be a good idea to turn the spotlight on wild vegetation, which normally gets little consideration, because plants play a vital role in our lives and one 【 to / nothing / that / with / do / has 】 homicide cases. A lot of problems will ensue if plants become cast as ②villains and so I would here like to come forward in their defense.

③Plants have saved an incalculable number of lives, and 【 it / them / for / not / were 】 the human life span could not have been extended as much as it has.

In Japanese there is a compound word, *yakudoku*, which joins the character for medicine with (A) for poison. Clearly there are many preparations, which can be either harmful or beneficial, (B) the way they are used. In our everyday lives there are many drugs which could not have been developed (C) making use of plants. A contraceptive pill was developed from a species of yam found in Mexico. This raw material, which grew widely on the slopes of the Himalayas in northern India, has largely disappeared as a result of overharvesting. ④In that case it 【 murdered / the / that / was / was / plant 】.

Elsewhere we find the drug quinine, which is especially effective against malaria, being 【 あ 】 from the bark of the cinchona tree; while the calmative drug aspirin was developed from elements taken from the white willow and other plants.

Up to about 30 years ago, infantile leukemia killed 4 out of 5 children who 【 い 】 from it. Now as many as 4 out of 5 are saved, thanks to a kind of short wild grass found on the island of Madagascar. Countless other drugs used throughout the world are synthetically produced, in the same way, from elements originally found in (D).

The original inhabitants of the Amazon forest use 1,300 kinds of plants for medical purposes. The poison with which they tip their blowpipe darts is now used as a muscle-relaxant during surgical operations.

All the above information is given in more (E) in a World Wildlife Fund report. Specialists say that the vegetation growing in tropical rain forests and other such places constitutes the equivalent of a pharmaceutical factory. However, there is a danger that these forests will disappear before their real value can be accurately 【 う 】.

We should be 【 え 】 to have lost sight of the way plants save lives, let alone continually harp on their use as murder weapons. To focus on ⑤this, rather than expressing a proper sense of gratitude, is surely to be barking up the wrong tree.

[問1] 文中の(A)～(E)に入る最も適切なものを，それぞれ(ア)～(エ)から1つずつ選び，その記号を書け。

A (ア) it (イ) ones
(ウ) that (エ) this

B (ア) depending on (イ) in spite of
(ウ) notwithstanding (エ) to say nothing of

C (ア) for (イ) in
(ウ) with (エ) without

D (ア) drugs (イ) medicine
(ウ) plants (エ) poison

E (ア) advance (イ) detail
(ウ) sudden (エ) sufficient

[問2] 文中の【 あ 】～【 え 】に入る最も適切な語を次の(ア)～(オ)から1つずつ選び，その記号を書け。ただし，各語はそれぞれ1度しか用いないこととする。

(ア) ashamed (イ) assessed (ウ) depressed
(エ) extracted (オ) suffered

[問3] 下線部②villainsの定義として最も適切なものを，次の(ア)～(エ)から1つ選び，その記号を書け。

(ア) substances used in curing disease

(イ) substances causing death or harm if absorbed by a living thing

(ウ) evil characters in a story, play, etc.

(エ) people who are admired by many for their noble qualities

[問4] 次の英語は，本文中のある単語の定義である。その単語を本文中より抜き出せ。

people who live in a particular place

[問5] 下線部①，③，④の【　　】内の語句を正しく並べ替えよ。ただし，解答は【　　】内のみ書くこと。

[問6] 下線部<u>⑤this</u>が表す内容として最も適切なものを，次の(ア)～(オ)から1つ選び，その記号を書け。

(ア) 森林が消滅する危険性があること

(イ) 植物が人殺しの道具として使われていること

(ウ) 植物によって人の命が救われていること

(エ) 植物がどのように生活に役立っているかということに，我々が気づいていないこと

(オ) 我々が感謝の気持ちを表明しないこと

[問7] 本文の内容と合うものを，次の(ア)～(カ)から2つ選び，その記号を書け。

(ア) A species of yam in the Himalayas has almost died out because of too much nutrition.

(イ) A kind of wild plant has enabled us to save about 80% of the children who have infantile leukemia.

(ウ) Thanks to the white willow, human beings have been able to get over malaria.

(エ) The people in the Amazon forest used so many plants for medical purposes that some kinds of them have disappeared.

(オ) According to this essay, some poison can be used as a drug for medical treatment.

(カ) Some specialists say that a pharmaceutical factory should be constructed in tropical rain forests.

(☆☆☆☆◎◎◎)

【2】次の英文を読んで，あとの[問1]～[問5]に答えよ。

One model of second language acquisition that was influenced by <u>①Chomsky's</u> theory of first language acquisition was Stephen Krashen's (1982) Monitor Model. He first described this model in the early 1970s, at a time when there was growing dissatisfaction with language teaching methods based on behaviourism. Krashen described his model in terms of five hypotheses.

First, in the *acquisition－learning hypothesis*, Krashen contrasts these two terms. We 【　あ　】 as we are exposed to samples of the second language we understand in much the same way that children pick up their first language － with no conscious attention to language form. We 【　い　】 on the other hand through conscious attention to form and rule learning.

Next, according to the *monitor hypothesis*, the acquired system initiates a speaker's utterances and is responsible for spontaneous language (　a　). The learned system acts as an editor or 'monitor', making minor changes and polishing what the acquired system has produced. Such monitoring takes place only when the speaker/writer has plenty of time, is concerned about producing correct language, and has learned the relevant rules.

The *natural order hypothesis* was based on the finding that, as in first language acquisition, second language acquisition unfolds in predictable sequences. The language features that are easiest to state (and thus to learn) are not necessarily the first to be acquired. For example, the rule for adding an -*s* to third person singular verbs in the 【　う　】 tense is easy to state, but even some advanced second language speakers fail to apply it in spontaneous conversation.

The *input hypothesis* is that acquisition occurs when one is exposed to language that is comprehensible and that contains i ＋ 1. The 'i' represents the level of language already acquired, and the '+ 1' is a metaphor for language (words, grammatical forms, aspects of pronunciation) that is just a (b) beyond that level.

The fact that some people who are exposed to large quantities of comprehensible input do not necessarily acquire a language successfully is accounted for by Krashen's *affective filter hypothesis*. The 'affective filter' is a metaphorical barrier that prevents learners from acquiring language even when appropriate (c) is available. 'Affect' refers to feelings, motives, needs attitudes, and emotional states. A learner who is tense, anxious, or bored may 'filter out' input, making it unavailable for acquisition.

Both psychologists and linguists challenged Krashen's model. Linguist Lydia White (1987) questioned one of his hypotheses in a paper called 'Against Comprehensible Input'. Psychologist Barry McLaughlin's 1978 article was one of the first to raise the question of whether the five hypotheses could be tested by empirical (d). For example, distinguishing between 'acquired' and 'learned' knowledge can lead to circular definitions (if it's acquired it's fluent; if it's fluent, it's acquired) and to a reliance on intuition rather than observable differences in behaviour.

In spite of lively (e) and debate, Krashen's ideas were very influential during a period when second language teaching was in transition from approaches that emphasized learning rules or memorizing dialogues to approaches that emphasized using language with a focus on meaning. Since then, COMMUNICATIVE LANGUAGE TEACHING, including IMMERSION and CONTENT-BASED INSTRUCTION, has been widely implemented, and Krashen's ideas have been a source of ideas for research in second language acquisition. ②Classroom research 【can / great / that / a / of / has / progress / confirmed / students / make / deal】 through exposure to comprehensible input without direct instruction. Studies have also shown, however, that students may reach a point from which they fail to make further progress on some features of the second language unless they also have access to guided (f). Some insights from learning theories developed in psychology help to explain why this may be so.

[問1] 文中の【 あ 】～【 う 】に入る適切な語を書け。

[問2] 文中の(a)～(f)に入る最も適切な語を，次の(ア)～(カ)から1つずつ選び，その記号を書け。ただし，各語はそれぞれ1度しか用いないこととする。

(ア) criticism (イ) instruction (ウ) input (エ) step
(オ) research (カ) use

[問3] 下線部②の【 】内の語句を正しく並べ替えよ。ただし，解答は【 】内のみ書くこと。

[問4] 下線部①の人物について述べたものを次の(ア)～(エ)から1つ選び，その記号を書け。

(ア) He is a researcher specializing in Child Second Language Acquisition, the theory of children learning a second language. He has one of the first books in this area. This study offers a fascinating account of how children learning a second language employ forms in the service of meaning

(イ) His research project investigated the measurement of explicit and implicit second language knowledge, the relationship of these two types of knowledge to second language proficiency, and the effects of providing instruction in explicit knowledge on the acquisition of implicit knowledge.

(ウ) He attempted to clarify a number of important issues in the area of second language learning. These include the ease and rapidity with which children learn a second language, the optimal age at which to begin second language instruction.

(エ) He considered language to be a species-specific property which is a part of the human mind. He studied the Internal-language, a mental faculty for language. His hypothesis about language acquisition influenced Stephen Krashen.

[問5] 本文の内容と合うものを，次の(ア)～(エ)から1つ選び，その記号を書け。

(ア) The ‘affective filter’sometimes enhances students’ motivation to acquire the second language, because the filter reduces learners’ tensions, anxieties, and boredom.

(イ) Krashen stated that some language forms that are considered to be the easiest to learn are not always acquired first as evidenced by the fact that some advanced second language speakers fail to apply simple rules in conversation.

(ウ) Linguist Lydia White was one of the first persons to have a question about a clear difference between ‘acquisition’ and ‘learning’ in the acquisition-learning hypothesis.

(エ) In the early 1970s, there was growing satisfaction with language teaching based on ‘communicative language teaching’, including ‘immersion’ and ‘content based language teaching’.

(☆☆☆◎◎◎◎◎)

【3】次の【問題】と【調査結果】は，平成23年11月に中学3年生3,000人を対象に国立教育政策研究所が実施した【特定の課題に関する調査(英語:「書くこと」)】の一部である。あとの[問1]，[問2]に答えよ。

【問題】

中学生のコウジ(Koji)と日本に来たばかりのカナダ人の留学生マイク(Mike)のそれぞれ＜　　＞に示された場面での会話です。

【内容A】 (　　)内の指示に従って＿＿＿＿の引かれた文を書きかえ，会話が成り立つようにしなさい。	【内容B】 ＿＿＿＿に必要な英語を書き，会話が成り立つようにしなさい。その際，(　　)内の語を適切な形で用いること。
<休憩時間に教室で> Koji: You speak Japanese very well. You studied it in Canada. (疑問文にしなさい。) Mike: Yes. I studied it every day.	<休憩時間に教室で> Koji: You speak Japanese very well. ＿＿＿＿＿＿ it in Canada? (study) Mike: Yes. I studied it every day.

【調査結果】

【解答類型ごとの反応率】

類型	解答類型（○：正答）	【内容A】反応率(%)	【内容B】反応率(%)
○1	Did you studyと解答しているもの（つづりの誤りや大文字・小文字の書き分けに不正確なところが見られるものを含む）	48.9	22.6
2	一般動詞の過去時制の疑問文としているが、誤っているもの、または一般動詞の現在時制の疑問文としているもの	26.4	14.4
3	疑問文になっていないもの	2.5	46.5
4	その他	15.6	8.1
5	無回答	6.6	8.4

[問1]【調査結果】から，内容Aと内容Bの反応率を比較し，あなたはどのようなことが生徒の課題と考えるか。40語以上の英語で書け。

[問2]　[問1]の課題を克服するために，あなたは中学校の英語教師として，どのようなことに留意して指導するか。具体的な指導例も含めて130語以上の英語で書け。

(☆☆☆◎◎◎)

【高等学校】

【1】次のAの英文は，インターネットの環境問題のサイトに寄せられた意見である。これが投稿された日の数日後，ある読者からBの英文が投稿された。これらを読み，[問1]～[問5]に答えよ。

A

Now many civic-minded Americans ask themselves not how to avoid buying stuff, but rather (①) to buy: that shiny new hybrid in the driveway, ⓐthe energy-efficient appliances in the kitchen, the right light bulb.

Does this pay off for the planet, or does the quest for efficiency distract from more effective approaches to cutting carbon output? What can consumers do that would be more effective?

B

To ask whether it is useful for consumers to focus on energy efficiency is like asking whether it is useful for consumers to focus on price. In practice, a cost-effective improvement in energy efficiency operates like a decrease in price. When you can drive (②) miles for every gallon of gas and run your household with (③) utility bills, the price of these energy services is lower. In many cases, energy efficiency saves you money — even if you don't care about the environment.

But what if you do care about the environment and want to reduce your carbon output by using less energy? Then you should also be aware of your potential behavioral response. Basic economics tells us that lower prices increase demand , meaning that people tend to drive more when it costs less to go each mile. People are also more likely to purchase and use things like air-conditioners when they cost less to operate. These so-called ⓑrebound effects eat into the initial energy savings of efficiency—because when things become more efficient, we tend to use them more.

While studies have shown that rebound effects are real and potentially important, they are not an argument for dismissing the importance of energy efficiency. Most of the evidence suggests that rebound effects offset only a fraction the environmental benefits. We should also not forget that beyond the benefit of saving money, people benefit from choices like driving more and keeping their homes at more comfortable temperatures.

Today, a lot of people purchase energy-efficient products. However, the most important question when it comes to energy efficiency is why consumers do not focus on energy efficiency more. This is the ©energy paradox. While there are many explanations for why it exists, a simple one is that most of us are unaware of efficiency when shopping for goods that we buy. One way to address this problem is improved product labeling that reports efficiency in terms that people care about — even money saved and pollution avoided. Recent changes to the * E.P.A.'s energy-efficiency labels for new vehicles and appliances are a step in the right direction and should help ⓓconsumers make more informed decisions.

* E.P.A.: United States Environmental Protection Agency

[問1]　本文中の(　①　)に入る最も適切な語を答えよ。

[問2]　下線部 ⓐについて，あなたの日常生活の中で見られる例を1つ日本語で答えよ。

[問3]　本文中の(　②　)，(　③　)に入る最も適切な語の組み合わせを，次の(ア)～(エ)から1つ選び，その記号を書け。

(ア)　②　more　③　higher　　(イ)　②　more　③　lower

(ウ)　②　fewer　③　higher　　(エ)　②　fewer　③　lower

[問4]　下線部 ⓑ～ⓓについて，それぞれわかりやすく日本語で説明せよ。

[問5]　英文Bの内容と一致するものを，次の(ア)～(エ)から1つ選び，その記号を書け。

(ア)　According to basic economics, lower prices increase our purchasing power and our awareness of environmental issues.

(イ)　If you are really concerned about the environment and want to reduce your carbon output, you should avoid buying energy-efficient products.

(ウ) Rebound effects do not deprive us of all the environmental benefits of energy-efficient products.

(エ) E.P.A. has just changed the way of producing new vehicles and appliances.

(☆☆☆◎◎◎)

【2】次の英文を読み，[問1]～[問11]に答えよ。

Globalization has already transformed how we live, work, and entertain, affected our views of relationships, and made salient the people who live thousands of miles away and were "(①)". As a social institution, education has been mostly a local entity, funded with local or national taxes, serving the purpose of the local community or the nation, preparing workers for the local economy, and passing on local values. [A] The idea of a local community has already become something of the past. We all live in a globally (②) community today. We can be certain that our children will live in an even more globalized world. [B] Their lives will be even more affected by others who live in distant lands and belong to different local communities. [C] Education, the traditionally local social institution, thus faces a number of significant challenges. [D] Here, I will discuss two significant challenges from among them.

One is what we can do to help our children secure jobs that will provide for them and their families. The death of distance has enabled businesses to consider their workforce globally. That is, employers can theoretically find the needed talents from anywhere on the globe when the job market is global. Not only can they move their businesses where the talents are found, but also they can directly move the talents to wherever they need them. In a strictly economic sense, businesses use two criteria to decide whom to employ, ⓐcost and quality, all other things being equal. To maximize profit, all businesses would like to pay as little as possible for their workforce provided that the workforce has adequate knowledge and skills for the tasks. One consequence of this is the fact that cheap labor in developing countries is responsible for many of the job losses and factory closures in developed countries. Therefore, schools in the developed nations must reexamine their curriculum and pedagogy to equip their students with the higher quality to justify the higher cost to employers.

The other challenge is what we can do to help our children live, work, and interact with people from different cultures and countries. One consequence of globalization is increased intensity and frequency of cross-cultural communications. As businesses become global and multinational, ⓑso do their workforces. Today, communications within a company often occur across many countries and cultures on a daily basis. External communications with customers, suppliers, government agencies, and other regulatory entities are similarly international. Even small business owners need talents that can help them navigate the cultural and linguistic differences when they enter the global economy. Therefore, the ability to interact effectively with people who speak different languages, believe in different religions, and hold different values has become essential for all workers. (③), what used to be required of a small group of individuals — diplomats, translators, cross-cultural communication consultants, or international tour guides — has become necessary for all professions. We call the set of skills and knowledge "global competence". ⓒAn essential ingredient of global competence is foreign language proficiency and a deep understanding of other cultures.

In the age of globalization, educational institutions will continue to be operated as local entities; (④), they will need to consider themselves as global enterprises because ⓓtheir products will need to function well in the globalized world in terms of competition for opportunities and collaboration with individuals from different cultures. Thus, schools need to adopt a global perspective in deciding what they should offer their students. This does not mean that schools should abandon their traditions. For example, schools should not seek global homogenization of curriculum, abandonment of local identities and traditions, disregard of local needs, and disrespect for student differences. Such actions are precisely the opposite of what is needed in the age of globalization. Globalization demands schools be different and unique so they can prepare students who will be able to discover their own ⓔniche. The term *glocalization*, which combines *globalization* and *localization*, suggests an excellent framework for the kind of education we need in the 21st century: ⓕlocal but with a global perspective.

[問1]　本文中の(　①　)に入る最も適切な英語を，次の(ア)～(エ)から1つ選び，その記号を書け。

(ア)　travel broadens the mind

(イ)　distance lends enchantment to the view

(ウ)　seeing is believing

(エ)　out of sight and out of mind

[問2]　本文中の(　②　)に入る語として，文脈から考えてふさわしくない語を次の(ア)～(エ)から1つ選び，その記号を書け。

(ア)　interdependent

(イ)　interconnected

(ウ)　interchangeable

(エ)　interactive

[問3]　次の英文は，本文中の[　A　]～[　D　]のいずれかに入る。文脈から考えて最も適切なものを選び，その記号を書け。

Schools must rise to them and prepare our children to live in the global society.

[問4]　下線部ⓐについて，その内容をわかりやすく説明せよ。

[問5]　第2段落で筆者が最も言いたかったことは，どのようなことか。最も適切なものを，次の(ア)～(エ)から1つ選び，その記号を書け。

(ア)　global communications in the job market

(イ)　global competitiveness in the job market

(ウ)　the death of distance in the age of globalization

(エ) the higher cost to employers in the age of globalization

[問6] 下線部ⓑについて，本文中に書かれている3つの具体例を日本語で説明せよ。

[問7] 本文中の(③)，(④)に入る最も適切な語または語句を，次の(ア)～(エ)からそれぞれ1つずつ選び，その記号を書け。ただし，下記の語または語句は文頭に来るものも小文字で記している。

(ア) however (イ) moreover (ウ) of course (エ) that is

[問8] 下線部ⓒを日本語で表せ。

[問9] 下線部ⓓは具体的に何を表しているか。日本語で答えよ。

[問10] 下線部ⓔが表す意味として最も適切なものを，次の(ア)～(ウ)から1つ選び，その記号を書け。

(ア) a job which is very suitable for someone

(イ) a tradition which is very important for someone

(ウ) a culture which is very unique to someone

[問11] 下線部ⓕの内容と矛盾するものを，次の(ア)～(オ)からすべて選び，その記号を書け。

(ア) Schools should adopt a global perspective in deciding what they should offer their students.

(イ) Schools should not seek global homogenization of curriculum.

(ウ) Schools should abandon the local identities and traditions.

(エ) Schools should not disregard local needs and disrespect student differences

(オ) Schools should not be different and unique.

(☆☆☆◎◎◎)

【3】次の(1)～(7)は，「英語表現Ⅰ」の授業において，与えられた日本文に対して生徒が黒板に書いた英文である。生徒の英文をできるだけ生かすという観点で，どのように直せばよいか。例にならって答えよ。

(例) 私はラジオは聴きません。実はラジオを持っていないんですよ。

I don’t listen on the radio. Actually I don’t have the radio.
a

(1)　一日の仕事が終わって，疲れて他に何もすることができなかったよ。

After a day’s work,I was too tired to do something else.

(2) 東京駅までの道はすごく混んでいて，私たちは列車に乗り遅れないかと心配しました。

The road to Tokyo Terminal was very busy and we were afraid to miss the train.

(3)　健二が試験に通ったら，みんなすごく驚くよ。

Every one will be greatly surprised if Kenji will pass the test.

(4)　次郎は喫煙にメリットがあるとは思っていないし，美樹もそうだ。

Jiro does not believe that smoking has any advantages, and so does Miki.

(5)　あのチームに多くの期待をすれば，ひどく失望することになるよ。

If you expect too much from that team, you’ll be sorely disappoint.

(6)　実咲はそんな必要がないのに2週間前からダイエット中なんだよ。

Misaki, though she doesn’t really need to, has been on a diet since two weeks.

(7)　私たちのオフィスではほとんどの人が車で通勤しているが，私は自転車に乗る方が好きだ。

Almost of the people at our office drive to work, but I prefer to ride my bicycle.

(☆☆☆◎◎◎)

【4】次の文は，平成21年3月に告示された高等学校学習指導要領「外国語」の中に示されている「コミュニケーション英語Ⅱ」についての「内容」の一部である。

聞いたり読んだりしたこと，学んだことや経験したことに基づき，情報や考えなどについて，まとまりのある文章を書く。

この趣旨を踏まえて，次の英文に続くパラグラフを作成し，まとまりのある英文を完成する授業を計画している。生徒に120語程度の英文で第2パラグラフを書くよう指導するとして，その模範例を作成せよ。また，語数を記入すること。

March 11th 2011 is a day we will not forget. On this day, the Great Eastern Japan Earthquake struck our country. A great many people in the Tohoku region suffered a lot of damage from this earthquake, the giant tidal wave which accompanied it and the ensuing nuclear accident. As time passed, the death toll rose higher and higher. Not only the people in Tohoku but the whole country was hit with confusion and anxiety. We all felt completely shocked by this unanticipated natural disaster.

(☆☆☆◎◎◎)

解答・解説

【中高共通】

【1】[Part 1]　No.1　(A)　No.2　(B)　No.3　(C)　No.4　(D)　No.5　(C)　No.6　(D)　No.7　(D)　No.8　(B)　No.9　(A)

[Part 2]　No.1　(D)　No.2　(C)　No.3　(B)　No.4　(A)

[Part 3]　No.1　To make him admit all the mistakes he had made during the past year.　No.2　To lose weight./ To stop smoking./ To be more productive at work. (以上から2つ書いていれば正答)　No.3　(It means) to take time to enjoy simple pleasures (instead of always being too busy and in a hurry).　No.4　(It means) not to worry or get angry about unimportant problems.　No.5　(He believes they reflect) the culture of the person.

〈解説〉スクリプトなし。リスニングでは，文字を媒体としたリーディングと違い，音声は流れるとともに消えていってしまうので，より効率の良い解答が求められる。そのため，受験する都道府県の出題内容や問題形式の傾向(例えば，放送は2度聞くことができるのか，質問文は問題用紙に記載されているのか，メモはとれるのか，など)をあらかじめ把握しておくことがとても重要である。また，近年は様々な訛りの英語が話される傾向もあるようなので，発音を選り好みせず，色々な英語に耳を慣らしておくとよい。実際のリスニング試験での一般的な心構えとして，①放送を聞く前に質問文や選択肢に目を通して聞かれる内容を把握しておく，②全ての単語を無理に聞きとろうとせず，どのような趣旨の英文なのか聞きとることをまずは優先する，③1度目と2度目の放送でそれぞれ何を聞きとればいいのか，目的を明確にして聞く，④必要に応じてメモをとることが必要である。どうしてもわからない場合は深く考えず勘で解答して，次の問題に答える準備をするという思い切りのよさも必要であろう。

【中学校】

【1】[問1] A (ウ) B (ア) C (エ) D (ウ) E (イ)
[問2] あ (エ) い (オ) う (イ) え (ア) [問3] (ウ)
[問4] inhabitants [問5] ① that has nothing to do with ③ were it not for them ④ was the plant that was murdered [問6] (イ)
[問7] (イ), (オ) (順不同)

〈解説〉[問1] A thatはthe characterの言い換え。薬毒(yakudoku)とは，薬(medicine)という字(character)と，毒(poison)という字を合わせたものだということ。 B depending on ～「～次第で」 薬は使い方次第で有益にも害にもなるということ。 C without ～ ing「～することなしに」 多くの薬は植物の利用なしに開発できなかったということ。 D 同段落最初の2文で，ある植物の発見により多くの子どもの命が救われたことを述べている。同様に，世界の薬の多くが植物からとれる成分をもとに作られているということを述べた文。 E in more detail「より詳しく」 [問2] あ being以下はマラリア特効薬のキニーネ(quinine)についての説明。キニーネはキナ皮(cinchona bark)から抽出(extract)される。 い children who suffered from itで「それで苦しんだ子どもたち」の意味。itはinfantile leukemia「小児白血病」を指す。 う assess「評価する」 植物の薬としての価値が評価される前に，森林がなくなってしまう危険性があるということ。　え　be ashamed to V「Vすることを恥に思う」　植物が命を救うその手立てを失ってしまったことについて我々は恥に思うべきだということ。　[問3] villain(s)とは「(劇や小説などに登場する)悪役や悪漢」のこと。もし植物を悪者として扱うと，多くの問題が起こってしまうので，弁護したいと思う，と述べた文。　[問4]　定義の訳は「ある特定の場所に住む人々」である。答えのinhabitantsは第6段落1文目にある。

[問5]　①　have nothing to do with ～「～とは関係のない」　関係代名詞のthatはその前のone(＝role)にかかる。　③　仮定法過去のifを省略したことで語順が変化したもの。もとはIf it were not for ～ で「もし～がなかったら」の意味。もし植物がなかったら人の寿命はこれほどに長くなかっただろうということ。　④　the plant was murderedをit is/was ～ that … の強調構文によりthe plantを強調した文。植物は人にとって害にもなるが，人の過剰収穫(over)によって絶滅してしまったヒマラヤのヤムイモ(yam)は，むしろ人によって殺されてしまったほうだ，ということ。　[問6]　thisは前文のcontinually harp on their use as murder weapons「人殺しの道具としての植物の使い道を引き続き唱えている」を指す。(様々な薬効をもたらす)植物に対し感謝の意を表すのでなく，このこと(＝植物が人殺しの道具だということ)に注目するのは，まさに見当違い(bark up the wrong tree)である，と述べた文。

[問7]　(イ)は第5段落にある内容(80％は4 out of 5の言い換え)。(オ)は第6段落にある内容(吹き矢の毒が医療に使われている)。(ア)はbecause of以下の理由が×。(ウ)のwhite willowは鎮静剤のアスピリンの原料。(エ)はthat以下の内容が本文にはない内容。(カ)は本文と全く関係がない。

【2】[問1]　あ　acquire　い　learn　う　present　[問2]　a　(カ)　b　(エ)　c　(ウ)　d　(オ)　e　(ア)　f　(イ)

[問3]　has confirmed that students can make a great deal of progress

[問4]　(エ)　[問5]　(イ)

〈解説〉[問1]　あ「習得」について説明した文。すなわち「言語形式を意識することなく，子どもが母語を覚える(pick up)のと同じように，理解した第二言語の表現(samples)にさらされて，我々は習得する。い　「学習」について説明した文。習得とは違い形式や規則を意識的に学ぶことを指す。　う　present tense「現在形」　3人称単数現在形の-sは説明は易しいが，習得するのは難しいという話。
[問2]　a　spontaneous language use「自発的な言語使用」　acquired system「獲得されたシステム」とはつまり文法知識のこと。この知識がモニター役として，発話産出と発話内容の監視の両方において機能するというのがモニター仮説である。　b　just a step beyond that level「そのレベルをほんの少し超えた」　「そのレベル」とは学習者の現在の言語熟達度(＝i)のことで，それより少し難しいインプットを与えるのが最も有効というのがこの仮説である。　c　when appropriate input is available「適切なインプットが与えられても」　情意フィルター仮説では，学習者が過度に緊張していたりすると，学習が阻害されるというもの。　d　empirical research「実証研究」　授業や実験を実際に行って，データ分析などをもとに仮説検証を行うような研究のこと。　e　In spite of lively criticism and debate「活発な批判や議論にもかかわらず」　批判はあるが，クラッシェンの仮説は今でも影響力が強い。　f　unless they also have access to guided instruction「教師主導の指導がなければ」　前文の理解可能なインプットを与えさえすればよいという意見に対し，この文は教師の適切な介入がなければ学習者の進歩は止まってしまうということを述べている。　[問3]　confirm that S V「SVであることを確証する」　make progress「成長する」　a great deal of ～「たくさんの～」　訳「教室で行った研究によって，生徒が直接指導なく理解可能なインプットにさらされると，大変な進歩を見せるということがわかった」　[問4]　Chomskyや彼の理論についての説明は本文にはない。彼は「普遍文法(Universal Grammar)」や「言語獲得装置(Language Acquisition Device)」という言葉を用いて，人間という種にのみ特有の(＝species-specific)言語能力を唱えた人である。

母語の習得過程を第二言語にもあてはめたKrashenは，彼の理論に影響を受けたということが第1段落に書いてあるが，選択肢にも同じことが書かれている。　[問5]　正解の(イ)は自然順序仮説(natural order hypothesis)を説明した文。第4段落の内容と一致。(ア)は情意フィルター仮説(affective filter hypothesis)についての説明。情意フィルターは本文では学習を阻害する負の要因として語られているが，ここでは逆の内容のため×。(ウ)の説明は心理学者Barry McLaughlinについてのもの。(エ)について，第1段落によると，1970年代初期はコミュニカティブな教授法ではなく，行動主義に基づいた教授法が主流だったとある。

【3】[問1]　48.9% of the examinees can write an acceptable English sentence following the grammatical instruction, whereas only 22.6% of the examinees can write an interrogative sentence in a particular situation and context. The problem appears to be that more students can only respond in grammatical terms rather than function used in context. (53語)

[問2]

I think that English teachers generally pay too much attention to the grammatical technical terms in their class, so that students can only respond in grammatical terms rather than function used in context.

To solve this problem, I recommend students ask questions more often in various contexts. For example, I always give Q and A activities after listening to a dialogue, a story or students speeches.

If students have more opportunities to ask questions in English, they come to reinforce some basic question forms in context. After the interaction, students write down the question forms in English. This way they learn to write interrogative English forms in appropriate context.

In conclusion, the research shows the importance of productive skills, not only writing skills but also speaking. The integration of both skills is needed in English lessons.　(136語)

〈解説〉[問1]　データを自分なりに解釈し作文しなければいけないため，

やや難易度が高い。調査結果の表で，内容Aと内容Bで極端に反応率が違うところを見つけて，原因を論じればよい。解答例は，類型1で内容Aの反応率が高いことについて言及している。他に目立つ違いとして，類型3で内容Bの反応率が高いことが挙げられる。これはおそらくYou studied itという解答が多かったためだろうが，そのなかに疑問文の作り方を理解していない生徒がいる可能性もある。指導課題として気をつける必要がある。　[問2]　ここでは1つか2つの指導例にしぼって，できるだけ具体的に説明することを心がける。問1の解答例では，生徒が言語形式(＝文法)にばかり気を取られ，様々なコンテクストにおける言語機能に無頓着であることを指摘した。上記の指導例においては，生徒同士での質問のやりとり，及びやりとり後の書く活動という2つのコンテクストを設けて，疑問文の機能を学習させようとしている。このように話す・書く活動(＝産出活動)を通して，学習者は自分の知識の穴に気づくことができるのである。

【高等学校】

【1】[問1]　what　[問2]　エネルギー効率の良い冷蔵庫　[問3]　(イ)　[問4]　ⓑ　エネルギー効率のよい商品を買うことが金銭的な節約につながり，結果的により多くの物を買ったり，エネルギーを消費したりすることになってしまうこと。　ⓒ　エネルギー効率が良い商品を買う人はたくさんいるが，彼らはそれほどそのことに焦点を置いて購入を決めているわけではないということ。　ⓓ　消費者が，お金を節約することや汚染をなくすことといったより多くの情報を踏まえて，商品購入を決定すること。　[問5]　(ウ)

〈解説〉[問1]　英語は並列した文構造を好む。not A but B構文のAにhow to Vという形があるので，Bにも同じ形(疑問詞＋to＋V)が入ると推測できる。コロン(：)の後に商品が並んでいることから，whatがあうと判断できる。　[問2]　ⓐは「キッチンにおけるエネルギー効率のよい(電気)器具」の意味なので，それに合うもの(省エネの電子レンジなど)を答えればよい。　[問3]　前文にあるように「コスト効率の向上＝価格の低下」である。問題の文で言えば，「1ガロンあたりより多くのマイルを運転できたり，より低い公共料金(utility bills)で家計をやりくりできたりする」ほうがコスト効率はよいと言える。

[問4]　ⓑ　rebound effectsがどんな効果を意味するのかは，下線部以前のlower prices increase demandや，下線部の後のwhen things become more efficient, we tend to use them moreからわかる。このあたりをうまくまとめて答えればよい。　ⓒ　paradoxとは一見矛盾した論理のこと。段落のはじめの2文の内容をつなげて説明すればよい。　ⓓ　下線部の訳は「客がより情報を得たうえでの決断をする」である。ここでいう「情報」とは，前文にあるようにmoney savedとpollution avoidedについての情報のことである。　[問5]　(ア)について，第2段落3文目の，Basic economics tells ～ の文で，「より低価格のものは需要を増す」と述べているが，「環境問題の自覚を増す」とは言っていないので×。(イ)について，rebound effectsを指して言っていると思われるが，消費行動に気をつけるべきというのが本文の主旨なので×。(ウ)は，第3段落2文目にrebound effects offset only a fraction the environmental benefits「環境的な利益をほんの少し相殺するのみである」とあり，「すべてを奪うわけではない」という(ウ)と一致する。(エ)はproducingではなくてlabelingである。

【2】[問1]　(エ)　　[問2]　(ウ)　　[問3]　D　　[問4]　従業員に支払う人件費と，従業員の仕事に対する知識や技術　　[問5]　(イ)

[問6]　企業内のコミュニケーションは，日常的に多くの国境や文化を越えて頻繁に行われている／取引先，納入業者，政府機関，そして他の監督機関との対外的なコミュニケーションも同様に多国間で行われている／中小企業の経営者でさえ国際経済に足を踏み入れると，文化や言語の違いに対処していく手助けとなる人材を必要とする。

[問7]　③　(エ)　　④　(ア)　　[問8]　グローバル人材として必要な能力に不可欠となる要素は，熟達した外国語運用力と深い異文化理解である。　[問9]　学生　　[問10]　(ア)　　問11　(ウ)，(オ)

〈解説〉[問1]　グローバル化によってどんな人が目立つか(salient)を説明した文。the people who以下の訳は「何千マイルも離れたところに住み，視界にも思考にもなかった(out of sight and out of mind)人々」となる。
[問2]　(ア)「相互依存の」，(イ)「関連し合う」，(エ)「相互に作用する」はいずれもグローバル化した共同体を言い表している。一方，(ウ)のみ「交換できる」という意味なので，文脈から考えて不適である。
[問3]　空欄Cの前まではグローバル化した社会の状況を述べており，Educationの文からそれをふまえた教育のあり方の話になっている。与えられた文は教育のあり方に関するものなのでDが適切。
[問4]　このcost and qualityは従業員を選ぶ2つの基準である。具体的な説明は次の文にあるので，その内容を使って簡潔に答えればよい。
[問5]　第2段落の主旨は，グローバル社会においては，労働力としての人間の価値もグローバルな視点でとらえられるということである。これに近いのは(イ)「労働市場におけるグローバルな競争」である。
[問6]　下線部の意味は「労働力もそう(＝グローバルで多国籍)である」。その具体例は続く3つの文に書いてある。それらを順に説明すればよい。　[問7]　③　空欄の前ではグローバルに仕事をするのに必要な能力(＝言語や価値観が違う人と意思疎通する能力)が述べられている。空欄の文では具体的な職業名(外交官，翻訳家など)を挙げて同じことを述べているので，つなぐ表現としてはthat is (すなわち)が適当である。
④　空欄の前では教育機関をlocal entities「ローカルな存在物」と言い，空欄の文ではglobal enterprises「グローバルな企業体」だと述べ，内容が逆になっている。よってhoweverが適当。　[問8]　文構造は難しくないので単語さえわかれば訳せる。essential「不可欠な」　ingredient「要素」　global competence「グローバルな能力(＝グローバルな人材に必要な能力)」　language proficiency「言語が熟達していること」
[問9]　their productsとは，教育機関をglobal enterprise「グローバル企業」とみなした場合の「商品」のこと(theirは教育機関のことを指す)。教育機関が産み出す商品(というのは言い方が良くないが)とは，生徒や学生のことである。　[問10]　nicheとは「(才能や力量に応じた)地位」

のこと。ここではグローバル社会における労働を題材にしているので，より具体的には「職」を指すと思われる。一致するのは(ア)である。

[問11]　(ア)は最後の段落の2文目Thus以下にある内容。(イ)と(エ)は同段落4文目For example, ～にある内容。一方，(ウ)は4文目の内容に反し，(オ)も6文目Globalization ～と一致しない。

【３】(1)　something→anything　(2)　to miss→of missing　(3)　will pass→passes　(4)　so→neither　(5)　disappoint→disappointed　(6)　since→for　(7)　Almost→Most

〈解説〉(1)　too ～ to …の構文「～すぎて…できない」には否定の意味が含まれている。not anyで「全くない」の意味。　(2)　be afraid to Vは「Vするのが怖くてできない」の意味。「～ではないかと心配する」はbe afraid of ～ing/that S Vで表す。　(3)　未来のことでもifを使った条件節ではwillは使わず現在形を使う(「～かどうか」を表す名詞節ではwillを使える)。文法書の「時制」を参照。　(4)　この「美樹もそうだ」は言い換えれば，「美樹も思っていない」のことで否定の意味を含んでいる。否定の意味ではsoではなくneitherを使う。　(5)　disappointは「～を失望させる」の意味の他動詞。人を主語にして「失望する(＝失望させられる)」という場合にはbe disappointedと受け身形にしなければならない。　(6)　現在完了の継続の文。sinceはsince the last weekのように起点を示すときに用いる。期間を表す場合にはforを使う。
(7)　almostは副詞なので，almost all the peopleのように後ろに形容詞が来ないといけない。Mostは代名詞の用法もあり，前置詞ofの前に直接置くことが可能。

【４】(解答例) After the earthquake, the depressing and distressing news related to it was repeatedly reported all over Japan, but there was also good news. Soon after the earthquake, seventeen countries from all over the world sent rescue teams to Japan. Many more countries, regions and international groups supported us by sending relief supplies and other contributions. We all felt grateful for the support from the international community. People all over the world took quick action beyond the barriers of race, culture and religion. This made us realize again what international contributions are. We will not forget that terrible day known as 3.11, and, more importantly, we must not forget our role in the international community.　(115語)

〈解説〉第1段落は大震災に起こった不幸について広く述べている。それに続く第2段落では，学習指導要領に従い，生徒が自分で体験したことや，新聞やインターネットなどから学んだ情報を中心に書かせたい。解答例では，大災害の最中見られた良いこととして，他国からの支援について書いている。語数が多いので，何について書くかしっかり計画してから書き始めよう。これは指導する際にも重要なことである。学習指導要領の解説では「まとまりのある文章」には「書く目的」が必要だとしている。生徒に指導する際にも，最終的にどういうメッセージをクラスメイトに伝えたいのか，はじめに考えさせるとよいだろう。

2012年度　実施問題

【中高共通】

【１】放送を聞いて，[Part 1]～[Part 3]の各問に答えよ。

[Part 1]

No.1

(A)　He can give his pen to her.

(B)　He can't lend his pen to her.

(C)　He wants more pens.

(D)　He doesn't need a pen.

No.2

(A)　She was out raising money for earthquake victims.

(B)　She was out helping earthquake victims rebuild.

(C)　She was out raising children victimized by the earthquake.

(D)　She was moving around some places hit by the earthquake.

No.3

(A)　She has no money.

(B)　She has to move.

(C)　She has another plan.

(D)　She went bowling last Sunday.

No.4

(A)　She doesn't mind getting wet.

(B)　She doesn't want to get wet.

(C)　She is already sick.

(D)　She lost her umbrella.

No.5

(A)　He understands why the woman didn't attend.

(B)　He couldn't understand the class at all.

(C) He thought the class was easy.

(D) He didn't understand the details of the class.

No.6

(A) She has a lot of things to do.

(B) She wants to see a weather forecast.

(C) She doesn't like the weather.

(D) She doesn't feel well.

No.7

(A) Studying management at college.

(B) Working in a restaurant.

(C) Opening her own restaurant.

(D) Taking classes at a cooking school.

No.8

(A) She needs to work out.

(B) She is inefficient.

(C) She is doing better.

(D) She has many problems.

No.9

(A) He is angry at the woman.

(B) He is surprised and upset.

(C) He thinks the plants died because of something he did.

(D) He knows why his experiment failed.

[Part 2]

No.1

(A) 2.9%

(B) 9%

(C) 11%

(D) 20%

No.2

(A) To conclude a treaty.

(B) To change the world's weather.

(C) To limit water pollution.

(D) There is no specific goal.

No.3

(A) It can prevent strokes from ever happening.

(B) It reduces the chances of another stroke.

(C) It reduces the heartbeat.

(D) It prevents first-time heart attacks.

No.4

(A) To raise the issue of rising fuel prices during almost every public appearance.

(B) To make a speech about fuel prices that are putting on some family budgets.

(C) To increase budgets that would be used for importing foreign fuels.

(D) To spend money developing renewable energy sources.

[Part 3]

Questions :

No.1 Why have working dogs earned a reputation?

No.2 According to some farmers, why are sheep dogs smart?

No.3 How does the Guide Dog Association in the UK get money to train dogs as guide dogs?

No.4 Why can detector dogs stop many people trying to bring illiegal goods into Australia?

No.5 What do you think is the most appropriate title of the passage?

(☆☆☆◎◎◎)

【中学校】

【1】次の英文を読み，[問1]～[問7]に答えよ。

For many people, mushrooms are strange, colorless, incomprehensible plants that should be avoided. Quaint tales and scary stories surround mushrooms because some are extremely poisonous. In reality, however, mushrooms are fungi that are simple plants without (A) roots, leaves, stems, flowers, or seeds. They grow in wetlands, grassy meadows, and woods. Certain types of mushrooms are delicious and are included as ingredients in many recipes and ①trendy snacks. For example, morels are considered one of the choicest foods, and truffles, related to morels, are highly (B) in Europe. Their shape is tubelike, and they remain entirely underground, a foot or more below the surface. In the old days, dogs and pigs were specially (C) to hunt them by scent.

Mushrooms stand out among other plants because they have no (②) and cannot generate their own nourishment. The part of the fungus that rises above the ground is the fruiting body, and the vegetative part that produces growth is (D) under the ground. It can be usually dug up in the form of dense, white tangled filaments, which, depending on the food supply and moisture, can live for hundreds of years. ③In fact, mushrooms, as well as the rest of the fungus genus species, are one of the few remaining simple plants that are believed to be among the oldest living organisms. When their environment is not conducive to growth, filaments stop proliferating and can lie dormant for dozens of years.

Although mushrooms are rich in flavor and texture, they have little food value. Picking mushrooms requires a thorough knowledge of environments where they are most likely to grow and an ability to ④tell between edible and poisonous plants.Most mushrooms thrive in temperatures from 68° to 86° F with plenty of moisture, and nearly complete darkness produces the best crop. The entire mushroom should be picked, the stem, the cap, and whatever part that is underground. Brightly colored mushroom caps usually indicate that the plant is not fit for consumption, and ⑤【the / attracts / more attention / the / mushroom】, the more poisonous it is. Mushrooms with beautiful red or orange spotted caps that grow under large trees after a good rain are particularly poisonous. If milky or white juices seep from a break in the body of plant, chances are it should not be picked. Old mushrooms with brown caps are also not very safe.

[問1]　文中の(　A　)～(　D　)に入る最も適切な語を，次の(ア)～(オ)からそれぞれ1つずつ選び，その記号を書け。

(ア)　prized　(イ)　trained　(ウ)　hidden　(エ)　converted
(オ)　developed

[問2]　下線部①を，ほぼ同じ意味を表す他の単語に置き換えるとき，最も適切な語を次の(ア)～(エ)から1つ選び，その記号を書け。

(ア)　soft　(イ)　experimental　(ウ)　fashionable　(エ)　tasty

[問3]　文中の(　②　)に入る最も適切な語を，次の(ア)～(エ)から1つ選び，その記号を書け。

(ア)　caps　(イ)　filaments　(ウ)　protein　(エ)　chlorophyll

[問4]　下線部③を日本語に直せ。

[問5]　下線部④を，ほぼ同じ意味を表す他の単語に置き換えるとき，最も適切な語を次の(ア)～(エ)から1つ選び，その記号を書け。

(ア)　narrate　(イ)　distinguish　(ウ)　say　(エ)　consider

[問6]　下線部⑤の【　　】内の語句を正しく並べ替えよ。ただし，解答は【　　】内のみ書くこと。

[問7]　次の(1)，(2)の質問の答えとして，最も適切なものを下の(ア)～(エ)からそれぞれ1つずつ選び，その記号を書け。

(1)　According to the passage, in what condition are mushrooms most likely to grow other than a moderate temperature?

(ア)　Plenty of moisture and nearly complete darkness.
(イ)　Rich soil with a lot of dead leaves.
(ウ)　A lot of rain and many pine trees.
(エ)　Plenty of sunshine and much dampness.

(2) According to the passage, what kind of mushrooms are not edible?

(ア) Mushrooms that attach to pine trees.

(イ) Mushrooms that remain entirely underground.

(ウ) Mushrooms that have plenty of water and good nutrition.

(エ) Mushrooms that have beautiful red or orange spotted caps.

(☆☆☆◎◎)

【2】次の英文を読み，[問1]～[問8]に答えよ。

Rachel Arenstein teaches English at Arazim in Maalot, Israel. Students in her school go to a networked 20-station computer laboratory once a week, and ①Arenstein decided to 【 have / portfolios / the time / create / use / the students / to 】 on the World Wide Web called Webfolios. In the laboratory, Arenstein worked with fifth- and sixth-grade students who had been studying English since the third grade. The students wrote and designed their Web pages in English themselves using Netscape Composer (a component of Netscape Communicator, 1999). Instructions on how to design the Web pages were given in Hebrew, but the software itself is in 【 A 】, so using it reinforced the students' language skills.

Topics and tasks for the portfolios corresponded to ②the specific elements of a portfolio recommended by the national English Inspectorate of Israel. For example,fifth graders are expected to copy correctly, so the students were asked to copy a jazz chant from their course book. Students are expected to be able to express their feelings in English, so they created a table of their likes, hates, and wants. For a piece of factual writing, students were asked to describe the weather.

[a] Some wrote directly on the screen, and others prepared their writing at home. Students also had free rein to choose the backgrounds and fonts for their sites from among those that the teacher had preselected and downloaded onto a graphics page.

Arenstein feels that the project has tapped students' multiple intelligences well. Students can use their artistic skills to design the pages, their writing skills to create the texts, and their interpersonal skills to plan the pages with their classmates. They are highly motivated, and they are learning English and computer skills simultaneously. A downside to the project is that it takes a good deal of time for the children to master the computer skills and carry out the tasks. Arenstein plans on continuing the Webfolio project, and she hopes that the children develop more creative sites after they complete some of the preliminary projects.

Markus Kneirum and Alexander Mokry teach English and social sciences at Georg-August-Zinn Comprehensive School in Kassel-Oberzwehren, Germany. They developed a Web publishing project for a seventh-grade English class based on the book K's First Case, a detective story about a case of murder.

According to Kneirum, most German students' writing experience is restricted to fill-in-the-gap exercises and 【　B　】 compositions. He and Mokry thus wanted to give their students the opportunity to develop their skill in writing for more natural and communicative purposes. At the same time, they did not want their students to become overwhelmed, so they began the project with exercises and tasks the students were familiar with, moved to guided but independent tasks, and ended by having the students working on their own with minimal teacher control.

[　　　　　b　　　　　] First, they wrote a short summary of the book, making use of a teacher-prepared worksheet with questions and useful expressions. The second writing activity was more open and collaborative, with students working in groups to develop their own ideas on a topic that built on the book's story. For example, some wrote newspaper articles and interviews about the characters, some wrote dialogues between characters, and others wrote TV news reports based on the book's events.

[　　　　　c　　　　　] They were told from the beginning that their writing would be published on the Web, and, according to Kneirum, this knowledge greatly increased their motivation to write well. The writing activities were complemented by other activities designed to foster additional skills. Students were given the option of recording audio or video versions of their written texts, and their work on developing these entailed a good deal of pronunciation practice. Students were also allowed to make their own Web sites and thus gained design and authoring experience. Finally, they wrote personal home pages that were included in the site.

The entire project was completed in a room with one computer for every three students. Although students sometimes had to wait their turn, this encouraged them to work collaboratively and help each other with their writing and Web design.

On the final day of the project, the children visited each other's Web sites and turned in their portfolios. Their grades for the project were based on the quality of their written product (correctness, creativity, and effort), their mark on a vocabulary test (based on vocabulary from the book and on other expressions the students had come across in reading and writing their essays), and an evaluation of their portfolio, which contained all versions of their texts.

According to Kneirum, the project was quite challenging for the students because it imposed new expectations on them. Instead of providing a teacher-centered classroom, the instructors demanded independence. Instead of handing out worksheets, the instructors expected creativity. And instead of working alone, as was usually the case, the students were expected to work in groups. But the fact that the students were working on their own projects to be published on their own home page, which would be subject to public scrutiny, brought out a great deal of motivation, commitment, and creativity, and the students completed the project with great success.

These projects are only a few of the many interesting examples. There is no single right way to use the Internet in English language teaching, just as there is no one way to use textbooks, tape players, or libraries. However, it is possible to learn from the successes of others, and there is a pattern of positive results being achieved from 【　C　】 computer work in the classroom.

[問1]　下線部①の【　　】内の語句を正しく並べ替えよ。ただし，解答は【　　】内のみ書くこと。

[問2]　下線部②の具体例を3点，日本語で書け。

[問3]　【　A　】に入る適切な語を書け。

[問4]　【　B　】に入る最も適切な語を，次の(ア)～(エ)から1つ選び，その記号を書け。

(ア)　guided
(イ)　free
(ウ)　creative
(エ)　open-ended

[問5]　【　C　】に入る最も適切な語を，次の(ア)～(エ)から1つ選び，その記号を書け。

(ア)　evidence-based
(イ)　form-based
(ウ)　grammar-based
(エ)　project-based

[問6]　文中の[　a　]～[　c　]に入る最も適切な文を，次の(ア)～(エ)からそれぞれ1つずつ選び，その記号を書け。

(ア)　Students had writing assignments for the project.
(イ)　Students met in groups to check the Web site their teachers had produced.
(ウ)　Students spent much time editing, revising, and rewriting their pieces.
(エ)　Students pursued a variety of strategies in creating the elements of their Webfolios.

[問7]　Arensteinの考えるThe Webfolio projectのデメリットはどのようなものか，40字程度の日本語で書け。

[問8]　Kneirumらのプロジェクトにおいて，Kneirumが生徒に期待したことは何か。簡潔に日本語で書け。

(☆☆☆☆◎◎◎◎)

【3】次は，平成20年10月に実施した和歌山県学力診断テスト〔中学校第1学年英語〕の問題の一部と，その採点基準及び各設問の生徒の正答率である。これを見て，あとの(1)，(2)に答えよ。

【問題】(本問題のために設問番号を変更して記載)

英語の授業で，あなたは自分の持ちものや飼っているペットなどについて3文以上で紹介することになりました。紹介したい持ちものやペットを1つあげ(次に示した例を用いてもかまいません)，下の指示にしたがって英文を書きなさい。

設問1　1文目は，I haveまたはThis isで始めること。

設問2　選んだ持ちものやペットについて，さらに2文以上で書くこと。

【採点基準及び正答率】

	設問1	設問2
採点基準	I haveまたはThis isで始めており，内容的に理解できれば，冠詞の脱落，綴りの誤り，大文字と小文字の混用，ピリオドの脱落等があっても可。	1文目で提示した内容と関連があり，2文以上書いていれば，冠詞の脱落，綴りの誤り，大文字と小文字の混用，ピリオドの脱落，複数形のsの脱落等があっても可。
正答率	83.9%	51.0%

(1)　この結果から，あなたは生徒の「書くこと」における課題をどのようにとらえるか。結果の分析も含めて40語以上の英語で書け。

(2)　(1)の課題を克服するために，あなたは中学校の英語教師として，どのような指導の工夫を行うか。具体的な指導例も含めて120語以上の英語で書け。

(☆☆☆☆◎◎◎◎)

【高等学校】

【1】命令文は，状況により異なった意味をもつ。次の(1)～(5)の発話における“do it now”は，それぞれどのような意味で使われているか。下の語群から最も適切なものをそれぞれ1つずつ選び，その記号を書け。

(1)　A:　What do you think?
　　B:　Do it now. Then it'll be dry when we come back.

(2)　A:　Do it now. There's somebody coming.

(3)　A:　Do it now.
　　B:　Yes, sir.

(4)　A:　Do it now, please. I want to go home.

(5)　A:　You need to turn it over very quickly. Do it now.

ア　warning　　イ　appeal　　ウ　advice　　エ　instruction
オ　command

(☆☆◎◎)

【2】次の英文を読み，[問1]～[問4]に答えよ。

Understanding and producing the new language involves empathy with other people, especially with individuals from the target culture.

Developing Cultural Understanding

Background knowledge of the new culture helps learners understand better what is heard or read in the new language. Such knowledge also helps learners know what is culturally appropriate to say aloud or in writing. Teachers should help students sharpen their cultural understanding by injecting short cultural discussions into classroom activities, and by comparing and contrasting behavior in the students' native culture and the target culture. Teachers should turn the language classroom into a cultural laboratory. In second language classes, where many nationalities may be represented and where students are learning the language of the (①) community, learners can bring in materials from their own cultural group to share and can discuss how their background differs from that of the culture in their new homeland. ⓐIn foreign language classes, where learners are learning a language from a distant country and are generally from a homogeneous cultural background, students can bring in cultural artifacts from traveling abroad.

(②) of the classroom, encourage students to find out all they can about the target culture through reading, going to lectures, or watching films in the target language. All these activities develop greater cultural awareness, which is necessary for achieving proficiency in the new language.

Here are some instances of developing cultural understanding. Paco, who is studying in England, listens to the BBC to try to get a flavor of the culture. Clem and his classmates sign up for a trip to Central America so they can learn about the culture in person as they speak the Spanish language. Lucretia looks at department store catalogs from France to understand more about French culture.

Becoming Aware of Others' Thoughts and Feelings

Learners can purposefully become aware of fluctuations in the thoughts and feelings of particular people who use the new language. Such awareness brings learners closer to the people they encounter, helps them understand more clearly what is communicated, and suggests what to say and do.

Observing the behavior of others during face-to-face communication often sharpens ⓑthis awareness. Listening carefully to what is said, and what is left unsaid, enables learners to become more aware of the mindset of other people. For instance, Rosalee carefully listens to the tone and expression of the mother in the Italian "host family," so that she can be more (　③　) to the mother's feelings. Ramon observes the physical signals and speech of his teacher, so he can be more aware of the teacher's mood and thoughts. With this knowledge, Rosalee and Ramon both understand better what they themselves should say.

In addition, learners can become aware of the feelings of others as expressed in writing. Students can sense the feelings of people with whom they communicate informally through letters, notes, or memos. (　④　) writing like novels, stories, and articles can be understood more easily when learners consciously try to "get (　⑤　) the skin" of the writer to understand the writer's point of view. For informal or formal writing, this awareness might mean reading on two levels: the literal, verbatim level and the (　⑥　), between-the-lines level. The literal meaning might be perfectly sensible in many instances, but sometimes meanings are expressed in both (　⑦　) and subtle ways, and learners need to read for both types of meanings. For example, Mickey reads the letter from his Asian friend on both levels to determine what is directly expressed and what is implied. This helps Mickey know how to respond in the next letter he writes to his friend. Sandy reads the Tredyakovsky poem in Russian, being aware of both possible levels of meaning.

[問1]　筆者は，生徒の「文化理解」を高めるための方策として，教員が行うべきことを2点述べている。それぞれ日本語で書け。

[問2]　下線部ⓐを日本語で表せ。

[問3]　下線部ⓑについて，分かりやすく日本語で説明せよ。

[問4]　本文中の(　①　)~(　⑦　)に入る最も適切な語を，次の語群からそれぞれ1つずつ選び，その記号を書け。(ただし，文頭に来る語も小文字で示してある。)

ア outside	イ sensitive	ウ covert	エ explicit
オ sensible	カ inside	キ nonverbal	ク formal
ケ informal	コ immediate		

(☆☆☆◎◎◎◎)

【3】次の英文は，新聞のコラムに掲載された問題提起と，それに対して寄せられたある有識者の意見である。これを読み，[問1]~[問8]に答えよ。

Do We Want to Be Supersize Humans?

Introduction

Advances in technology and improvements in (①) have produced remarkable physiological changes in the human body over a relatively short period.

Debate over the causes and implications of those changes has been raised anew by the Nobel Prize-winning economist Robert W.Fogel and his co-authors in a forthcoming book titled, "The Changing Body." "In most if not quite all parts of the world," they argue, "the size, shape and longevity of the human body have changed more substantially, and much more rapidly, during the past three centuries than over many previous millennia."

If ⓐthe pattern holds and humans become taller, bigger and longer-living, will that always represent progress?

Our Hunter-Gatherer Bodies

Many humans today are taller, heavier and live longer than our grandparents, great-grandparents and other distant relations. We are also more (②). Since I was born in 1964, the world's population has doubled to nearly 7 billion.

These changes unquestionably reflect advances in agriculture, medicine and sanitation that have rapidly and profoundly changed how humans obtain and use energy. Like all organisms, humans must spend effort to acquire energy, which we then apportion*1 into growth, maintenance and reproduction. Because many humans today have abundant supplies of food and nutrients, and because we spend (あ) energy in fighting illness or getting food, we have (い) energy to grow and reproduce.

Whether our species' increased height, longevity, girth and fecundity represent progress depends on the lens one uses to assess the meaning of progress.

To many economists, progress represents more of something good like wealth, health or leisure. So by this measure, yes, our changing bodies reflect progress.

But in the context of evolutionary biology, progress is a meaningless term since evolution doesn't have any goals. Evolution just happens, sometimes by natural selection, sometimes by other chance mechanisms. Nature doesn't make judgments.

And there's one reason not to crow*2 about progress. It's the realization that ⓑour species' recent gains have also come with ⓒcosts, some of them alarming. Humans, as a species, have been around for approximately 10,000 generations, and the human genus has been around for more than 100,000 generations. For all but the last 600 generations, our ancestors were hunter-gatherers. Accordingly, the bodies we inherited are still mostly adapted to a hunter-gatherer way of life, which includes plentiful exercise, and a diet (③) in protein and fiber, but (④) in saturated fat and simple sugars.

Today's well-fed children may grow (う) than a typical hunter-gatherer, and they have a much (え) chance of dying young. But as standards of living rise throughout the world, so do obesity rates and related illnesses that are virtually unknown among hunter-gatherers such as adult-onset diabetes, coronary heart disease and cancer.

The optimists among us hope that our ever inventive minds will eventually devise new solutions to ⓓthese challenges just as we have the power to conquer hunger, polio, and the need to do physical labor. I hope ⓔthey are right, but I suspect that human cultural capabilities are nowhere near as powerful as millions of years of natural selection. Future progress for the human body -- that is, gauged by an economic lens -- may require that we eat and exercise more like the hunter-gatherers we evolved to be.

＊1:apportion　配分する　＊2:crow　誇らしげに言う

[問1]　本文中の(①), (②)に入る最も適切な語の組み合わせ

を，次の(ア)～(エ)から1つ選び，その記号を書け。

(ア)　①　nutrition　　②　numerous

(イ)　①　nutrition　　②　crowded

(ウ)　①　intelligence　　②　numerous

(エ)　①　intelligence　　②　crowded

[問2]　下線部ⓐについて，分かりやすく日本語で説明せよ。

[問3]　下線部ⓑ，ⓒについて，それぞれ具体的に日本語で説明せよ。

[問4]　本文中の(　③　)，(　④　)に入る最も適切な語の組み合わせを，次の(ア)～(エ)から1つ選び，その記号を書け。

(ア)　③　rich　　④　rich

(イ)　③　rich　　④　low

(ウ)　③　low　　④　rich

(エ)　③　low　　④　low

[問5]　本文中の(　あ　)～(　え　)に入る最も適切な語を，次の語群からそれぞれ1つずつ選び，その記号を書け。

ア　higher　　イ　lower　　ウ　more　　エ　less　　オ　taller

カ　shorter

[問6]　下線部ⓓに対して，筆者はどのようにすればよいと考えているか，日本語で説明せよ。

[問7]　下線部ⓔが表すものを，本文中から抜き出して書け。

[問8]　本文中には，“progress”に対する2通りの解釈が述べられている。このことについて，具体的に日本語で説明せよ。

(☆☆☆☆◎◎◎)

【4】次の(1)～(8)は，「英語表現Ⅰ」の授業において，与えられた日本文に対して生徒が黒板に書いた英文である。生徒の英文をできるだけ生かすという観点で，どのように直せばよいか。下の例にならって答えよ。

(例)　地図を持ってきてよかったよ。とっても便利だ。

It's a good thing we brought a map. It's been very <u>convenient</u>.
useful

(1)　若い頃にアフリカに行った時，ライオンを見ましたか。

Have you ever seen a lion while you were traveling around in Africa when young?

(2)　その車が，なぜライトをつけたままでここに止められているのか分からない。

I don't know why is the car parked here with its lghts on.

(3)　私はラジオを聴きません。実はラジオを持っていないんです。

I don't listen to the radio. Actually I don't have the radio.

(4)　その夜は，とても疲れていたので10時に寝ました。

I was so tired that night that I slept at ten o'clock.

(5)　その少女は私に微笑みかけた。まるで私のことを知っているかのように。

That girl smiled to me, as if she knew me.

(6)　契約者たちの4つの新しい提案に対して，社長はどれも断わると言っている。

The president refuses to accept either of the four new proposals made by the contractors.

(7)　約10人に1人が花粉症になる可能性がある。

About one person in ten is the potential to become hay fever.

(8)　国連の目的は，広い意味で言うと，平和と安全を維持し，人権尊重を促進することだ。

The purpose of the United Nations, broad speaking, is to maintain peace and security and to encourage respect to human rights.

(☆☆☆☆◎◎◎)

【5】次の文は，平成21年3月に告示された高等学校学習指導要領「外国語」の中に示されている「英語表現Ⅰ」の「内容」の一部である。

発表の仕方や発表のために必要な表現などを学習し，実際に活用すること。

この趣旨を踏まえ，生徒が英語で発表するために必要な表現を指導するため，「科学技術の恩恵」というテーマについての発表の模範例を作成することとした。

その際，下の(1)と(6)は必ず，(2)～(5)は必要に応じて用いながら，120語程度の英文を書け。ただし，語数を記入すること。

(1)　導入：　Today I would like to present...

(2)　順序：　first of al1, next, finally 等

(3)　例示：　for example, such as 等

(4)　追加：　moreover, in addition, furthermore 等

(5)　分析：　Let me go into detail about why...

(6)　結論：　in conclusion, therefore 等

(☆☆☆☆◎◎◎◎◎)

解答・解説

【中高共通】

【1】[Part1]　No.1　B　No.2　A　No.3　C　No.4　A　No.5　D　No.6　D　No.7　B　No.8　C　No.9　B　[Part2]　No.1　C　No.2　A　No.3　B　No.4　D　[Part3]　No.1　Because they are extremely loyal and also have the ability to learn practical skills.

No.2　Because they can not only herd sheep but count sheep.

No.3　It gets money by donation.　No.4　Because they are trained to sniff out fresh fruit as well as meat and even live animals hidden in people's bags.　No.5　“Dogs Working in Different Fields”

〈解説〉スクリプトなし。質問を放送前に確認できる問題は，質問や選択肢に目を通して，聞きとるべき内容を予め整理するとよい。確認できない場合は，2度放送されるなら，1度目で必ず質問内容を理解すること。また，適宜メモをとるなどして，記憶への負担を軽減しよう。リスニングで意味内容に十分な注意を向けるためには，音を無意識かつ

正確に聞きとれる力が必要である。日ごろからディクテーションやシャドーイングをして，音声を聞き取る力を伸ばしておきたい。

【中学校】

【1】[問1]　(A)　(オ)　(B)　(ア)　(C)　(イ)　(D)　(ウ)
[問2]　(ウ)　[問3]　(エ)　[問4]　実は，キノコは，他の菌類種同様，最も古くから存在すると思われている有機体で，今なお生き残っている数少ない単純な植物の1つである。　[問5]　(イ)
[問6]　the more attention the mushroom attracts
[問7]　(1)　(ア)　(2)　(エ)

〈解説〉[問1]　(A)　without developed roots, leaves, ～ or seeds「発達した根，葉，～，種を持たない」　(B)　highly prized「非常に価値のある」　(C)　trained「訓練された」　(D)　hidden under the ground「地下に隠れた」，生殖機能を持つfruiting bodyが地表に表れている(rise above the ground)ことと，成長機能を持つvegetative partが地下に隠れていることは，対比された内容である。　[問2]　trendy「最新流行の(＝fashionable)」　[問3]　chlorophyll「葉緑素(＝光合成に必要な色素)」，直後のcannot generate their own nourishment「自分自身の栄養を生成することができない」から，栄養を作りだす力を持つ何かが入るとわかる。　[問4]　as well as ～「(～と同様に)」は挿入句。that以下はplantsにかかる関係代名詞節。fungus genus species「菌類種」，remaining「現存する」，be among ～「～の1つ」　[問5]　tell (the difference) between A and Bで「AとB(の違い)を見分ける」という意味。同じ意味はdistinguish A and／from B　[問6]　「the 比較級 S＋V, the 比較級 S＋V」で「～であればあるほど，…」　[問7]　(1)　質問は「適度な温度以外に，どのような条件においてキノコはよく育つでしょうか」という意味。正解の(ア)は，最後の段落，Most mushrooms thriveから始まる1文に書いてある内容である。　(2)　質問は「どのようなキノコが食用に適さないか(not edible)」という内容。正解の(エ)の内容は，最後の段落の下線部⑤の後の文にある。spotted「斑点模様の」，capはキノコの笠の部分を指す。poisonous「有毒な」。

【2】[問1]　use the time to have the students create portfolios

[問2]　・英文を正確に書き写すこと　・英語で感情を表現すること　・事実に基づいて書くこと　[問3]　English　[問4]　(ア)

[問5]　(エ)　[問6]　[a]　(エ)　[b]　(ア)　[c]　(ウ)

[問7]　子どもたちがコンピュータの操作を習得し，課題を実行するのにかなり多くの時間がかかること。　[問8]　教師から自立し，創造的に，グループで力を合わせて学習すること。

〈解説〉[問1]　3つの他動詞(have, create, use)にどの目的語(portfolios, the time, the students)を続けるかが並び替えのポイントとなる。目的語を一番選びそうなcreateにまず目をつけ，これにはportfolios(個々の生徒の作品などをまとめて整理しておくフォルダ)が続く。また，文脈からuseの目的語がthe studentsとは考えにくいのでthe timeが目的語と見当をつけ，あとはhave＋O＋Vを用いて「OにVさせる」を表せることに気づけば並び替えが完成する。　[問2]　具体例は次文以降に，are expected/asked to ～の形で示されているので，それらを簡略化して書けばよい。copyは書き写すこと，factual writingは事実について書くことをそれぞれ指す。　[問3]　前の2つの文から，生徒たちは英語を学んでいることがわかり，the software itself is in 【A】ということが，生徒の言語技術(＝この場合は英語)を高めると言っているので，答えはEnglish。　[問4]　guided compositionsは書く内容が定められた作文のことで，fill-in-the-gap exercisesと同種の活動である。これらはfree/creative/open-ended compositionsとは真逆のものである。

[問5]　直前のpositive resultsから，筆者が有意義だと考えている活動のタイプ(＝プロジェクト型の活動)を入れればよいとわかる。there以下の訳は「教室におけるプロジェクト中心のコンピュータ活動から得られている良い結果にはパターンがある」　[問6]　[a]は段落の主題文を探せばよい。画面背景やフォントを自由に選ぶといった本文の内容が，選択肢(エ)のa variety of strategies in creating ～と一致する。

[　b　]から始まる4つの段落では，writing projectの一連の手順が説明されている。その手順とは，①short summaryを書く→②groupでideasをdevelopする→③空欄[　c　](書いたsummaryの修正等)→④home pageを作成→…である。　[問7]　答えが表れている文は，第4段落の後ろから2文目(A downside to ～)にあるので，この文の内容を40語以内に要約して書けばよい。downside「悪い面」，a good deal of ～「多くの～」，master「(技術などを)修得する」，carry out「実行する」

[問8]　Kneirumが生徒に期待したこと(expectations)は最後から2番目の段落にある。キーワードは，independece「教師からの自立」，creativity「創造性」，work in groupsの3つ。解答ではこれらを文の形でまとめればよい。

【3】(1)　Although about 80% of the first year students can write one sentence in English about what they have, about 30% of them can't add two more relevant sentences to the first sentence. Students are not used to writing three or more English sentences about a topic.　(46語)

(2)　To solve the problem I mentioned above, I will suggest two points as follows.

First, whenever I ask a Yes-No question about a topic to students, I will have them add one or more pieces of information about the topic after they answer the question. Then students will get used to adding more information about a topic.

Second, I will give students more opportunities to write three or more sentences about one topic in English. For example, I will do an activity called "Show and Tell". In this activity students present something in front of other students and explain it using some English sentences.

Through these activities I mentioned above, students will improve their skills in writing some English sentences about a topic.　(123語)

〈解説〉(1)　設問1に比べて，設問2の正答率が約30%低くなっている。このことから，3割程度の生徒にとって同じ題材について内容を拡張して書くことが難しかったことがわかる。これらの内容を40語以上(3文前後)の英語で書けばよい。 (2) 先述の課題を克服するためには，同じ題材について，内容を膨らませて書いたり話したりする活動を，数多く行う必要がある。その例として，自分の意見(Yes/No)に対して理由を述べさせたり，Show and Tellで身近な事柄について複数の内容を述べさせるといった方法がある。120語ならば，こうした具体的な指導例を2～3点挙げる必要があるだろう。

【高等学校】

【1】(1) ウ (2) ア (3) オ (4) イ (5) エ

〈解説〉(1) Then it'll be dry when we come back.から，ここのDo it now.は「今洗濯したほうがいいよ」を表すと思われる。したがってadvice「助言」が正しい。 (2)「誰かが来るから今やったほうがいいよ」はwarning「警告」に最も近い。 (3) BがYes, Sir.と答えていることから，AはBにとって目上の者だとわかる。よってcommand「命令」が最も近い。 (4) pleaseがあることから，appeal「懇願」しているとわかる。 (5)「素早くひっくり返してください」とやり方を説明してからDo it now.と言っているので，instruction「指導」に近い。

【2】[問1] ・教室での活動に，文化に関わった短いディスカッションを導入すること。 ・「生徒自身の国の文化」と「目標言語が話されている国の文化」における行動様式を比較したり，対照させたりすること。 [問2] 外国語学習の場では，学習者は遠く離れた国の言語を学び，一般的に均質な文化的背景をもっているが，そのような状況では，生徒は海外旅行で手に入れた文化と関わりのある物を持ち込むことができる。 [問3] 目標とする言語を使っている人たちの思考や変化に意図的に気づけるようになること。 [問4] ① コ ② ア ③ イ ④ ク ⑤ カ ⑥ ウ ⑦ エ

〈解説〉[問1] 1つ目は，本文第1段落目のby injecting以下に，2つ目は同文のby comparing以下に書いてある。これらをそれぞれ日本語に訳せ

ばよい。　[問2]　where以下はforeign language classesを説明した関係副詞節。homogeneous「均質の」，bring in ～「～を持ち込む」，artifacts「人工の物(工芸品など)」　[問3]　this awareness「この気づき」は前段落のfluctuations in ～を指している。fluctuation in～「～における変化」，who以下はparticular peopleを修飾した関係代名詞節である。
[問4]　①　immediate community「身近な地域」　②　outside of the classroom「教室の外では」　③　sensitive「敏感な(cf. sensible「分別のある」)」　④　formal writing「形式ばった書き物(例：novelsやarticlesなど。反対にinformalなのがmemosなど)」　⑤　get inside the skin of the writer「筆者の皮膚の下に入る(「筆者の真意を読む」を隠喩的に表現したもの)」　⑥　covert, between-the-lines level「隠れた，行間を読むレベル」(⇔literal, verbatim level「文字通り，言葉通りのレベル」)　⑦　explicit「明白な(「微妙な」を意味するsubtleとは逆の意味)」

【3】[問1]　(ア)　[問2]　世界のほとんどの地域で人間の体型と寿命は，この300年間で，それまでの何千年と比べて，より大きく，しかも急速に変化してきたこと。　[問3]　ⓑ　人間の体が以前と比べて大きくなり，寿命が延び，人口が増えたこと。　ⓒ　我々が狩猟採集民だった時代には，ほとんど知られていなかった病気が増加してきたこと。　[問4]　(イ)　[問5]　あ　エ　い　ウ　う　オ　え　イ
[問6]　筆者は，狩猟採集民により似かよった食事や運動をすることがよいと考えている。　[問7]　the optimists　[問8]　経済学においては，progressとは，富，健康，娯楽といった何かしら人間に利益をもたらすことである。しかし，進化生物学においては，progressとは，それ自体は目的を持たず，自然淘汰や偶然などによって引き起こされることである。
〈解説〉[問1]　①に関して，remarkable physiological changes in the human body「人間の体における目を見張る生理的変化」は，次の段落からsize, shape and longevity「大きさ，形状，寿命」に関することだとわか

る。したがってintelligence「知能」よりもnutrition「栄養」のほうがふさわしい。②に関しては，numerous「数が多い」は人を主語にすることができるが，crowdedは「(場所や乗り物などが)混み合った」の意味なのでここでは使えない。　[問2]　the pattern「その傾向」は，前段落の本の引用部分(In most ～ over many previous millennia.)を指すので，ここを日本語に訳せばよい。In most if not quite all ～は「全ての～とは完全には言えないまでも，大部分の～」の意味。　[問3]　ⓑは，これまで何度か繰り返されているように，身体の成長や寿命の延び，及びそれに伴う人口の増加を指す。文中ではour species' increased height, longevity, girth and fecundityなどが参考になる。ⓒのcostsはここでは「犠牲」の意味。人類の進歩(progress)の代償として懸念されていることは，最後から2番目の段落のBut as standards of living rise以下に具体的に書かれている。ここを要約して解答すればよい。　[問4]　どんなdiet「食事」が，現代と特徴を異にする，狩猟採集的(hunter-gatherer way)な食事なのかを考えればよい。それは，たんぱく質(protein)や食物繊維(fiber)を豊富に含み(＝rich)，脂肪(fat)や糖類(sugar)をあまり含まない(＝low)食事である。　[問5]　あい　病気と闘うことや食物を得ることに使うエネルギーがより少なければ(spend less energy)，成長や生産のために使えるエネルギーは増える(more energy)。　うえ　現代の栄養十分な子供たち(well-fed children)の特徴を表すように空欄を埋めればよい。すなわち彼らは，昔の狩猟採集民よりも背が高く(taller)，若くして死ぬ確率が低い(lower chance of dying young)。　[問6]　these challengesは問3のⓒで答えた内容を指している。それへの対処法を筆者は，記事の最後の1文，require that以下に示している。ここを日本語に訳せばよい。　[問7]　optimistは「楽観主義者」のことで，彼らは「私たちのこれまでの発明の心が，最後には新しい解決法を考え出してしまうだろう」と気楽に考えている。それに対し筆者は，but I suspect ～と疑いの念を表している。new solutionsはその具体的な内容がわかっていないため，筆者がI hope they are rightと意見を述べるのは考えにくいので，答えとしては不適切。　[問8]　経済学と進化生物学におけるprogressの捉え方の違いは，To many economistsから始まる段落と，その次のBut in the context of evolutionary biologyから始まる段落にそれぞれ説明されている。ここを要約して答えればよい。natural selectionは「自然淘汰」の意。

【4】(1)　Have you ever seen→Did you see　(2)　is the car→the car is
(3)　have the radio→have a radio　(4)　slept→went to bed
(5)　smiled to→smiled at　(6)　either→any　(7)　ten is→ten has, become→develop　(8)　broad→broadly, respect to→respect for

〈解説〉設問の「生徒の英文をできるだけ生かすという観点で」は，言い換えれば「不必要な修正は行わずに」という意味なので，より高度な表現を考える必要はなく，純粋に文法的に誤っている箇所のみ訂正すればよい。　(1)　while ～の節では，明らかな過去の一時点が述べられているため，完了形は用いることができない。　(2)　why以下は間接疑問なので，SVの語順となる。　(3)　最初のthe radioは総称としてのラジオを指すのでtheでよいが，後のradioは個人の所有物として数える名詞の扱いとなるので不定冠詞のaが適当。　(4)　sleepは「寝る」という行為全体を指し，「就寝する」ことだけを述べたい場合にはgo to bedを用いる。　(5)「～に微笑みかける」はsmile at ～となる。
(6)　eitherは「(2つのうち)どちらか」の意味。ここは4つのproposalがあるのでanyが適当。　(7)　has the potential to V「Vする可能性がある」, develop ～「(～の病気)にかかる」　(8)　broadly speaking「広く言うと」, respect for ～「～に対する尊敬」

【5】(解答例)

Today I would like to present how the recent development of technologies has improved our personal relationships.

First of all, the spread of new technologies has made person-to-person communication possible to an unexpected degree. With mobile phones, for example, you can reach anyone at any time and at any place. Various barriers of time and space kept us from direct communication in the past, but most of them have been broken down now. Moreover, new technologies have brought about different ways of communication. You can tell other people what you can't say in some situations, by using e-mail via computers or mobile phones.

In conclusion, advanced technologies have enabled us to build up better and deeper personal relations with each other.　(121語)

〈解説〉「英語表現」は現行指導要領では英語科のみの対象だった科目だが，今回の改訂で普通科などでも実施可能になった。「英語表現」の目的は，解説によると「『話すこと』及び『書くこと』に関する技能を中心に論理的に表現する能力の育成を図る」こととなっている。授業における課題は「論理的に表現する能力」をどのように育てるかである。このため教師は，1文対1文の機械的な作文練習だけではなく，まとまった量の論理的文章を生徒に書かせる指導を行っていかなければならない。採用試験受験者に，「例示」「追加」といった様々な論理形式を使って文章を組み立てる力があるかどうかを試す問題は，近年では出題されやすいところである。しっかり準備しておきたい。

2011年度　実施問題

【中高共通】

【1】放送を聞いて，[Part 1] ~ [Part 3]の各問に答えよ。

[Part 1]

No. 1

(A) He will have Thai food for dinner today.

(B) The newspaper headlines described a typhoon.

(C) The weather will probably get worse later.

(D) There was news about a headstrong man.

No. 2

(A) Reservations for seats are not accepted here.

(B) It's too early to make a reservation.

(C) Window seats won't be available until Wednesday.

(D) He thinks that Saturday is not a good day.

No. 3

(A) He finally got used to his new car.

(B) He usually uses his new car.

(C) He doesn't use his new car daily.

(D) He drives his new car only on campus.

No. 4

(A) Luke's German is not as good as Andy's.

(B) Andy and George write better than Luke.

(C) Luke's essays are worse than George's.

(D) George writes as well as Luke does.

No. 5

(A) He would like some iced coffee.

(B) He wants to stop drinking coffee.

(C) A drink seems like a good idea.

(D) He wants to stop his coughing.

No. 6

(A) She's been looking for 15 minutes.

(B) Her sight has been declining.

(C) She's late for her flight.

(D) She needs to get a taxi.

No. 7

(A) He reported that the time for the budget meeting had been set.

(B) He is always late in submitting his accounting figures.

(C) He manages to budget his time well.

(D) He is never too late in turning in his reports.

No. 8

(A) There are many books on physics in the library.

(B) Last year, she passed the course.

(C) She can show how to find passages about physics.

(D) He should have studied harder.

No. 9

(A) He is staying in this hotel.

(B) He keeps going to bed late.

(C) He lives by himself in this house.

(D) He started early and finished late.

[Part 2]

No. 1

(A) Because the Asian Games will be held in the biggest city in China.

(B) Because Japan has the most kinds of sports in Asia.

(C) Because three sports will make their Asiad debut.

(D) Because some Japanese traditional sports will be added to the Asian Games.

No. 2

(A) Since fiscal year 1988.

(B) For 13 years.

(C) Since March 31.

(D) For 4 years.

No. 3

(A) She made a pink yacht by herself.

(B) She criticized a journey that spanned the globe.

(C) She erupted into cheers in Sydney.

(D) She sailed around the world by herself.

No. 4

(A) Because more natural gas is being used than in the past.

(B) Because the water supply in many areas has been reduced.

(C) Because the climate gets warmer and colder in natural cycles.

(D) Because people are polluting the atmosphere.

[Part 3]

Questions:

No. 1 In ancient times, an eclipse was a terrifying religious experience, but how is an eclipse likely to be viewed these days?

No. 2 From a scientific point of view, what is the dark spot streaking across the earth?

No. 3 What are the specific things that scientists can study only during an eclipse?

No. 4 How long do people have to wait if they want to see an eclipse again in the same place?

No. 5 If the moon were smaller, what would eclipses be like?

(☆☆☆◎◎◎◎)

【中学校】

【１】次の英文を読み[問1]～[問7]に答えよ。

①Human memory, formerly believed to be rather inefficient, is really much more sophisticated than that of a computer. Researchers approaching the problem from a variety of points of view have all concluded that there is a great deal more stored in our minds than has been generally supposed. Dr. Wilder Penfield, a Canadian neurosurgeon, proved that by stimulating ②their brains electrically, he could elicit the total recall of complex events in his subjects' lives. Even dreams and other minor events supposedly forgotten for many years suddenly (　A　) in detail.

③The memory trace is the term for whatever is the internal representation of the specific information about the event stored in the memory. Assumed to have been made by structural changes in the brain, the memory trace is not subject to direct observation but is rather a theoretical construct that we use to speculate about how information presented at a particular time can cause performance at a later time. Most theories include the strength of the memory trace as a variable in the degree of learning, retention, and retrieval possible for a memory. One theory is that the fantastic capacity for storage in the brain is the result of an almost unlimited combination of interconnections between brain cells, (　B　) by patterns of activity. Repeated references to the same information support recall. Or, to say that another way, improved performance is the result of strengthening the chemical ④bonds in the memory.

Psychologists generally divide memory into at least two types, short-term and long-term memory, which combine to form working memory. Short-term memory contains what we are actively focusing on at any particular time, but items are not (　C　) longer than twenty or thirty seconds without verbal rehearsal. We use short-term memory when we look up a telephone number and repeat it to ourselves until we can place the call. On the other hand, long-term memory can store facts, concepts, and experiences after we stop thinking about them. All conscious processing of information, as for example, problem solving, involves both short-term and long-term memory. As we repeat, rehearse, and recycle information, the memory trace is (　D　), allowing that information to move from short-term memory to long-term memory.

[問1]　文中の(　A　)~(　D　)に入る最も適切な語を，次の(ア)~(オ)からそれぞれ1つずつ選び，その記号を書け。

(ア)　changed　　(イ)　retained　　(ウ)　emerged

(エ)　stimulated　　(オ)　strengthened

[問2]　下線部①を，文中のthatの指す語を明らかにして，日本語に直せ。

[問3]　下線部②を，theirが指す語を明らかにして，日本語に直せ。

[問4]　下線部③について，本文中で述べられている内容と一致しないものを，次の(ア)~(エ)から1つ選び，その記号を書け。

(ア)　It is probably made by structural changes in the brain.

(イ)　It is able to be observed.

(ウ)　It is a theoretical construct.

(エ)　It is related to the degree of recall.

[問5]　下線部④を他の語に置き換えるとき，最も適切な語を次の(ア)~(エ)から1つ選び，その記号を書け。

(ア)　influences　　(イ)　informations　　(ウ)　connections

(エ)　reactions

[問6]　次の(1)，(2)の質問の答えとして，最も適切なものを下の(ア)~(エ)からそれぞれ1つ選び，その記号を書け。

(1)　What is the main topic of this passage?

(ア)　Chemical experiment.

(イ)　Problem solving.

(ウ)　Neurosurgery.

(エ)　Human memory.

(2)　How did Dr. Wilder Penfield elicit dreams and other minor events from the past?

(ア)　By electric stimulation.

(イ) By surgery.

(ウ) By chemical stimulation.

(エ) By repetition.

[問7] short-term memoryとはどのようなものか。本文中から例を挙げて簡潔に説明せよ。

(☆☆☆☆◎◎◎)

【2】次の英文を読み，[問1]～[問7]に答えよ。

When students write or speak in lessons they have a chance to rehearse language production in safety, experimenting with different language in different genres that they will use on some future occasion away from the classroom.

When students are working on their language production, they should be operating towards the communicative end of the communication continuum. Activities at the non-communicative end of the continuum — such as language drills — are excluded from the category of productive skills even though they may be done orally.

Similarly, the writing of sentences to practice a grammar point may be very useful for a number of reasons, but such exercises are not writing skill activities. This is because language production means that students should use all and any language at their disposal to achieve a communicative purpose rather than be restricted to specific practice points.

However, skill training is not always communicative in itself, since teaching people to take turns or use correct punctuation, for example, is often fairly controlled -- and may involve quite a lot of teacher intervention.

One of the chief advantages of production activities is that they provide evidence for students and their teachers to assess how well things are going. ①【 seeing / the / the / of / greater / freer / the task / the chance 】 how successful a language learning programme has been.

Reception and production

The teaching of productive skills is closely bound up with receptive skill work. The two feed off each other in a number of ways.

●[　a　] : when a student produces a piece of language and sees how it turns out, that information is fed back into the acquisition process. Output becomes input.

Such input or feedback can take various forms. Some of it comes from ourselves, whether or not we are language learners. We modify what we write or say as we go along based on how effective we think we are being. Feedback also comes from the people we are communicating with. In face-to-face spoken interaction our listeners tell us in a number of ways whether we are managing to get our message across. On the telephone listeners can question us and/or show through their intonation, tone of voice, or lack of response that they have not understood us.

Teachers can of course provide feedback too, not just when a student finishes a piece of work but also during the writing process, or when as prompters or as a resource teachers offer ongoing support.

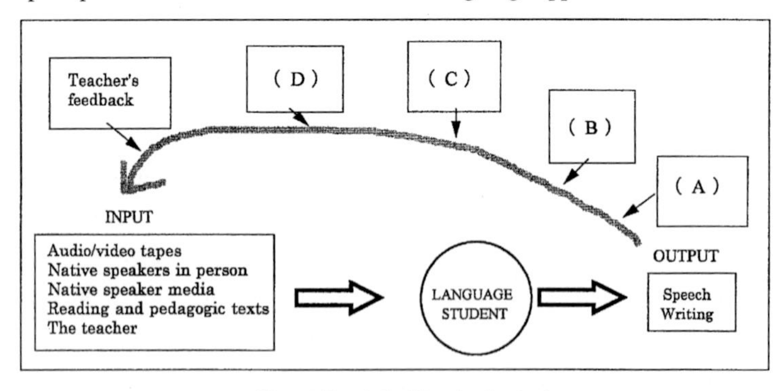

Figure: The circle of input and output

●[　b　] : especially where students are working with genre-focused tasks, written and spoken texts are a vital way of providing models for them to follow. One of the best ways of having students write certain kinds of report, for example, is to show them some actual reports and help them to analyze their structure and style; ②to get students to give spoken directions they will benefit from hearing other people doing it first.

Productive work need not always be imitative. But students are greatly helped by being exposed to examples of writing and speaking which show certain conventions for them to draw upon.

●[c] : a lot of language production work grows out of texts that students see or hear. A controversial reading passage may be the ③ springboard for discussion, or for a written riposte in letter form. Listening to a tape or disk in which a speaker tells a dramatic story may provide the necessary stimulus for students to tell their own stories, or it may be the basis for a written account of the narrative.

●[d] : in many situations production can only continue in combination with the practice of receptive skills. Thus conversation between two or more people is a blend of listening and speaking; comprehension of what has been said is necessary for what the participant says next. In writing too what we write often depends upon what we read. Letters are often written in reply to other letters, and e-mail conversation proceeds much like spoken dialogues. Indeed, in the case of chat rooms and MOOs (permanent spaces on the Internet where a number of users can meet in real time in virtual rooms), the computer discourse takes place, like spoken conversation, in real time.

④ The fact that reception and production are so bound up together suggests strongly that we should not have students practice skills in【　　】even if such a thing were possible. That is why many of the examples in this book show integrated skill sequences, where the practice of one skill leads naturally on to other linked activities.

● Production enables reception : productive skill work is a way of helping students with their receptive skills. ⑤ Students can apply the insights【 from / to / gain / their reading / they / their writing work 】. When they have tried to speak within certain genres, they are better attuned to understanding other people speaking in the same context.

[問1]　本文で述べられている1anguage productionの定義を，60字程度の日本語で書け。

[問2]　本文で述べられている内容と順序に従い，Figureの(　A　)～(　D　)に入る最も適切なものを，次の(ア)～(オ)からそれぞれ1つ選び，その記号を書け。

(ア)　Other students' feedback

(イ)　Other students participate

(ウ)　Student sees how it turns out

(エ)　Student modifies his/her understanding

(オ)　Student tries to work on their language production

[問3]　文中の[　a　]～[　d　]に入る見出しとして最も適切なものを，次の(ア)～(カ)からそれぞれ1つ選び，その記号を書け。

(ア)　Structuring discourse

(イ)　Reception as part of production

(ウ)　Process and product

(エ)　Output and input

(オ)　Text as stimuli

(カ)　Text as models

[問4]　下線部①，⑤の【　　】内の語を正しく並べ替えよ。ただし，解答は【　　】内のみ書くこと。なお，文頭の語も小文字で示してある。

[問5]　下線部②について，具体的に80字程度の日本語で説明せよ。

[問6]　下線部③の語の意味を説明する英文として最も適切なものを，次の(ア)～(エ)から1つ選び，その記号を書け。

(ア)　Something that helps you to start doing something.

(イ)　Something that helps you to know where you are.

(ウ)　Something that you hope to achieve something.

(エ)　Something that you hope to use in communications.

[問7]　下線部④の【　　】に入る最も適切な語を，次の(ア)～(エ)から1つ選び，その記号を書け。

(ア)　reverse　　(イ)　isolation　　(ウ)　mesh　　(エ)　neutral

(☆☆☆☆☆◎◎◎)

【3】下の2つの【グラフ】は中学2年生を対象にした英語に関する調査結果の一部である。この結果を見て，次の(1)，(2)に答えよ。

(1)　これら2つの【グラフ】から読み取れる課題を30語以上の英語で書け。

(2)　(1)の課題を克服するために，あなたは中学校の英語教師として，どのようなことに留意して指導するか。課題に対する考えを含め，130語以上の英語で書け。

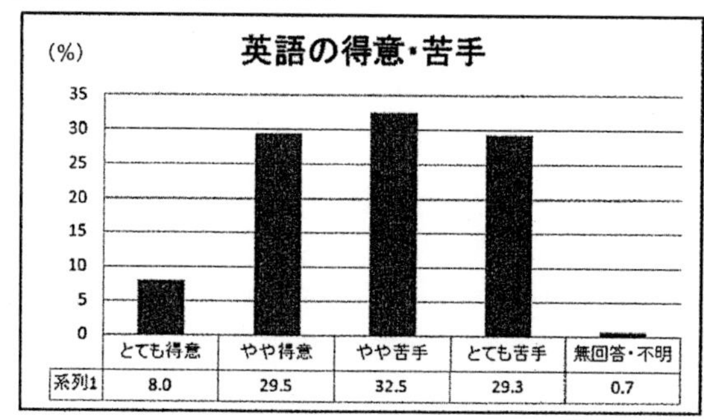

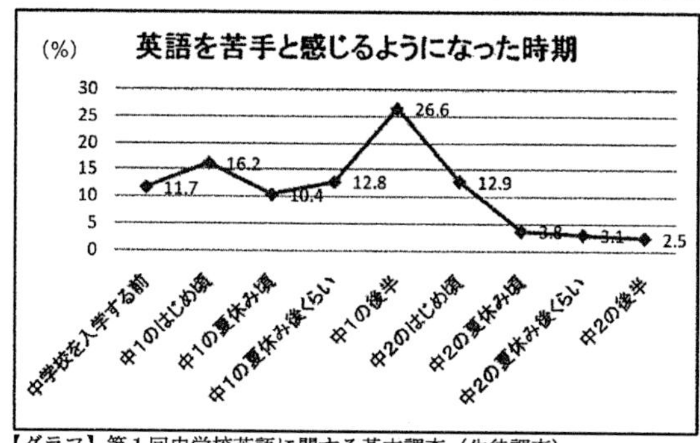

【グラフ】第1回中学校英語に関する基本調査（生徒調査）
（Benesse 教育研究開発センター 2009 年 1 月～2 月実施）

(☆☆☆◎◎◎)

【高等学校】

【１】次の英文を読み，[問1] ～ [問5]に答えよ。

"What words do you want to test?"

If the purpose of a test is to give an estimate of a learner's total vocabulary size, then some method is needed to sample from all of the words the learner might know. For lower-level learners, frequency lists up to the 10,000-word level are suitable, because such students are unlikely to know many words beyond this. In fact, sampling from the most frequent 1,000 and 2,000 levels is often sufficient, especially for beginners. But, for very advanced learners it is necessary to sample from all the words in a language. In this case, ⓐ the dictionary method is often used. This involves systematically choosing words from a large dictionary, for example, the 5th word from every 10th page. These words are then fixed on a test. The percentage of correct answers is then multiplied by the number of words in the dictionary to arrive at an estimate of vocabulary size. Unfortunately, this method has several problems, the main one being that the resulting total size estimate will depend on the size of the dictionary used. Also, direct sampling will result in skewed results, so some adjustments in the sampling procedure need to be made.

Another problem is that the number of words finding their way onto the test compared to the total number of possible words is very low. This issue of ⓑ sample rate is an important one in vocabulary testing. Let us say that the purpose of a test is to measure knowledge of the most frequent 1,000 words of English, and it includes a sample of 100 of those words. The 1 in 10 sample rate is probably sufficient for us to infer the degree of knowledge of the whole 1,000 word set. But if the test included only 20 words (1 in 50), we would be much less confident that these accurately reflected knowledge of the set. In general, higher sample rates and greater numbers of words make for a better vocabulary test.

Sample rate has direct effects on the three major criteria in language testing: *validity*, *reliability*, and *practicality*. Validity is a complex issue, but for our purposes here, it refers to how well a test measures what it is supposed to measure. In other words, do learners' responses to the test items represent their actual knowledge of the target words, both those on the test and the others in the set that did not make it onto the test? For example, a vocabulary test in which a target word is embedded in a sentence or paragraph is supposed to measure knowledge of that word. But in order to answer that item, a learner must also know the other words in the context, as well as be able to read. So the test item is tapping other knowledge in addition to knowledge of the target word. Many test types wish to capture this integrated interaction of multiple linguistic aspects, but if a test purports to measure mainly vocabulary knowledge, these other aspects can (①) the vocabulary scores in ways that are difficult to determine. This can compromise validity. Of the many things that influence the validity of a vocabulary test, sample rate is important in that higher rates obviously allow a more representative sample of the total target word pool.

Reliability concerns the stability or consistency of a test's behavior over time. If an examinee took a test several times, without his or her ability changing, the test would (②) produce the same score on each administration. In the real world, the test scores would vary to a certain degree, because of such factors as examinee alertness or fatigue, motivation, the testing environment, and the test itself. If the test scores varied wildly, we would have no idea which particular score most closely corresponded with the examinee's true ability. (③), the more items a test contains, the more reliable the test is.

Therefore, in terms of validity and reliability, longer tests are better. But [ ] in terms of practicality; for example, tests with hundreds of words are unlikely to be of much use in the classroom. Thus, there is always tension between having a test long enough to be valid and reliable, yet short enough to be administered. A useful rule of thumb is that the more important the consequences of a test, the longer and more carefully constructed it should be.

High-stakes tests that greatly affect the lives of examinees obviously need to be more comprehensive than tests that have a relatively minor effect.

The bottom line is that we are often dealing with large sets of words when assessing learners' total vocabulary size, and the larger the vocabulary set we wish to measure, the lower the sampling rate is likely to be. Thus, it is an advantage if an item format can be answered quickly, allowing the maximum number of items to be placed on a test.

[問1]　下線部ⓐは，どのような方法か，具体的に日本語で説明せよ。

[問2]　下線部ⓑについて，分かりやすく日本語で説明せよ。

[問3]　本文中の(　①　)～(　③　)に入る最も適切な語句を，次の(ア)～(エ)からそれぞれ1つずつ選び，その記号を書け。

① (ア) increase　(イ) affect　(ウ) obtain　(エ) measure

② (ア) realistically　(イ) linguistically　(ウ) semantically　(エ) ideally

③ (ア) For example　(イ) However　(ウ) In general　(エ) Moreover

[問4]　本文中の[　　]に入る最も適切なものを，次の(ア)～(エ)から1つ選び，その記号を書け。

(ア) unreasonably intensive tests often exist

(イ) unreasonably extensive tests often fail

(ウ) unreasonably intensive tests often fail

(エ) unreasonably extensive tests often exist

[問5]　筆者はvalidity, reliability, practicality の観点をふまえた上で，sample rateを上げるためには，どのような語彙テストがよいと述べているか，具体的に日本語で書け。

(☆☆☆☆◎◎◎◎)

【2】次の英文を読み，[問1]～[問9]に答えよ。

A major concern of L2 teachers is how to generate rich and meaningful interaction in the classroom which will facilitate SLA. Many teachers find it difficult to engage students in interaction, especially ⓐ in teacher-fronted settings. From some research findings a number of pedagogical implications have been made clear. First, when students fail to respond to the teacher's question, it may be because the questions were too complex, inappropriately phrased or contained difficult vocabulary items. If the question is too complex, then the modifications should be '[　A　]', such as paraphrasing difficult words, simplifying syntax and making the main point salient. If it is inappropriately phrased, then the modifications should be 'response-oriented', such as rephrasing into several simple questions to which the students can respond more easily. One effective way is to ask teachers to video-tape their own lessons and examine questions which fail to (　①　) responses. For example, in an L2 lesson the teacher put on the board a newspaper headline 'Police to pursue crooked cabbies' and asked the students 'What *is* it? Never mind what it means but what *is* it?' When no response was forthcoming, he modified it as 'Where would you find this?' However, after 8.5 seconds there was still no response. Finally, he changed the question to 'How can you tell that that belongs in the newspaper?' In the post-observation discussion, the teacher said that he was not sure why ⓑ his subsequent modification did not work. Upon examining the possible interpretations of the modified question, it became clear to him that the question could mean 'Where would one find police pursuing crooked cabbies?' or 'Where would this line appear?' ⓒ The discussion helped to raise the teacher's awareness of the importance of introspecting on his own use of language [the students, than, blaming, for, rather, passive, being] .

It is also very useful to examine instances of successful modification of questions and discuss why they are successful. For example, in a primary L2 classroom, the teacher read out a sentence describing a dog. She said 'So that's a very good descriptive sentence. It tells you exactly what the dog looks like. [　　　] ?' The teacher realised that the use of the verb 'picture' might be a bit beyond the pupils' ability level. Therefore, she modified the question to 'If I were to ask you to draw the dog, would you be able to draw the dog?' As a result of her lexical modification, the students immediately responded in chorus by saying 'yes, yes'.

Not giving enough wait-time for learners to process a question and formulate an answer is another reason for the lack of response from students. Many teachers fear that lengthy wait-time slows down the pace of teaching and leads to disruption in the classroom, or that they might appear to be inefficient and incompetent. Therefore ⓓ they often answer their own questions. A study showed that if the teacher allowed longer wait-time after a learner made a mistake or after the teacher posed a question, the learner was much better able to respond correctly. This does not mean that lengthening wait-time necessarily improves students' responsiveness. In a study of teachers' action research, it was found that excessive lengthening of wait-time exacerbated anxiety amongst students. To alleviate L2 learning anxiety, from which many L2 learners (②), the teacher can provide opportunities for learners to rehearse their responses to a teacher's question by comparing notes with their partners or group members, or writing down their responses before presenting them to the rest of the class.

The way a teacher allocates turns in the classroom can also affect students' classroom interaction. In classrooms where interaction is highly controlled by the teacher, as in many Asian classrooms, patterns of turn-allocation is an important factor. In a study of his own turn-allocation behaviour by recording the number of turns he allocated to which learner, a teacher found that, contrary to his perception of himself as allocating turns evenly, he frequently allocated turns to the same learners. On reflection, he realised that these learners were those who [B], and that he subconsciously turned to these learners whenever he wanted to progress quickly. To ensure more even turn-allocation, he kept a class list and put a tick against a student whenever he allocated him or her a turn.

The above pedagogical practices to improve classroom interaction must be implemented with the teacher's awareness of L2 learning as a psychologically unsettling and potentially face-threatening experience which can generate debilitating anxiety. The teacher needs to be sensitive to the psychological state of the students and to be supportive and appreciative of any effort made by the students to learn the target language. Only then will the teacher be able to generate the kind of classroom interaction which will facilitate meaningful and enjoyable learning.

(注)　L2 = second language, SLA = second language acquisition

[問1]　本文中の(　①　)，(　②　)に入る最も適切な語を，次の(ア)～(オ)からそれぞれ1つずつ選び，その記号を書け。

(ア)　elicit　(イ)　prevent　(ウ)　modify　(エ)　suffer

(オ)　tolerate

[問2]　本文中の[　A　]に入る最も適切な語を，次の(ア)～(エ)から1つ選び，その記号を書け。

(ア)　interaction-oriented　(イ)　vocabulary-oriented

(ウ)　comprehension-oriented　(エ)　production-oriented

[問3]　本文中の[　B　]に入る最も適切なものを，次の(ア)～(エ)から1つ選び，その記号を書け。

(ア)　would think of his turn-allocation

(イ)　would try to find their own answers

(ウ)　could rarely give appropriate answers

(エ)　could usually answer correctly

[問4]　下線部ⓐとほぼ同じ意味で用いられている表現を，本文中から抜き出して答えよ。

[問5]　下線部ⓑが表すものを具体的に述べている箇所を，本文中から抜き出して答えよ。

[問6]　下線部ⓒが，本文の流れに合うように，[　　]内の語句を並べ

かえよ。

[問7]　本文の流れに合うように，文中の[　　　]に，ふさわしい英語を書け。

[問8]　下線部@について，その理由を具体的に日本語で書け。

[問9]　本文の最終段落に述べられている筆者の考えを，120字以内の日本語で書け。

(☆☆☆◎◎◎◎)

【3】下の(1) ～ (7)は，「英語表現Ⅰ」の授業において，与えられた日本文に対して生徒が黒板に書いた英文である。生徒の英文をできるだけ生かすという観点でどのように直せばよいか。次の例にならって答えよ。

(例)　あす天気がよければ，ピクニックに行こう。

If it will be sunny tomorrow, we'll go picnic
is　go on a picnic

(1)　君のメールは届いてないよ。

Your e-mail doesn't come.

(2)　地図を持ってきてよかったよ。とても便利だ。

It's a good thing we brought a map. It's been very convenient.

(3)　新幹線の泣き所は，雨や雪に弱い点だ。

Shinkansen's trouble is that it is weak in snow or rain.

(4)　私がその田舎町で過ごした5日間は，とても心休まるものでした。

The five days that I lived in the local town was very peaceful.

(5)　最初は，10日もあれば，自転車で九州を一周できるだろうと思っていた。

For the first time, I thought I would be able to travel around Kyushu by a bicycle for 10 days or so.

(6)　昔に比べて最近の子どもは本を読まなくなったのは確かだ。

It is sure that children today don't read more than former days.

(7)　私は空港までの道を鈴木君に教えてやるように言われた。

I was said to teach Mr.Suzuki the way until the airport.

(☆☆☆◎◎)

【4】次の文は，平成21年3月に告示された新高等学校学習指導要領「外国語」の中に示されている「英語表現Ⅱ」についての「内容」の一部である。

論点や根拠などを明確にするとともに，文章の構成や図表との関連，表現の工夫などを考えながら書くこと。また，書いた内容を読み返して推敲すること。

この趣旨をねらいとした授業において，あなたは生徒に「小学校における英語教育についてどう考えるか」といったテーマで，150語程度の英語で作文を書かせた。

次の英文は，その課題に対してある生徒が提出してきたものである。この授業のねらいをふまえて，この生徒の英作文に対するコメントやアドバイスを150語以上の英語で書け.

① I think that it is a good idea to teach English in elementary schools. ② English is an international language. ③ The number of foreign people living in Japan has been increasing recently. ④ Furthermore, if we can speak English, we can enjoy our trips more when we travel abroad. ⑤ So it is very important for children to learn English. ⑥ There are many people who cannot speak English even if they have studied English for over 6 years. ⑦ This is a big problem.

⑧ However, children in elementary schools already have too much to learn. ⑨ For example, they study about ten subjects such as Japanese, math and so on. ⑩ If they have to learn English too, it will be too much for them. ⑪ However, the younger we are, the more easily we can master a language. ⑫ Therefore, in my opinion, only English conversation should be taught in elementary schools.

(注)　各英文の文頭に付した①, ②...は，便宜上，英文の順序を示すものである。

解答にあたって生徒の英文を取り上げる際には各英文をthe 1st sentence, the 2nd (sentence)... で表記すること。また，語数を記入すること。

(☆☆☆◎◎◎◎)

解答・解説

【中高共通】

【1】[Part 1]　No.1　(C)　No.2　(B)　No.3　(C)　No.4　(A)　No.5　(C)　No.6　(D)　No.7　(B)　No.8　(D)　No.9　(B)

[Part 2]　No.1　(C)　No.2　(B)　No.3　(D)　No.4　(D)

[Part 3]　No.1　It is likely to be viewed as a tourist attraction.

No.2　It is the shadow of the moon.　No.3　They are the corona and other dim things that are normally lost in the sun's glare.　No.4　They have to wait for 375 years on average.　No.5　They would not be possible.

〈解説〉リスニング能力の向上には毎日少しずつでも時間を取って英語を聞くことが重要であるが，ラジオ講座のように内容のわかりやすいものも，ニュースなど毎日内容の変わるものも，それぞれの面で効果がある。試験の際には，メモ取りが許可されているのであれば，数字，曜日，列挙された物の名前などのキーワードを，関連する内容と共に必ずメモしながら聞くこと。

【中学校】

【1】問1　(A)　(ウ)　(B)　(エ)　(C)　(イ)　(D)　(オ)

問2　以前はむしろあまり役に立たないと思われていた人間の記憶は，実際にはコンピュータの記憶よりかなり精巧である。　問3　ペンフィールド博士の被験者の脳　問4　(イ)　問5　(ウ)

問6　(1)　(エ)　(2)　(ア)　問7　私達が電話番号を調べて電話を

かけるまで，頭の中で何度も番号を繰り返すような短い期間の記憶のこと

〈解説〉問1 (A) 「長年の間，忘れ去られたと考えられた夢やその他のささいな出来事が，突然詳細に～」で「出現した」があてはまる。
(B) “result” 以下は：「行動パターンにより(B)された，脳細胞同士の相互連結のほとんど無限の組み合わせの結果」の意。「行動パターン」は複数形で「様々な行動パターン」というニュアンスであることから，「いろいろな行動パターンによる刺激を受け，複雑な組み合わせの記憶を貯めていく」意味と推察できる。 (C) 「短期的記憶」についての説明なので，「20～30秒より長く記憶に留めて置かれることはない」の意味と推察できる。 (D) 「私達が情報を繰り返し，何度も使うことによってその情報についての記憶が強化され，短期的記憶が長期的記憶となることを促す」の意で「強化する」があてはまる。
問2 この文の骨組みは “Human memory is more sophisticated that that of a computer. (ヒトの記憶はコンピュータのそれよりも洗練されている)” で，ここから「それ(that)」が「記憶」であると判断し，訳に反映させる。 問3 下線部②を含むフレーズ：“by stimulating their brains electrically” は強調のため前に持ってきているが，一般には最後に置かれるという点を考慮すれば，“their” が “his subjects'” と同義であると判断できる。 問4 同じパラグラフの2行目に “the memory trace is not subject to direct observation (記憶痕跡は観察対象とはならない)” とあり，(イ)と逆のことを論じている。 問5 “chemical bonds” は「化学的結合」の意。選択肢で「結合」の意味を表すのは “connection” である。他の選択肢はそれぞれ，(ア)影響，(イ)情報，(エ)反応の意。
問6 (1) 英文の論文では，冒頭に記事の主題を持って来るパターンが非常に多い。冒頭が「人間の記憶は」で始まる一文であり，これが主題であると先ず推察できるが，全文をざっと読み，他の選択肢が主題の説明・例示部分で論じられている点を確認すること。 (2) 第1パラグラフの “Dr. Wilder Penfield ……” で始まる一文に，“by stimulating their brains electrically” とある。 問7 第3パラグラフ2行

目に，“short-term memory”の定義的説明が書かれており，3行目にその生活上の用途が例示されている。問題が「どのようなものか」と，具体的説明を求めているので，後の方の例示部分を解答にあてる。

【2】問1　特定の学習事項のプラクティスに制限されるのではなく，コミュニケーションを達成することを目的としながら，自由に言語を駆使すること。(64字)　問2(A)　(ウ)　(B)　(エ)　(C)　(イ)　(D)　(ア)　問3a　(エ)　b　(カ)　c　(オ)　d　(イ)
問4　①　The freer the task the greater the chance of seeing　⑤　they gain from their writing work to their reading　問5　指導者がクラスルームイングリッシュを使用するなかで，ある学習者が，指導者の指示どおり反応する他の学習者の姿を見て，それをモデルにして反応することができる。　問6　(ア)　問7　(イ)
〈解説〉問1　第3パラグラフの最後のセンテンス“language production means”に続く部分に定義が書かれているので，その部分を制限文字数にまとめる。　問2　長い文の読解問題は，先ず各パラグラフの冒頭部分および見出しを拾い読みすることで，アウトラインがつかめるであろう。本問では「自分からの発信がコミュニケーションの相手その他の他者からの反応(フィードバック)として返って来ることで，受動的なスキルが向上する」というストーリーをある程度つかみ，それに沿ってAからDへの流れに沿った現象をあてはめるとよい。
問3　各パラグラフごとに，ほぼ選択肢と同じかたちのキーワードが含まれている。見出しの語やフレーズを選択する問題は，面倒でもざっと通読して捜すのが一番速い解き方である。　問4　①　カッコ内に形容詞の比較級が2つ，(名詞についたthe以外に)theが2つあるので，[the比較級，the比較級]の構文を先ず想起する。語義から，freer－task，greater－chance，chance-of-seeing，という繋がりが発見できれば並べ替えは完了。The ～，the ～.”の構文の意味は「～なほど～だ」で，それぞれの動詞が共通しているならば，動詞を完全に省いてもよく(例：The sooner, the better.)，また設問の場合のように，後ろだけに動詞を持ってくるケースもある。 ⑤ 問題箇所の前の文：「productive skill workは生徒のreceptive skillsの向上の助けとなる方法である。」から，“from their writing work to their reading” という流れをつかむ。残った “they gain” は” insights (洞察力)” を修飾する形容詞節なので，insight の直後，語群の冒頭に置く。 問5 問題箇所を含むパラグラフ冒頭に「特に，生徒が分野(genre)重視の課題に取り組んでいるとき，書かれた，また口頭による文章は，見習うべき見本(model)を生徒に提供するための重要な方法である。」とある。問題箇所はその具体例であるから，単に訳すのではなく，この冒頭部分の内容が伝わるようにまとめる。 問6 問題箇所を含む文は，「論議を呼ぶような文章の一節は，ディスカッションや，レター形式の気の利いた反論へのspringboard (踏み切り台／きっかけ)となるかもしれない。」の意であるから，「何かを始める手助けとなるもの」を意味する(ア)があてはまる。
問7 問題箇所を含む文は，「reception と production が非常に緊密に組み合わさっているという事実は，私達が生徒に(両方の)スキルを，もしそうすることが可能であったとしても，【～のようなかたちで】練習させるべきではない，ということを強く示唆している」のように訳せるであろう。前半の「緊密に組み合わさっている」に対し，後半は “should not” で論じられており，後半は前半と逆の意味を含むと判断できることから，空欄には，“in isolation (分離して)” があてはまると判断できる。

【3】(1) More than 60% of the second year J.H.S. students think that they are not good at English, and about 80% of them think that they started to feel that way when they were in their first year at Junior High. (40 words)

(2) It is a serious problem that more than half of the second-year students don't think that they are good at English. I will discuss one of the reasons why they think so and a possible solution.

While learning a foreign language, we make a lot of mistakes. Through mistakes students acquire English in the classroom. However both teachers and students tend to focus just on accuracy. So when students make some mistakes, they feel disappointed and don't think that they are good at English.

To help solve this problem. I would accept students' mistakes positively during class Then I would correct the students' mistakes little by little. After that I would help the students recognize what they are becoming able to do using English. Once they recognize their improvement, they will probably think that they are getting better at English. (140words)

〈解説〉自分の考えを英語で記述する問題は必ず出題されるが，英語教育について，特に本設問のように，実際の教育活動についての意見を記述させる問題は頻出されている。解答に際しては，自分の論点を明確にし，文法上のミスを避けるためひとつひとつのセンテンスを短く簡潔に書く事が大切であるが，主旨の選択は自由である。例えば本設問(2)であれば，中学1年生の文法や語彙を自然に身につけられるような工夫についてや，毎日の復習をうまく習慣づけるための方法を論じる等も考えられる。英文を書く問題では，本来の自分の考えだけでなくいろいろな側面から問題を分析できる柔軟性を持つことにより，自分の英語表現のレパートリーの範囲で無理のない文を書くことが可能になる点も覚えておいてほしい。

【高等学校】

【1】問1　大辞典から，10ページごとの5番目の単語といったように，規則的に単語を選び，試験に出す方法。　問2　語彙テストにおける，出題範囲全体の語彙数に対する語彙数の割合。　問3　①　(イ)　②　(エ)　③　(ウ)　問4　(イ)　問5　解答するのに時間がかからず，可能な限り問題数を多くしたテスト。

〈解説〉問1　下線部ⓐに続き，代名詞“This”で始まる文がある。代名詞は通常直前の名詞の代わりとなるものであるから，この文が“dictionary method”の説明となっていると判断できる。　問2　問題箇所を含むフレーズは“This issue of sample rate”とあり，すでに述べられた事について，さらに述べている箇所であるとわかる。遡って読むと，“issue” とほぼ同義の単語 “problem” があるので，その部分が問題箇所の定義となっていることが判断できる。　問3　①　問題箇所は逆接の接続詞 “but” に導かれており，それに先行する文意の対照をなす。すなわちここでは，前の部分とは逆にある特定の語についての知識を問うことを意図する場合について述べており，先行する文で言われている方式が純粋な語彙テストに否定的な影響を及ぼす点を指摘している。to tap は，ここでは「利用する」の意，to purport は「意図する」，affect は「影響を及ぼす」の意で使われている。　②　パラグラフ冒頭に「Reliability (信頼性)は “stability (安定性) あるいは consistency (一貫性)” と関連する」とあり，それを受けて「受験者の力に変化がなければ，(理想的には)試験施行のたびに同じスコアがあがるだろう」と述べている。選択肢アは「現実的に」で，推測を述べているここ(would)ではあてはまらない。またイ，ウについては文中に言及がない。　③　問題箇所の前後の文：「試験結果のばらつきが大きいと，どの結果が受験者の実力と対応するか判断できない」と，「テストがより多くの事項を含むほど，そのテストはより信頼性がある」を繋げる語の選択。後者は前者の関連事項であり，例示でもアンチテーゼでも強調でもないので(ア，イ，エ)は当てはまらない。
問4　パラグラフ冒頭の文で，「有効性と信頼性という点では長大なテストの方がよい」と述べつつ，But と続けているので，セミコロンまでであれば，反論となる選択肢(イ)と(エ)が可能だが，for example として「数百語によるテストは教室で役に立ちそうにない」と述べており，(エ)は例示とならないので不可。　問5　“The bottom line is …… (結論として)” に続く最後のパラグラフを読んで行くと，“Thus (従って)” というキーワードがあるので，そこに主題が述べられていると判断する。

【2】問1　①　(ア)　　②　(エ)　　問2　(ウ)　　問3　(エ)
問4　In classrooms where interaction is highly controlled by the teacher
問5　Where would you find this?　　問6　rather than blaming the students for being passive　　問7　Can you picture the dog　　問8　待ち時間を

長くすることにより，授業のペースが遅くなって教室が混乱するとか，自分自身に能力がないように思われると教師が考えるから。

問9　教師は，第2言語学習において学習者が感じている不安感などに対して敏感であり，言語習得に対する努力について支持的，肯定的である必要がある。そのようになって初めて，教室内で意味のある楽しい相互的な学習活動を生み出すことができる。(112字)

〈解説〉問1　①「返答を～することに失敗した質問を検証する」という文脈で，“elicit (引き出す，導き出す)”があてはまる。　②“from which learners ……”という構文から，“from”と共に群動詞を構成し，anxietyを目的語とし得る動詞として suffer があてはまる。“suffer from anxiety”で「不安に悩まされる」の意。　問2　問題箇所に続く部分に「例えば難解な語を置き換える……」等とあるので「理解に焦点を宛てた修正がなされるべき」とする(ウ)があてはまる。　問3　ブランクに続く文に「彼(教師)は，速く(授業を)進めたいときはいつも，無意識にこれらの学習者(生徒)に宛てていると気づいた」とあることから，正解を答えて時間的無駄を作らない生徒の意味で「ほぼいつも正しく答えることの出来た(生徒)」の(エ)があてはまる。　問4　ⓐは「教師が仕切る状態(設定)となっているクラス」というほどの意味。同じ意味合いの箇所を意識しながら通読するしかないが，たとえば situation , classroom などのキーワードを念頭に置いて捜すのもひとつの方法かもしれない。　問5　“subsequent (続く，次の) modification”は最初の質問に引き続いて発した，修正された2番目の質問を指している。

問6　語の並べ替えの際は，先ずセットフレーズや繋げることが可能な語で形成された小グループを作る。“rather than”，“being passive”，“blaming the students”の塊ができれば，“blame ～ for ……ing”という構文と組み合わせ，さらに“rather than ＋ 名詞”の構文から“rather than blaming”と繋げ，並べ替え完了。　問7　問題箇所に続き「教師は picture という動詞の用法が生徒の能力レベルを超えていたかもしれないと察した」とあるので，“picture (頭に思い描く)”を使用した文をあてはめればよい。　問8　下線部ⓓは“Therefore (従って，それだから)”で始まっているので，遡って読んで行けば具体的な説明をしている箇所を発見できる。　問9　問題に「本文の最終段階に述べられている」とある通り，最後のパラグラフに結論部分があるので，120字以内にまとめればよい。

【3】(1)　Your e-mail doesn't come.
hasn't come (yet)

(2)　It's a good thing we brought a map. It's been very convenient.
useful

(3)　Shinkansen's trouble is that it is weak in snow or rain.
The trouble with the Shinkansen　easily affected by

(4)　The five days that I lived in the local town was very peaceful.
spent　provincial

(5)　For the first time, I thought I would be able to travel around Kyushu by a bicycle for 10 days or so.
At first　by　bicycle　in

(6)　It is sure that children today don't read more than former days.
certain　read less　than in former

(7)　I was said to teach Mr. Suzuki the way until the airport.
told　tell　to

〈解説〉(1)「まだ届いていない」の意味なので，現在完了に修正。

(2)　品物が“convenient”なのは属性として便利なのであり，ある特定の機会において「便利だった」という使い方はしない。　(3)“one's trouble”とすると，「新幹線自身の悩み」のニュアンスになる。この場合は「新幹線における問題点」という使い方に修正する。また，“weak in ……”とすると，「……が苦手」という意味合いになる。

(4)“live”はある程度長いスパンで「生活する」の意味。5日間程度だと「時を過ごす」という意味合いの“spent”を当てるべき。また“local”は「局所の，ある一地域の」という意味であり，「郊外の，田舎の」という意味では必ずしもない。主語は“five days”であるから，be動詞は複数形に。　(5)“For the first time”は「初めて」の意味で，ここで述べている「当初はそう考えていた」という意味には当てはまらない。「ある自転車で」ではなく，機能面での「自転車で」と言いたいので無冠詞。“for”は時間の長さについて言う場合に使うがこの場合は「10日間で」なので“in”とする。 (6) “sure”は「確信している」の意味合いであり，客観的に「確かである」なら“certain”とする。主語を変更して，“I am sure …….”とするなら可。“don't read more”だと「それ以上読まない」の意。“than former days”とすると，その「日々」自体を別の「日々」と比較する表現になってしまう。
(7) “I was said……”は「私は……だそうだ」のような意味合いになる。「道を教える」は“tell the way to ……”が決まり文句。“until”は，時間的な「～まで」であり，空間的な「～まで」の意味では使用しない。

【4】Good job, but your essay has some good points and bad points.

In writing an essay of about 150 words, it should be composed of two or three paragraphs. So the structure of your essay is good. Each paragraph of your essay has a topic sentence and supportive sentences. This is also good. Moreover you use various discourse markers, so your readers can understand your essay easily.

Then what should you have been more careful about in writing this essay? In the 1st sentence, you say ‘teaching English in elementary schools is good,’ but in the 12th, you refer to ‘English conversation.’ In this case, your readers may be confused about which is your opinion. Do you realize your essay is logically incoherent in some parts? For instance, in the 5th and the 6th sentences of the 1st paragraph and the relationship between the 1st paragraph and the 2nd paragraph.

Lastly, I advise you to examine the outline of your essay more carefully before you start.

〈解説〉英語で論説やコメントを書く設問は，いろんな場面で頻出されるので，制限語数でまとめられるよう，日頃から50語，100語，150語，200語，300語以上，等の設定で文章をまとめる練習が必要である。本番では文法的誤りを犯さないよう，個々のセンテンスは短く，また文の主旨は簡潔にわかりやすく伝わるように心がけることが大事である。

●書籍内容の訂正等について

弊社では教員採用試験対策シリーズ（参考書，過去問，全国まるごと過去問題集），公務員試験対策シリーズ，公立幼稚園・保育士試験対策シリーズ，会社別就職試験対策シリーズについて，正誤表をホームページ（https://www.kyodo-s.jp）に掲載いたします。内容に訂正等，疑問点がございましたら，まずホームページをご確認ください。もし，正誤表に掲載されていない訂正等，疑問点がございましたら，下記項目をご記入の上，以下の送付先までお送りいただくようお願いいたします。

① **書籍名，都道府県（学校）名，年度**
（例：教員採用試験過去問シリーズ　小学校教諭 過去問　2025年度版）
② **ページ数**（書籍に記載されているページ数をご記入ください。）
③ **訂正等，疑問点**（内容は具体的にご記入ください。）
（例：問題文では"ア～オの中から選べ"とあるが，選択肢はエまでしかない）

〔ご注意〕
○ 電話での質問や相談等につきましては，受付けておりません。ご注意ください。
○ 正誤表の更新は適宜行います。
○ いただいた疑問点につきましては，当社編集制作部で検討の上，正誤表への反映を決定させていただきます（個別回答は，原則行いませんのであしからずご了承ください）。

●情報提供のお願い

協同教育研究会では，これから教員採用試験を受験される方々に，より正確な問題を，より多くご提供できるよう情報の収集を行っております。つきましては，教員採用試験に関する次の項目の情報を，以下の送付先までお送りいただけますと幸いでございます。お送りいただきました方には謝礼を差し上げます。
（情報量があまりに少ない場合は，謝礼をご用意できかねる場合があります）。

◆あなたの受験された面接試験，論作文試験の実施方法や質問内容
◆教員採用試験の受験体験記

送付先
○電子メール：edit@kyodo-s.jp
○FAX：03-3233-1233（協同出版株式会社　編集制作部 行）
○郵送：〒101-0054　東京都千代田区神田錦町2-5
協同出版株式会社　編集制作部 行
○HP：https://kyodo-s.jp/provision（右記のQRコードからもアクセスできます）

※謝礼をお送りする関係から，いずれの方法でお送りいただく際にも，「お名前」「ご住所」は，必ず明記いただきますよう，よろしくお願い申し上げます。

教員採用試験「過去問」シリーズ

和歌山県の
英語科 過去問

編　集　© 協同教育研究会
発　行　令和5年11月25日
発行者　小貫　輝雄
発行所　協同出版株式会社
〒101-0054　東京都千代田区神田錦町2－5
電話　03－3295－1341
振替　東京00190－4－94061
印刷所　協同出版・POD工場

落丁・乱丁はお取り替えいたします。